D0152095

FORSYTH LIBRARY - FHSU
2 1765 0052

Turkish Folk Music from Asia Minor

NUMBER 7
IN THE NEW YORK BARTÓK ARCHIVE
STUDIES IN MUSICOLOGY

THE NEW YORK BARTÓK ARCHIVE

Benjamin Suchoff, *Trustee*

The Béla Bartók Archives:
History and Catalogue

Rumanian Folk Music
I Instrumental Melodies
II Vocal Melodies
III Texts
IV Carols and Christmas Songs (*Colinde*)
V Maramureş County

Turkish Folk Music from Asia Minor

Béla Bartók Essays

TURKISH FOLK MUSIC FROM ASIA MINOR

by

BÉLA BARTÓK

edited by

BENJAMIN SUCHOFF

with an afterword by

KURT REINHARD

PRINCETON UNIVERSITY PRESS

1976

Library of Congress Cataloging in Publication
data will be found on the last
printed page of this book
This book has been composed in Monotype
Bembo, with Augustea initial letters

PRINTED IN THE UNITED STATES OF AMERICA
BY THE STINEHOUR PRESS, LUNENBURG, VERMONT, AND
THE MERIDEN GRAVURE COMPANY, MERIDEN, CONNECTICUT

Contents

List of Plates

Turkish Folk Music
from Asia Minor

Editor's Preface

THE sequence of events which ultimately were to lead Béla Bartók to the writing of his last ethnomusicological study —this publication of his Turkish folk music collection— apparently began in December of 1935. It was on the first day of that month that László Rásonyi, a Hungarian-born philologist and professor at the newly founded University of Ankara, wrote the first of a series of letters to Bartók, in which he extended a preliminary invitation to travel to Ankara for the purposes of lecturing and collecting local musical folklore.[1]

Bartók's exhilaration over the possibility of widening the range of his ethnomusicological studies is hardly concealed in his affirmative and lengthy reply. Indeed, Bartók was also willing to perform in concert without fee, providing that the voyage would not be made at his own expense. With characteristic integrity he questioned the propriety of his lecturing on the relation between Hungarian and Turkish folk music, since knowledge of the latter material—other than previous Turkish editions that were essentially Arabic in character—was lacking in Hungary. On the other hand, he was aware of the assertion made by the Turkish ethnomusicologist Mahmud Raghib Gazimihâl that "the genuine Turk-

1. D. Dille, ed., *Documenta Bartókiana* (Budapest: Akadémiai kiadó, 1968), 3:179–183 (hereafter cited as *DocB 3*). Rásonyi asks Bartók to lecture on three questions: (1) the connection between Hungarian and Turkish music, (2) the development of Hungarian music and its apparent state, and (3) how a Turkish national music could develop.

ish folk music includes many pentatonic melodies."[2] Bartók, however, found this statement "predicated on scanty material which does not permit one to draw broad inferences," and he asked Rásonyi to send the Turkish folk song publications edited by Gazimihâl and to arrange for his visit to the music folklore center in Istanbul, prior to his lecture in Ankara, "because I shall only be able to give useful hints after having been informed what was done till now and what was neglected."[3]

The next year, in April, Bartók received an official invitation from the Ankara Halkevi[4] to visit there in May and lecture on "methods for the study of folk music in general, and the principal elements of your School in particular."[5] Bartók, committed to a series of concert performances in April and May, suggested a postponement until October and offered a five-point "program" for Ankara which would include three lectures, a concert with orchestra, the collecting of Turkish folk music, and "conversations with the competent people on future tasks."[6]

Bartók availed himself of Rásonyi's presence in Hungary that summer for help in learning Turkish. He found the undertaking more difficult than he had presumed, particularly "the twisted sentences, contracting in one sentence what is expressed in other languages by ten. Fortunately, this rarely occurs in the texts of the folk songs; now I shall be busy with the pertinent part of the Kúnos collection."[7]

2. *Zenei Lexikon* (Budapest, 1931), 2:621.

3. János Demény, ed., *Bartók Béla levelei* (Budapest: Zenemukiado, Vallalat, 1955), 3:406–408 (hereafter cited as *Lev. 3*). Written from Budapest, the letter is dated 18 December 1935.

4. The designation of the social institutes set up throughout Turkey.

5. *DocB 3*, p. 190.

6. *Lev. 3*, pp. 411–412.

7. *Lev. 3*, p. 413. Bartók brought with him to New York, in 1940, a Turkish primer for the second grade (*Okuma Kítabı*, Istanbul, 1936), which contains his annotations in Hungarian and French. The Kúnos collection of Turkish folk song texts (see the listings in the Bibliography below), published in Budapest, was copied by Bartók in a small notebook, also with Hungarian and French annotations.

In October Bartók completed and mailed to Ankara the promised three lectures,[8] and in a humorous letter to a former pupil residing in Ankara, added this postscript: "I learned a little Turkish and can already make very interesting statements in this language, for example, 'At deveden çabuk gider' or 'Kedi köpekden küçüktür,' etc.! But I am not as yet on friendly terms with the literary language! They use terribly long expressions and an appalling number of participles!"[9]

Following his stay in Istanbul during the first week in November, Bartók had the opportunity to listen to a number of the sixty-five double-faced records (produced by Columbia and His Master's Voice, since 1930, on commission from the city) of performers—mostly peasants—who had been brought there for recording purposes. He voiced a number of objections to the collection of almost 130 melodies: (1) since the material was not collected on the spot, it was not possible to determine systematically what should be collected and, subsequently, which pieces should be recorded; (2) the performers were itinerant musicians and, therefore, could not be very authentic sources of village music linked to the site; (3) the recorded melodies had not been notated nor were the texts written down. And, in the latter case, since the performers were no longer available, deficiencies in the recordings could not be corrected. In fact, even the Turks themselves were unable to understand the texts on some of the recordings that were played for Bartók during his Istanbul visit.

During the following week Bartók presented his lectures and a concert in Ankara. A short collecting trip had been planned for him, following these appearances and prior to a repetition of the concert program on 17 November, but illness prevented its realization. After a full recovery and with his obligations met, Bartók

8. Published in Ankara (1936) under the title "*Halk müziği Hakkında,*" and in Hungarian translation (by László Rásonyi) in *Új Zenei Szemle* (Budapest, 1954).

9. János Demény, ed., *Bartok Béla levelei* (Budapest: Művelt nép könyvkiadó, 1951), 2:119–120; hereafter cited as *Lev. 2*. The translation of Bartók's Turkish phrases is: The horse is faster than the camel, The cat is smaller than the dog.

had approximately ten days remaining for field work. His companions were the composer A. Adnan Saygun, whose task was the collecting of data from the performers as well as the jotting down of the texts, and two composition teachers from the Ankara Conservatory of Music, who were to witness how musical folklore is collected on the spot.

Having been warned by his Turkish escorts that it would be necessary to fraternize with the peasants for weeks before they finally would be induced to sing, Bartók set out with mixed feelings. As the result of their conversation concerning words common to the Hungarian and Turkish languages, Saygun suggested to Bartók that they construct a sentence that would be almost the same in both tongues. Then, whenever they met peasants who were intimidated by the presence of a stranger, Saygun would say that the Hungarians were only Turks who had settled somewhere else, that they had always spoken Turkish, but that evidently in the course of centuries their accent had become more or less different. Then Bartók was to repeat the sentence that had been concocted. The amusing sentence (in English translation: *In the cotton field are much barley and many apples, camels, tents, axes, boots, and young goats*) was understood by all and provided the researchers with the means to facilitate the collection.[10]

In a summary[11] of the results of his trip Bartók indicated that what had been achieved did not come up to his standards of perfection. One great shortcoming, for example, was his inability to obtain all the relevant information about the collected material: designation of the songs, how they had been handed down, and so

10. A. Adnan Saygun, "Bartók in Turkey," *Musical Quarterly*, 37(1951):8–9. The sentence in Hungarian: *Pamuk tarlón sok árpa, alma, teve, sátor, balta, csizma, kicsi kecske van.* In Turkish: *Pamuk tarlasinda çok arpa, alma, deve, çadir, balta, çizme, küçük var.*

11. Béla Bartók, "*Népdalgüjtés Törökországban*" [On Collecting Folk Songs in Turkey], *Nyugat* (Budapest, 1937) pp. 173–181. This article, an expanded version of the lecture given by Bartók on Budapest Radio (11 January, 1937), appears in revised form in English in *Béla Bartók Essays*, ed. Benjamin Suchoff (London: Faber & Faber, 1976).

forth. And, in a number of cases the obtained data were either incorrect or contradictory; there was not enough time to thoroughly check these data and simultaneously pursue the recording of the available performers. He was also considerably handicapped by linguistic problems: he could not talk to the peasants directly. Communicating through an interpreter, he was unable to discover whether two or more performers ever sang together and, if they had, on what occasions. The fact is that he could never get people to sing together, not even those who lived together in the same village: "All my trials resulted in a complete failure, which would indicate that singing in chorus was unknown in this part of the world. But even that statement should be accepted with caution. It is almost unthinkable that Turkish people should never sing together, never form a chorus (if only in one part)." The greatest shortcoming of all, however, was Bartók's inability to record songs performed by women: Moslem women did not sing in public, especially not in the presence of a stranger. And, lastly, it was not always possible to write down the complete texts on the spot, with the result that they were for the most part preserved only on the phonograph records.

Saygun's memoirs present yet another circumstance that hampered the research. The old Edison recording machine that Bartók brought with him from Budapest could not clearly record both voice and accompanying instruments at the same time.[12]

No sooner had Bartók returned to Budapest when he set to work transcribing the sixty-four cylinders he had recorded. In fact, he reported that a quarter of them had been completed by the first week in January. In this report, the first in a brief series of exchanges with Saygun, Bartók wrote that he was "anxiously expecting" the promised French translation of the Turkish poetic texts, and that with one exception—a recording in which "the

12. Saygun, "Bartók in Turkey," p. 7. Saygun also recalls that the tempo of each song was verified by means of a metronome, and the register of the voice by means of a pitch pipe.

singer has performed changes which were not written down (and which—it goes without saying—I cannot understand)"—the words of the original Turkish texts were written down very exactly.[13]

By the following week Bartók had researched his material to the extent that he was able to list these conclusions: (1) the peasant music in the Adana region of Turkey has little in common with the music (possibly Arabic-influenced) in the Turkish cities; (2) rhymed prose hardly can be found in rural music; (3) Aeolian, Dorian, and, sporadically, Mixolydian modes occur; (4) deviations from the pure intonation of the diatonic scale do not exceed Hungarian ones in particular and those of east Europeans in general; (5) augmented seconds are rarely encountered.[14]

In May Bartók had completed the major part of his transcriptions and, looking ahead to an edition of the work, had initiated steps to obtain a joint Turkish-Hungarian publication.[15] Later that month he received his first reply from Saygun who reported that difficulties had been encountered in transcribing the texts and the *taksim* (improvisations) that precede the dance. Saygun was doubtful that these improvisations were folk products, especially when performed throughout the record, and in cases where the *taksim* preceded the dance, it would no longer be an improvisation if the same *taksim* were to be played alike by all performers.[16]

On 20 June Bartók responded to Saygun's letter with the an-

13. Letter dated 2 January 1937. Written in French, a photocopy of this letter is in the correspondence files of the New York Bartók Archive (hereafter cited as *NYBA*). In German translation in *Béla Bartók Ausgewählte Briefe*, ed. János Demény (Budapest: Corvina Press, 1960), pp. 170–171 (hereafter cited as *BBAB*).

14. *Lev. 3*, p. 419, letter to János Bán (Hungarian professor of Turkish linguistics and author of the article on Turkish art music in *Zenei Lexikon*), dated 8 January 1937.

15. Ibid., pp. 423–424, letter to Rásonyi, dated 13 May 1937. Bartók's futile attempts to achieve publication of his Turkish material offer another example of the failures and frustrations that plagued him throughout his ethnomusicological career. The interested reader will find a detailed description of these setbacks in Victor Bator's Foreword to *Rumanian Folk Music*, ed. Benjamin Suchoff (The Hague: Martinus Nijhoff, 1967), 1:viii–xix.

16. *DocB 3*, p. 210, letter dated 27 May 1937.

nouncement that the latter's text translations had arrived, along with Turkish folk music material collected by Saygun in the northeastern (Black Sea area) part of the country. The greater part of Bartók's letter was devoted to a critique of Saygun's transcriptions, of which the following remarks are worthy of quotation here:

> There were practical reasons that prompted us to select g^1 as the final tone. Because this tone is—up to the present time—applicable to melodies *of all peoples*. A lower tone (for example, f^1 or d^1) would be impossible for many Western European melodies, since they often descend as much as an octave below the final tone. A higher tone, on the other hand, would present inconveniences, since many Turkish and Hungarian melodies go higher than the final tone by as much as thirteen steps! With g^1 as the final tone we have at our disposal the compass of g through c^3 or d^3. . . .
>
> You asked me whether or not the "improvisations" should be notated. You are right if it is a matter of a genuine improvisation, then one cannot consider it to be a "folk melody." However, if improvisations of this kind are in vogue among the peasant musicians of the villages, one must collect them, from the folkloristic viewpoint. This is my opinion, and, as a matter of fact, I myself have collected pieces of this kind (by the way, they are quite rare here). In your country it is only necessary to check whether the improvisators are truly permanent village residents or are wandering troubadors. In the latter case one must consider their improvisations with suspicion, with distrust.[17]

The hiatus of more than nine months in Bartók's correspondence concerning his Turkish collection was probably due to a number of disparate factors. The principal one, perhaps, was composition: the Sonata for Two Pianos and Percussion was written during July and August, the Violin Concerto No. 2 was com-

17. *NYBA* Correspondence File. See also *BBAB*, pp. 176–177. The letter closed with Bartók's report that he was busy with the study of the Turkish texts, aided by Saygun's translations, and that he would like permission to use the latter's work in a French-language edition of the collection which was in preparation for publication in Hungary.

menced in August (and completed at the end of the next year), and the *Contrasts* for violin, clarinet, and piano was sketched prior to the end of September. The second factor was the matter of preparation for concerts and recitals: he and his wife, Ditta, gave the world premiere of the Sonata for Two Pianos and Percussion on 16 January 1938 in Basel; Bartók then went on alone to play recitals in Luxembourg, Brussels, Amsterdam, The Hague, and London. The third and most significant factor was the German occupation of Austria in March: Bartók resolved to leave Hungary and began making preparations for his exile.[18]

A letter from Saygun in April, which informed Bartók that Saygun's book[19] on the music, instruments, and dances of towns in northeastern Anatolia had been forwarded to Budapest, may have prompted Bartók to return to his Turkish collection.[20] For his own reasons Bartók broke off contact with Saygun and turned to Lászlo Rásonyi for help with the Turkish texts:

> Alas! it did not come off by any means to have the Turkish texts checked: nor could I busy myself with them! . . . Under the impact of your letter I resumed with difficulty the task of making fair copies of the texts; we completed half of them, I enclose them herewith.
>
> One more request: in the Turkish texts kindly underline the words of Arabic origin in blue pencil, those of Persian origin in green pencil; in particular those which are in public use; underscoring once the fully acclimatized words, and twice, the words used only in more educated circles.—That would have great importance for me, since I could then infer many things.[21]

18. See Ralph Hawkes's recollections in *A Memorial Review* (New York: Boosey & Hawkes, 1950), pp. 14–17. Hawkes flew to Budapest a few days after the Anschluss and obtained from Bartók an agreement for publication of his future works.

19. A. Adnan Saygun, *Rize, Artvin ve Kars Havâlisi, Türkü, Saz ve Oyunları* (Istanbul: Nümune Matbaasi, 1937).

20. *DocB 3*, pp. 219–220, letter dated 6 April 1938. According to Saygun's article in *Musical Quarterly* ("Bartók in Turkey," p. 9) he received a typewritten letter from Bartók, shortly after the Anschluss, asking whether a position could be found in Turkey that would enable Bartók to establish permanent residence there.

21. *Lev. 3*, pp. 429–430, letter dated 28 April 1938.

In May Bartók sent the remainder of the Turkish texts to Rásonyi, with additional instructions concerning orthographical matters: "The difficulty is with *ğ* and *y*, since even the Turks confound them (for example, değil, deyil, eğlemek, eylemek!); how could I, poor Hungarian, know which to use?!" And, after a remark that he ought to emigrate, he makes this statement concerning the fate of his Turkish collection: "It would be of great importance that the Halkevi enter into negotiations with Rózsavölgyi [Bartók's Hungarian music publisher]: I am afraid that otherwise, in view of the general slump, they would drop altogether the publishing project."[22]

In his response, dated 3 June, Rásonyi informed Bartók that examination of the texts disclosed very few Arab and Persian words, and that those that occurred were in common usage. Rásonyi added that he noticed fluctuations of the phonetic notation but that he refrained from altering them, since the pronunciation *i̥* and *u* might vary.[23]

The political and economic climate in 1938 and 1939 was hardly conducive to the publication of such esoteric works as Bartók's Turkish folk music collection. Fully resolved to emigrate, and counting on his new publishers in England for assistance, Bartók prepared the fair copy of the Turkish music examples on master sheets and a typescript draft of the Turkish texts (see description below, p. 16).[24] The prefatory study, originally planned as a French-language version and at that time apparently unwritten in any form, was temporarily deferred. His creative energies, on the other hand, continued unabated: composition of the *Divertimento* for

22. *Lev. 3*, p. 431, letter dated 12 May 1938.

23. According to the Hungarian passage quoted in Lászlo Somfai's letter to the editor, dated 8 June 1971. This and three other unpublished letters from Rásonyi to Bartók are in the Budapest Bartók Archivum (dated 22 April 1936, 1 September 1936, and 24 January 1937); also contained there, and annotated by Somfai for the editor, are five unpublished letters from Saygun to Bartók (dated 7 February 1937, 13 March 1937, 1 September 1937, 24 November 1938, and 19 March 1939).

24. He probably had the help of a former pupil, Jenő Deutsch, for the autography (cf. *Rumanian Folk Music*, 1:2).

string orchestra and String Quartet No. 6, and completion of the Violin Concerto No. 2 and the monumental *Mikrokosmos* for piano. He was also feverishly at work preparing the fair copies of his Rumanian folk music collection, an enormous undertaking which resulted in the production of almost 900 master sheets by the time Bartók made his first visit, in 1940, to the United States for concert and lecture purposes.

The second voyage, with Bartók as emigrant, was made in October. Taking up residence in New York, he commenced a busy schedule of public appearances as recitalist and lecturer (for the most part on tour of the United States); as research follow at Columbia University, where he transcribed recordings of the Milman Parry Collection (owned by Harvard University) of Serbo-Croatian folk music; and as ethnomusicologist, simultaneously preparing prefatory studies for his vast collection of Rumanian material and the newly acquired, less extensive Serbo-Croatian women's songs.

Although he was able to obtain a contract for the publication of the latter work, finding a publisher for *Rumanian Folk Music* (he had completed separate volumes of instrumental and vocal melodies in December, 1942) proved to be an unrealizable venture.[25] Prior to this attempt, however, Bartók completed his Serbo-Croatian study (in February) and several of the series of lectures he planned as newly designated visiting lecturer at Harvard University. These lectures exhausted him and led to his breakdown and subsequent hospitalization, beginning in mid-March, for a period of seven weeks. But the indefatigable Bartók, abhorring indolence, was "poring over some Turkish poems with the help of a handwritten Turkish-Hungarian dictionary that he himself had compiled. The poems, scattered about on his bedspread, were also in his handwriting, together with his attempts at translation. Dissatisfied

25. The contract for *Serbo-Croatian Folk Songs* (with Albert B. Lord as co-author) was signed in July, 1943; the posthumous publication, by Columbia University Press, was in 1951.

with the efforts of some philologists on his behalf, he was now having a try at it single-handed."[26] In fact, between April and June Bartók had "prepared for publication my Turkish material, again with a 100 pp. introduction, etc. All this was very interesting for me. The trouble is that extremely few people are interested in such things, although I arrived to [*sic*] highly original conclusions and demonstrations, all proved by very severe deductions. And, of course, nobody wants to publish them. . . ."[27]

During this period of time Bartók was also undergoing frustrating negotiations with the New York Public Library for the publication of his two volumes of Rumanian folk music material. That institution's enthusiasm for the undertaking quickly waned when cost estimates were presented by their printer, and they withdrew their offer of publication.[28] It was perhaps then that the idea occurred to Bartók to offer the much smaller Turkish collection in place of the rejected Rumanian project. He had taken with him the various drafts of the Turkish material when he left the city for a summer convalescence in Saranac Lake, New York, at the end of June. By the time he was to return to New York, in mid-October, he had completed the fair copy of the extra-musical portion of the work (introduction, texts and translations, marginalia) and, moreover, the sketch of the *Concerto for Orchestra*.[29] On 3 October he wrote to the Library that

> . . . nothing can be done with the Rumanian material for the time being. Fortunately, however, I have another work, to offer for pub-

26. Joseph Szigeti, *With Strings Attached*, 2nd ed. (New York: Alfred A. Knopf, 1967), p. 271.

27. *NYBA* Correspondence File, letter to Ralph Hawkes, dated 31 July 1943. The use of the word "them" refers also to the two volumes of *Rumanian Folk Music* mentioned in a preceding paragraph in this letter which, as a matter of fact, probably was intended as an indirect approach to Boosey & Hawkes to publish both studies.

28. *NYBA* Correspondence File, letter from the NYPL to Bartók, dated 30 June 1943.

29. See below, p. 15, for details concerning this manuscript.

lishing, about less than half the size of the Rumanian one. It is the "Turkish rural folkmusic from Asia Minor. . . ."

This work contains the first collection of rural Turkish folkmusic ever made by systematic research work, and ever published. The Introduction contains a description of how to determine the approximate age limit of rural folksong material, in certain specific cases. Such problems have never yet been described and published. Therefore, this feature of the book has an international significance. Besides this, many other highly interesting questions are treated in the Introduction.[30]

The Library's rejection of the Turkish book on 15 October, coupled with Hawkes's 8 September letter that a Boosey & Hawkes publication of the Rumanian volumes must await the end of the war, prompted this reaction from Bartók:

As for the bad ones [news]—I mention only a few. First: the impossibility of publishing my scientific works (Rumanian, Turkish folk music material). Of course my Essay on Serbo-Croatian folk songs is going to be published by the Columb. University Press, perhaps next fall it will be issued. But for the others, there is not much hope. What made my [*sic*] especially angry was the unfair way negociation [*sic*] with the New York Public Library were conducted. It would take too much space and it is not worth wile [*sic*] to describe the details of these unhappy dealings.[31]

On 14 December Bartók deposited the master-sheet draft of the first two volumes of *Rumanian Folk Music* (and, on 1 July 1944, *Turkish Folk Music from Asiá Minor*) "at the Columbia University Music Library—there they are available to those few persons (very few indeed) who may be interested in them."[32]

30. *NYBA* Correspondence File.

31. *NYBA* Correspondence File, letter to Wilhelmine Creel Driver, dated 17 December 1943. See also *Lev. 2*, p. 181.

32. Ibid.

THE MANUSCRIPTS

The source materials fall into two basic categories for editorial purposes: Music (Part One) and Texts (Part Two). The first category comprises those manuscripts related to the music examples, the notes to the melodies, and the prefatory and miscellaneous materials. The second category has to do with the poetic texts, the notes to the texts, and the various reference materials Bartók used to prepare the text translations and the introductory remarks.

The music examples. The first draft of the melodies is contained in the first seventy-five pages of Bartók's field sketchbook, a small (12 × 17 cm.) cloth-covered music manuscript notebook in which the melodies are notated basically in the order of accession (1–93).[33] A second set of numeric designations, with or without parenthetic lowercase letters to indicate subparts, and numbered from 1 to 60, serve as pointers to the appropriate cylinder on which each melody is recorded. Several of the notations have underlying texts; many have descriptive commentaries.

The second draft is composed of 122 pages, which Bartók left behind when he emigrated to the United States in 1940. Notated on the basis of the phonographed melodies, this material contains the author's Hungarian annotations.[34]

The third draft consists of ninety-eight pages of Ozalid prints

33. The collected material is preceded by two pages of notations made by Bartók from recordings he heard at the Istanbul Conservatory of Music (see p. 5, above). This interesting document (*NYBA* MS. code no. 80FSS1) has, additionally, the first draft of Bartók's *Concerto for Orchestra.*

34. According to the description of Dr. Kurt Reinhard, Professor of Ethnomusicology at the Free University of Berlin, who had access to a facsimile of this draft (and a taped copy of the recordings), which had been sent from Budapest to the Berlin Museum für Völkerkunde. His detailed study of the facsimiles enabled him to provide the answers to several problems that arose during the editorial process. (A facsimile of melody No. 21b. appears facing p. 16 in his book *Türkische Musik*, which was published by the Museum in 1962.)

Another draft is reported by Lászlo Somfai in his letter to the editor, dated 27 April 1971. Contained in the Budapest Bartók Archivum, it "consists of 115 sheets (330 × 196 mm.) . . . the whole material is a carbon copy of Bartók's handwriting [except for melody No. 16 which is written with green ink]. . . ."

reproduced from master sheets (Draft 4). Addenda in the form of designation and classification symbols appear in pencil. Corrigenda were entered in separate steps by means of red, green, and blue crayon. This draft, prepared in New York, contains indications as to how the original master sheets are to be cut up and reassembled in uniform page-length format.

The fourth draft—the third chronologically, and fifth in terms of Bartók's preparation of the music examples for publication purposes—is represented by 115 pages of master sheets written with black ink.[35] Originally prepared in Budapest as ninety-eight pages of varying length, it was cut up and reassembled by Bartók, using transparent cellulose tape, after he had arrived in New York. Editorially emended, this draft constituted the version used in the present publication.

Notes to the melodies. Here, too, the first and second drafts are embodied in the respective drafts of the melodies.

The third draft—in Hungarian and apparently extracted from the annotations made in the second draft of the melodies—consists of ten fragments which, for the most part, originally were letters addressed to Bartók between 1936 and 1937. The autograph clearly indicates that the draft was written on at least two different occasions and then corrected at a later time.

The fourth draft is placed as pages 116–129 in the first compilation of the complete work.[36]

The fifth draft appears as pages 116–126 in the second compila-

35. The basic music notation was probably autographed by Jenő Deutsch, a former Bartók pupil, who prepared the clean copies of Bartók's Rumanian folk music material (see fn. 24, above). As mentioned above (p. 14), the master sheets were deposited by Bartók in the Columbia University Music Library; they were photostated there prior to the preparation and subsequent facsimile printing of the manuscript for this publication.

36. The order of parts is as follows: introduction to the melodies, pp. i–xlix; music examples (master-sheet drafts), pp. 1–115; notes to the melodies, pp. 116–129; introduction to the texts, pp. 129–130; notes to the texts, p. 131; bibliography, pp. 131–132. The texts and their translations are in separate compilations, ordered according to the respective melody numbers (see description below).

tion of the complete work.[37] Editorially emended, it served as the final copy for this publication.

Introduction to the melodies. The first draft is placed as pages i–xlix in the first compilation (see fn. 36), and the second draft as pages i–xli in the second compilation (see fn. 37). The latter, editorially emended, served as the final copy for this publication.

The poetic texts. The first version, alluded to in the historical narrative that precedes this chapter, is in two parts: the relatively few text lines that underlie the melody sections in Bartók's field sketchbook (the first draft of the melodies), and the jottings made on the spot by A. Adnan Saygun.[38]

What appears to be the second draft is a small (12×18 cm.) cloth-covered notebook containing ninety-three numeric designations which basically indicate the order of accession. Seven designations (55, 71–72, 76–79) are followed by the word *hangszeres*—Hungarian for instrumental [piece]—and three of them are missing (45–46, 54).[39] Since fifteen of the texts (Nos. 6, 8–15, 22–23, 50–53) are in several different autographs and the remainder are holographic, this draft may have been assembled by Bartók, before he left Turkey, from the above-mentioned Saygun text jottings. Bartók's annotations, apparently made at different time intervals, appear in ink, pencil, and red crayon.

The third draft, therefore, would be the underlying texts in the second draft of the melodies (see fn. 34, above).

The fourth draft clearly indicates how thoroughly Bartók worked and reworked its contents. Except for the holographic

37. The order of parts is as follows: introduction to the melodies, pp. i–xli; music examples, pp. 1–115; notes to the melodies, pp. 116–126; introduction to the texts, p. 127; texts and translations, pp. 128–167; notes to the texts, bibliography, p. 168.

38. For certain reasons this draft was not available for examination, nor was it feasible to obtain a detailed description of its contents.

39. As Bartók indicates here, No. 45 appears with the respective melody in the field sketchbook. No. 46 is missing, and No. 54 appears in typescript form on a separate leaf that had been folded and placed inside the notebook.

text Nos. 7b., 34, and 53–54, this typescript collection of cut up pieces or glued fragments was probably drafted originally in two parts.[40] Each text shows four ordinal designations, of which the first three (typescript, ink, then pencil numerals, with or without parenthetic lowercase letters) are struck out. Typescript or holographic annotations in French are, except in the many cases where they have been cut out, struck out and replaced by English comments. It was undoubtedly a carbon copy of this draft in its original form that Bartók prepared in Budapest, on separate occasions, and sent to László Rásonyi for checking.[41]

The fifth draft is the fair copy in black ink that Bartók deposited in 1944 in the Columbia University Music Library. This version of the texts, unretouched (see pp. 22-23 and fn. 45, below), served as final copy for facsimile reproduction.

The text translations. The first rendition is either Bartók's Hungarian and French translations of selected words in the second draft of the texts, or Saygun's French translation of the complete Turkish texts (see p. 17, and fn. 38, above.)

The available correspondence permits no more than conjecture as to the nature of the third draft: Bartók probably prepared a typescript copy of Saygun's translations and sent them to Rásonyi for checking.[42]

Since Bartók writes in his Introduction (p. 215, below) that the English translations were "made by Mrs. G. Kresz on the basis of a

40. The holographs were written on paper which bears an American watermark. The remainder of the material shows a watermark of a sailboat within a circle, or joined leaves bearing acorns and what appears to be a berry.

41. See p. 10, above. Bartók stapled together the various-sized papers, totalling seventy-six pieces, in five sets: text Nos. 1a.–8e., 9–16, 17a.–32, 33–48b., and 49–59. Emendations appear in blue ink, pencil, and red and blue crayon. Here and there are found black ink additions which clearly indicate that Bartók used this draft to prepare the fair copy of the texts (Draft 5).

42. In his letter to Rásonyi (see other details on p. 11, above), dated 12 May 1938, Bartók writes: "[ ] designates in the French text the complements necessary for full understanding, while (=) denotes the explanation of certain expressions in the text." It is also possible but probably doubtful that Bartók sent the Saygun translations (Draft 1 or 2) for evaluation.

literal French and Hungarian translation," there is the possibility that a Hungarian version of the Turkish texts was intended.[43]

As for the English rendition just mentioned, the details concerning preparation of its preliminary version are as yet unknown. On hand, however, is a typescript draft, consisting of forty-nine leaves, in which the texts are placed in their final order; the total impression is that of a fair copy.[44] But there are a number of cut-out sections as well as emendations in pencil and blue ink. Additions in black ink indicate that Bartók used this draft to prepare the final form of the English translations.

The fair copy of the English translations is composed of those pages, written in black ink, which face the respective pages in Draft 5 of the Turkish texts. This version of the text translations, unretouched (see pp. 22-23 and fn. 45, below), served as final copy for facsimile reproduction.

Introduction to the texts. The first draft is placed as pages 129–130 in the first compilation (described in fn. 36, above), and the second draft as page 127 in the second compilation (see fn. 37). The latter, editorially emended, served as final copy for this publication.

Notes to the texts, Bibliography. Other than the difference in pagination, the same remarks made in the preceding description of the Introduction to the texts are applicable for these sections.

Miscellaneous reference material. Two Turkish reference items have already been mentioned: first, the primer *Okuma Kítabı* with Bartók's pencilled marginalia; and second, the self-compiled

43. According to Lászlo Somfai's letter to the editor, dated 27 April 1971, there are seven packages of text translations in the Budapest Bartók Archivum. From Somfai's descriptions the following information is available: autograph manuscript of the complete texts in Hungarian translation; autograph manuscript, incomplete, of side-by-side Turkish and French texts; carbon copy of the typescript Turkish texts, corrected by Bartók and other hands; carbon copy of the typescript English translation of the texts; original and two carbon copies of the French translation of the texts, corrected by Bartók and by other hands.

44. The watermark (Whiting Mutual Bond) is the same one that appears on the four holographic Turkish texts (Draft 4, see fn. 40, above) and on pp. 116–132 of the introduction and notes to the texts (see fn. 36). Therefore, the probable year of preparation is 1943.

Turkish dictionary and reference notebook (spiral bound, 12× 19 cm., written in pencil and ink) containing Hungarian translations. The third item is a compilation of English phrases used by Bartók in his Turkish and Serbo-Croatian studies: three letter-size sheets of bond paper, each folded in half, in which Bartók's originally conceived expressions appear side by side with their idiomatically correct equivalents.

ADDENDA AND CORRIGENDA

The editorial emendations which are listed below represent the results of a thorough comparative survey of all the Turkish materials found among Bartók's papers, including, moreover, other reference sources that are listed in the preceding discussion of manuscripts. The marginalia indicate editorially derived emendations; all other addenda and corrigenda were made on the basis of the author's proofreading of his work, which, for one reason or another, had not been entered in the fair copy when that ostensibly final draft was deposited in the Columbia University Music Library on 1 July 1944.

ADDITIONS TO THE MUSICAL PART

Melody No.	Staff	Measure	Description
2	3	2	[♭3] [a]
6	2	2	*Extensor to* lin [b]
8b.	1	1	*
8c.	12	1	*Apostrophe to* Ekmeğñ
11	4	3	*Wavy underline to* ye
12	7,11	1	n *to read* ñ
17a.	1	1	** [c]

a. Caesura symbols, here and in the author's Introduction represented by half-brackets and boxes, are in the form of semi- and full circles in the manuscript.

b. Editorial addition.

c. Editorial addition, in accordance with the respective Note ** to this melody.

Melody No.	Staff	Measure	Description
21a.	4–5,		
	9–10,		
	14–15	1	*Vertical brace*
	9	1	-rin *to read* -rı̆n
	12	3	*Wavy underlines* [d]
22	9	2	Ayagı̆na *to read* Ayağı̆na
	12	1	(r.)
31	5,6	2	-ga *to read* -ğa
34	2	4	[1]
35	3	1	-gi *to read* -ği
36	1	4	7 *to read* [7]
	2	2	[♭3]
40	3	2	[1]
	4	2	[1]
43b.	1	1	**
43c.	1	1	* [e] *and* 1[a] volta
48a.	3,4,7,		
	8,12,13	3	r.
48b.	3	3	[1]
	3,4,7,		
	13,14,		
	17,18	3	r.
	8–10	1	(r.?){
52	5–6	1	(r.){
	11	1	(r.)
55d.	5	1	-gi *to read* -ği
57	3	3–4	(r.)
60	1	1	Kemençe
61	1	1	1[a] volta
App. I, II, III, IV, V	1	1	* [e]

d. Editorial addition, in accordance with the given syllabic structure of eleven syllables (see the further evidence offered in the underlying text of the following line, m.3).

e. Editorial addition, in accordance with the respective Note * to this melody.

The other corrections required in the music examples are described in the following list:

No. 8c. In line 2, second measure, the author's text-line extensor was converted to hyphens, in accordance with the syllabic structure of the underlying text.
No. 12 One asterisk was deleted above the first measure of the skeleton form of the melody, as were the parentheses enclosing *ñ* in the last word of the second line, all in accordance with preliminary draft instructions.
No. 15 The range designation was altered from a plus sign to a dash.
No. 18 In accordance with preliminary draft instruction, the single asterisk following the county name in the data section was deleted.
No. 41 In the first measure of the fifth stanza the word *Vay* had been marked with a wavy underline. Since the function of this word exactly fits the author's description of a Turkish performance peculiarity (see p. 49, below), in which certain rhythm-altering syllables are placed on the first downbeat of a measure, the wavy underline was replaced by a bracket.
No. 45 In accordance with the final copy of the texts, the refrain designation (*r.*) in the first measure of the fourth and ninth lines was emended to read, respectively, (1.*r.*) and (2.*r.*). The refrain designation in line 14, however, indicated by the author as 1. *refr.* in the texts, was emended to read (3. *r.*), since this refrain differs from the other two in terms of text content, syllabic structure, and melodic contour.
No. 49d. In accordance with the final copy of the texts, the hyphen appearing between the first two words of the eighth text line was deleted.

In view of the calligraphic quality of Bartók's autographed Turkish texts and translations, it was decided to reproduce them in facsimile rather than typeset form—and without editorial emendation of the manuscript.[45] The reader is therefore advised to enter the following additions and corrections in the pertinent texts (pp. 216–249).

No. 1a. Line 2: zĭndan.
No. 6 Line 6: Circassian.
No. 7a. English title: Lullaby.
No. 7b. Line 3: (2. refr.).
No. 9 Line 3: bağĭşladĭ.
No. 14 Line 3: ğavuş/tur.
No. 15 Line 1: İstanbuldan.
Line 2: gĭ/zĭna.
No. 16 Line 8: Işte.
No. 17a. Line 11: İstanbuldan.
Line 12: sevdiğĭ.
No. 17b. Line 8: ağĭz'.
No. 17c. Line 13: 2).
No. 19 Line 4: İzmiri.
Line 16: İstanbulu.
No. 20 Footnote: 6) ölmeyile.
No. 21a. Line 13: ğa/tar.
No. 22 Lines 8, 12: (refr.).
No. 23 Line 15: zalĭm.
No. 28 Line 6: İki.
No. 31 Line 1: kürd.
No. 32 Line 2: greeted.
Line 9: İki.
No. 38 Line 5: 3. = 2.[46]
No. 41a. English title: Rain-begging Song.

45. Any attempt to enter certain corrections would have marred the calligraphy or damaged the manuscript.

46. Editorial addition. Melody No. 38 shows the third melody stanza underlaid with the second text stanza.

No. 45 Line 13: 3. refr.[47]
No. 47 Line 14: 7.
Line 16: 8.
No. 49a. Line 26: içelim.
Line 30: 30.
Line 31: thighs.
No. 56 Lines 5, 13: Circassian.
No. 58 Line 9: diyoñ.

Although Bartók stresses the importance of repetition in his discussion of text-stanza structure (below, p. 197), he neglected to provide nine texts with repetition signs (|: :|): Nos. 4, 14, 17b., 23, 45, 48a.b., 58, and 59. These signs should be added to those text lines whose counterparts are underlaid in the respective melodies.[48]

The following discrepancies between the Turkish texts and their counterparts underlying the respective melodies are listed here for the convenience of the reader:

No. 4 text = *geliyor*; melody = *geliyo'*.
No. 18 text (st. 1) = |: *yareli* :|; melody = *yareli, yaralī* (*sic*).
text (st. 2) = |: *berk benim* :|; melody = *berk benim, berk beni.*
No. 21b. text (st. 1) = |: *gelir* :|; melody = *geli, Gelir,* |: *gelir* :|.
text (st. 2) = *Durnadan-mī*; melody = *Durnudan* (*sic*)-*mi*.
text (st. 2) = |: *gelin* :|; melody = *gelin, Gelin,* |: *gelin* :|.
No. 22 text (st. 2) = |: *sürmelim* :|; melody = *sürmelim, sürmeli.*
No. 30 text (st. 2, refrain) = *sürmelim, dost*; melody = *sürmeli, dost* (this last word bears a wavy underline).
No. 37 text (st. 1) = *işledim*; melody = *işledim, Aman, işledim.*
text (st. 2) = *dişledim*; melody = *dişledim, Aman, dişledim.*

47. Instead of: 1. refr. See the remark on p. 22 concerning the editorial treatment of the respective melody.

48. In fact, in a marginal note (below, p. 197), Bartók refers to repetitions in text No. 23, and on p. 198 he mentions repeats occurring in text Nos. 45, 47, 48a.b., 58, and 59.

text (st. 2) = *dişineyn*; melody = *dişineyn, Aman, dişineyn.*
text (st. 3) = *silamĭ*; melody = *silamĭ, Aman, silamĭ.*
text (st. 4) = *yarĭmĭ*; melody = *yarĭmĭ, Aman, yarĭmĭ.*
text (st. 4) = *yaşĭnan*; melody = *yaşĭnan, Aman, yaşĭnan.*

No. 38 In stanza 1 the melody shows *sözüne* as a repeated word, and in stanza 2 of the melody *gözüme* appears three times.

No. 39 Text words ending in *-dür* or *-ler* (st. 1, 3) seem to end in *-dün* or *-en* in the melody (or perhaps *-dü, -e?*).

No. 47 In the fourth and fifth stanzas the second text line is repeated in the melody, not the first text line, and it also contains the syllables *la la*.

No. 51 In all seven lines of the melody the syllable *oy* occurs as double or triple repetitions, not one or two repetitions (line 6 has none) as shown in the text.

Nos. 55b.c. text (st. 2) = *güzelin*; melody = *gözelin.*

No. 55d. text (st. 3) = *memeleri*, melody = *memelerey.*

No. 56 The last line (st. 4, refrain) of this text does not appear in the melody.

Turning next to the Notes to the Melodies section, the following remarks describe the editorial emendations involved:

No. 13b. ** to read ***.
No. 17a. Notes * and ** were added.
No. 21b. Note ** was added.
No. 22 *** to read ****.
No. 55d. Note * was added.
No. 62 No. 21 to read No. 21b.[49] Note *** was added, and the Note that had been designated with three asterisks was transferred (as designated) to No. 63.
No. 63 Notes *, **, and *** were added.
Appendix Single asterisks were added to each Note.[49]

49. Editorial addition.

As regards the author's Introduction, few additions and corrections were needed, other than the usual orthographical, grammatic, and idiomatic lapses that occurred here and there. Format improvements, such as tabulations, follow the procedures used in editing Bartók's *Rumanian Folk Music* volumes. Certain emendations, however, should be placed on record, since they are of editorial origin.

In the descriptive tabulations of melody classes the entry for Class 17 originally listed one melody as representing this category (No. 48). There are actually two variants to this melody; therefore, the a. and b. designations have been added to the numerical one, and the number of melodies for this class has been changed to two. The total number of melodies, eighty-seven, stands as originally listed by Bartók. Alphabetical designations (a.b.c.d.) were also added to Class 18 melodies, originally listed as No. 49, in order to provide the reader with an explanation of why this class comprises four melodies. In marginal note 10 to this tabulation Bartók had erroneously indicated the flattened form of "dotted" rhythm as a pair of eighth-note/quarter-note figures, although the preliminary draft of the Introduction shows the second figure in the correct, reversed order of notation.

The author's references to the then unpublished manuscripts of his studies of Slovak, Serbo-Croatian, and Rumanian folk music have been emended to include publication details and, where possible, pagination references. All of the source materials quoted by Bartók, moreover, will now be found in the Bibliography (below, p. 253), similarly emended.

Omissions discovered in the list of refrains (below, p. 199) have been corrected as the result of comparative study of the melodies and their respective texts. The following melodies have been added to the list: Nos. 7b., 46, 48a.b., 52, and 57. These additions, together with a check of the author's statistical data, mandated a change in wording from "The first six of these eighteen refrains" to "The first seven of these twenty-three refrains."

Bartók's explanations to certain texts (pp. 209–210), curiously enough, are not exact duplications of the published text translations, although he italicized the pertinent words. It was not possible, however, to editorially resolve the discrepancies here.

In the list of Counties, Villages, Performers, and Other Data (below, pp. 53–55) the melody number for the village of Kelköy has been changed from 14 to 13a.; for Çardak, from 43 to 43d.; and for Ankara, from 48 to 48b. Italicization of patronymics, omitted by the author, was provided for the names Cuma (village of Çardak), Karakuş (Kelköy), and Kĭr (Tabaklar).

In the Explanation of Signs Used in the Music Notations (below, pp. 58–61) section 20 has been added (based on the author's own explanation) as a convenience to the reader.[50]

The Explanation of Signs Used in the Texts (below, pp. 212–213), represents an editorial amplification of Bartók's prefatory remarks to the texts and translations. These remarks originally incorporated the first two of the eleven sections now comprising the explanatory remarks to the texts. The remainder were derived from the author's Introduction, extracted from the similar listing in Bartok's *Rumanian Folk Music*, 3:xl, c, or based on special procedures Bartók followed in the Turkish texts.

Concerning the editing of the Bibliography, see the remarks made above (p. 26). And, finally, it should be noted that the last two paragraphs of the author's Preface were originally placed by him in the Introduction (following the Conclusions section) in the manuscript drafts. In view of their content as acknowledgements, and taking into consideration the rather abrupt termination of the original form of Bartók's Preface, it seemed advisable to transpose these two paragraphs to their present position.

The photographs of Anatolian peasant performers were furnished by Kurt Reinhard. I am further indebted to him for his

50. Derived from the similar listing (section 13) in the Introduction to Part Two of Vol. IV (Rumanian Carols and Christmas Songs [*Colinde*]) of Bartók's *Rumanian Folk Music*, p. 70.

assistance in regard to my comparative survey of the source materials related to the editorial process.

A special acknowledgement is tendered to Jack Heller, Professor of Computer Science, the State University of New York at Stony Brook, for his guidance and encouragement in the construction of the computerized indexes that form the appendices to this book, and to Lászlo Somfai and Adrienne Gombocz, of the Budapest Bartók Archivum, for annotations of correspondence and descriptions of source materials.

My gratitude is extended also to Philip Winters and Richard Tószhegy for editorial and translation services, and last—but surely not least!—my previously expressed thanks to my wife are iterated here for her help in the preparation of this work.

New York BENJAMIN SUCHOFF

Preface

by Béla Bartók

IN 1936, as a result of a suggestion by Dr. László Rásonyi, teacher at the University of Ankara, I was invited by the Ankara branch of the political party Halkevi to give a few lectures there, appear as soloist with the Ankara orchestra, and do some research work on Turkish folk music in appropriately chosen villages. I very gladly accepted the invitation as I had long desired to investigate Turkish folk music at first hand and, especially, to find out if there was any relation between Old Hungarian and Old Turkish folk music. It became more and more imperative to obtain an answer to this question, since a comparison between Old Hungarian folk music on the one hand, and the folk music of the Cheremiss (Mari) people[1] and the Turko-Tartar inhabitants of the Kazan area[2] in Russia on the other hand, resulted in the establishment of a definite relationship between the folk music of these various peoples. It seemed highly important to know whether Turkish folk music contained a similar stock of melodies, for this would suggest the possibility of far-reaching conclusions.

The period available for the research work was unfortunately rather short; we had only nine or ten days at our disposal. In Ankara the plans for our journey were thoroughly discussed, es-

1. The Cheremiss people live on the banks of the upper Volga and are of Finno-Ugrian racial origin (but they were subject to considerable Old Turkish influence on their language and civilization about a thousand to fifteen hundred years ago).

2. Their language is very closely related to that of the Turks of Asia Minor.

pecially the question concerning which area of the rather extended Turkish territory should be chosen for the work. Again on the suggestion by Dr. Rásonyi, we finally decided on the winter quarters of the so-called Yürük tribes, a nomadic people living in the Taurus mountain regions during the summer and, during the winter, in the environs of Osmaniye, a place not far from the southern seashore, about fifty or sixty miles to the east of Adana (Seyhan). The presumption was that people exhibiting such ancient migratory customs may have better preserved their old musical material than a more settled people.

The Ankara branch of the Halkevi political party appointed Mr. Ahmed Adnan Saygun as my interpreter, who also undertook the notation of the texts on the spot. In addition, two "observers," Mr. Necil Kâzim and Mr. Ulvi Cemal, both from the Ankara music school, came with us.

Prior to the journey to the Adana area we did some occasional collecting work twice in Ankara, on 16 and 17 November. The next day I left the capital for Adana, accompanied by these three gentlemen, and with great expectations for the discovery of at least a few melodies belonging to the above-mentioned characteristic old stock of material—expectations which were heightened by the discovery of two melodies of a similar type during the preliminary research on 16 November.

I feel obligated to express my innermost gratitude to all those who assisted in the achievement of this research work. First of all, to the leaders of the Ankara branch of the Halkevi, who organized the journey and gave me every possible help; to Dr. Lázló Rásonyi, the *spiritus rector* of the enterprise; to His Excellency Zoltán Máriássy, at that time the Hungarian minister; to Dr. Hamid Zübeyr, head of all the museums in Turkey; to Mr. Ali Riza Bey, director of the Adana Museum; and to the Hungarian Academy of Sciences in Budapest, for their assistance.

Thanks are also due to Mr. Ahmed Adnan Saygun who made the transcriptions of the texts on the spot and obtained their

French translation for me, which served as a basis for the English version; and, finally, to an expert in Budapest, who prefers to remain anonymous, who took great care in revising the texts and in ascertaining the meaning of a considerable number of dialectical words.

Bartók with nomadic tribesmen in Osmaniye

PART ONE

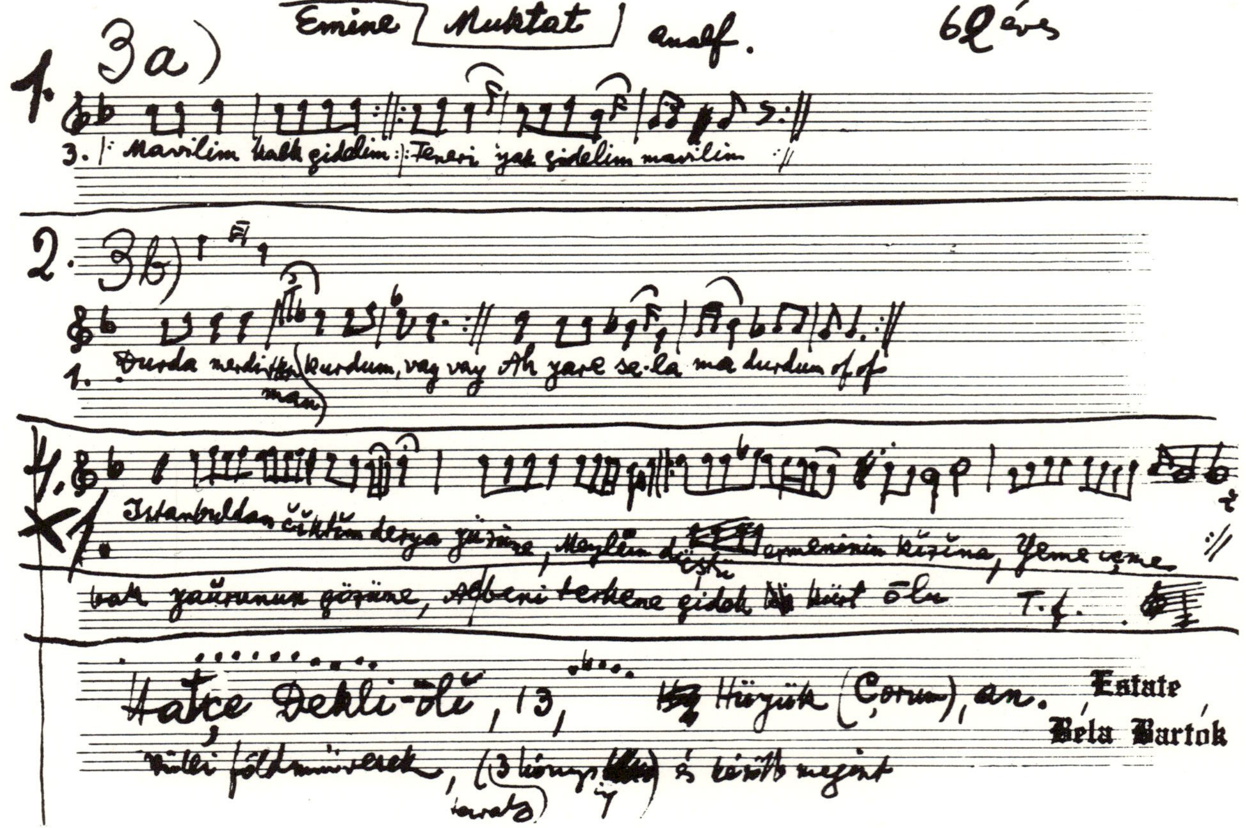

Page from Bartók's Turkish field sketchbook

Introduction to Part One

STRUCTURE OF THE MELODIES

DESPITE the small number of the melodies—seventy-eight vocal and nine instrumental pieces—it seemed advisable to group them according to a certain system. A detailed description of the system cannot be given for lack of space.[3] The principles used in grouping will, however, distinctly appear to anyone perusing, with sufficient attention, the material as published here. Nevertheless, some of the procedures used must be explained.

In order to facilitate the comparison of these or other folk melodies, each of them is transposed into a pitch which presents g^1 as the final tone. The original pitch is indicated by a black note without stem at the beginning of each melody; this note always refers to g^1. Certain symbols are used:

(a) I to VII for the scale degrees g–f^1, 1 to 12 for g^1–d^2;

(b) Arabic figures followed by a comma for the syllabic number of the melody sections;[4]

(c) Scale-degree symbols described in a), separated by a dash, for range (ambitus) of the melodies: the first figure indicating the lowest degree, the second the highest.

3. See my description of similar methods in B. Bartók and A. B. Lord, *Serbo-Croatian Folk Songs* (New York: Columbia University Press, 1951) which contains seventy-five music examples from the Milman Parry Collection of records at the Widener Library of Harvard University.

4. That is, a portion of the melody generally corresponding to a text line.

The grouping of the melodies resulted in the establishment of the following main Classes:

Class	Description of the Melodies	Melody No.	No. of Melodies[5]
1.	*Parlando*[6] isometric[7] four-section, with 8-syllable sections	1–9	*15*
2.	*Parlando* isometric four-section, with 11-syllable sections	10–23	*18*
3.	*Parlando* isometric three-section, with 11-syllable sections	24	*1*
4.	*Parlando* isometric two-section, with 8-syllable sections	25–26	*2*
5.	*Parlando* isometric two-section, with 11-syllable sections	27–29	*3*
6.	*Parlando* isometric two-section, with 14-syllable sections	30	*1*
7.	*Parlando* isometric four-section, with 7-syllable sections	31	*1*
8.	*Parlando* isometric four-section, with 9-syllable sections	32	*1*
9.	*Parlando* isometric three-section, with 8- (= 3+2+3) syllable sections	33	*1*
10.	*Parlando* isometric three-section, with 10- (= 5+5) syllable sections	34	*1*
11.	*Parlando* heterometric[8] four-section	35	*1*
12.	*Parlando* heterometric three-section	36–39	*4*
13.	*Tempo giusto*[9] isometric four-section, with "dotted"[10] rhythm and 7- or 7+7-syllable sections	40–44	*7*
14.	*Tempo giusto* heterometric four-section, with "dotted" rhythm	45	*1*
15.	*Tempo giusto* isometric four-section	46	*1*
16.	*Tempo giusto* isometric three-section	47	*1*

5. Variants are counted separately.
6. *Parlando* means a kind of free rhythm.
7. Isometric means melody sections (text lines) with equal syllabic number.
8. Heterometric means melody sections with unequal syllabic number.
9. *Tempo giusto* means a more or less rigid rhythm.
10. "Dotted" rhythm is a combination mostly of ♪♩. and ♩.♪ patterns or—as their flattened form—of ♪♩ and ♩ ♪; ♩ ♩ will also occur in the first case, ♫. in the second case.

Class	Description of the Melodies	Melody No.	No. of Melodies
17.	*Tempo giusto* heterometric four-section	48	*2*
18.	Rain-begging songs (with motif structure)	49	*4*
19.	Melodies with indeterminable structure or of suspicious origin	50–59	*13*
20.	Instrumental pieces	10b., 43c., 60–66	*9*
	Total:		**87**

If the isometric classes contain more than one melody, their melodies are further grouped into subclasses and groups according to the pitch of the final tone of their melody sections, considering first the tone of the second section (main caesura, marked by □), then the tone of the preceding (first) section marked by ⌉), and finally that of the following (third) section (marked by ⌈).[11] Classes 1 and 2, containing thirty-three melodies (forty-three percent), obviously form the most important part of the material.

The characteristics of Class 1 (about twenty percent of the collected vocal material) are as follows:

(1) Eight-syllable melody sections in *parlando* rhythm which may be considered as a derivation from supposedly original equal eighth values: ♪♪♪♪ | ♪♪♪♪ ‖ ; the transformation of the values results in the most varied—though not always stable—rhythmical formations, showing as a general feature the rather considerable prolongation of section final tones or, at least, that of the second and fourth section.

(2) More or less richly ornamented, with melismatic groups of various kinds.

(3) A scale with minor third, for the most part in Dorian mode (in four cases the Aeolian mode: melody Nos. 1b., 2, 3, 4), in which the second (sometimes the sixth) degree is frequently unstable (↓).

11. In three-section melodies the main caesura (□) will be at the end of either the first or the second section.

(4) The main caesura (final tone of the second section) is ♭3 in four cases, 4 in three cases, 5 in seven cases, and 8[12] in a single case. The secondary caesuras (final tone of the first and third sections) are 5 in eight, 4 in two, and ♭6, 7, ♭10[12] in single cases; ♭3 in eight, 5 in three, 4 in two, and 7, 8[12] in single cases. The position of section final tones on the ♭3, 4, 5, 7, and 8 degrees (excepting only ♭6 in melody No. 2), that is, exclusively on the degrees of the pentatonic scale , offers adequate evidence of the latent pentatonic structure existing in these melodies.

(5) The fact that 5 is the most frequent final tone in the first melody-sections, and ♭3 in the third sections, already shows the prevalence of a so-called "descending" structure of the melodic line, which means that the first half of the melody is placed approximately in the upper half of the octave, the second half (or last quarter) of the melody in the lower half.

If we compare these characteristics with those of the Old Hungarian melodies with eight-syllable sections,[13] we will see that they are practically identical. The only differences are as follows:

a) the Turkish melodies in question never touch the VII degree which, however, occurs rather frequently in the Hungarian melodies;

b) the Hungarian melodies show more clearly the pentatonic structure, not only in the final tones of the melody sections, as the Turkish melodies do, but even in their melodic line;

c) the so-called "transposing" structure (a variety of the "descending" structure), comparatively frequent in the Hungarian material, in which the second half of the melody is a repetition of the first half a fifth lower, does not appear in the Turkish melodies.

12. These exceptionally high degrees evidently are the result of the exceptional range (1–11) in melody No. 9.

13. See their detailed morphological description in B. Bartók, *Hungarian Folk Music* (London: Oxford University Press, 1931), pp. 14–25 (hereafter cited as *Hung. Folk Music*).

Incidentally, as a circumstance of minor importance, it can be stated that the relationship between the Turkish and Hungarian materials is particularly conspicuous in the melodies found in central Hungary (the area situated between the south bend of the Danube River and the western border of Transylvania), designated in *Hung. Folk Music* as dialect region III.

In addition to this striking similarity in the characteristic features of the Turkish and Hungarian *parlando* melodies with eight-syllable sections, is the occurrence of decided Hungarian variants in most of the nine Turkish melodies or variant groups of Class 1. The complete Hungarian material of about 13,000 melodies, kept in Budapest, is unfortunately not available to me at the present time.[14] I can therefore quote only four Hungarian variants in the Appendix (pp. 178–179), and refer to a fifth, published in *Hung. Folk Music* as mus. ex. No. 62, as a variant of melody No. 15 of this volume. Even these few examples provide enough evidence to indicate the closest relationship or, as I would put it, the identity of both materials. This identity is an irrefutable proof of the age of these melodies: it shows the way back to the sixth or seventh century. During that period the ancestors of the Anatolian Turks lived somewhere on the borders of Europe and central Asia, in the neighborhood of other Turkish tribes; the ancestors of the Hungarians occupied an area between the Caspian Sea and the Black Sea.

We have long had evidence of Old Turkish linguistic influences, exerted by some Turkish people[15] on the Finno-Ugrian Hungarian language. We have known for several decades that the ancient Székely-Hungarian alphabet, a kind of runic or scored alphabet (*rovásírás*), first discovered in a document in the church of the Székely-Hungarian village Énlaka (Transylvania), is in close relation to a similar alphabet found in inner Asia, at the dwelling place of certain ancient Turkish tribes (inscriptions from A.D. 500–

14. See the author's commentary in *Rumanian Folk Music*, 1:20.
15. Probably by the so-called Bulgaro-Turks.

700). And now, in step, musicology brings proof of the identity of the Old Hungarian and the Old Turkish music, proof corroborated by the specimens of the mentioned Cheremiss and Kazan-Turkish folk music, which show a related music structure and even near-variants of Hungarian melodies. Considering the historical fact that these peoples lived near each other twelve to fifteen centuries ago, later moved apart to rather distant territories, and could not have had any contact with each other since their separation, it is evident that this musical style must be at least fifteen hundred years old. The fact that such a statement is at all possible makes this subject of international importance, for there is no other instance known in the world, to my knowledge, which offers the possibility of this kind of irrefutable determination of the age of folk music traced back for so many centuries. As a case in point, the northern and southern Slavs also divided during the sixth or seventh century. However, no vestiges of an ancient common Slav folk music can be discovered in their actual folk melodies.[16]

There is one argument that could possibly arise counter to the assertion that the relationship of the Old Hungarian and Old Turkish folk music can be traced as far back as the sixth or seventh century. It is common knowledge that central and southern Hungary were invaded by the Turks and occupied from the middle of the sixteenth century for more than 150 years; thus, it could be hypothesized that these one and a half centuries of occupation might have provided an occasion for the imbuement of Hungarian folk music with Turkish elements. This possibility, however, is out of the question: the Turkish occupation had an exclusively military character; indeed, Turkish settlements or villages were never founded, and there was no social interaction between the Turkish army of occupation and the Hungarian nationals. In fact, a great many Hungarians fled from the invaded territories,

16. Except for some extremely slight traces, only tentatively admitted as such in *Serbo-Croatian Folk Songs*, pp. 54, 75–76, 86–87.

leaving vast areas entirely uninhabited.[17] The only visible purpose of the occupation was to gather taxes and firmly hold the military power in Turkish hands.[18] In addition, mercenary troops composed of all kinds of people could not develop a homogeneous musical style—the only way by which any essential influence could be exerted.

The melodies of Class 1 are from the above-mentioned Yürük and adjoining areas.

Class 2—twenty-three percent of the collected vocal material—although in near relationship to Class 1, nevertheless shows some important deviations which are as follows:

(1) Eleven-syllable melody sections in *parlando* rhythm, supposedly derived from the schema .

(2) A more extended range: 1–♭10 in nine cases, 1–11 in three, 1–12 in one, 1–(♭) 9 in two, 1–8 in three; that is, generally a range of one and a third octaves.

(3) In accordance with the wider range the final tone of the first melody section is placed on a high degree: [8] in six cases, [7] in five, [9] and [♭10] one each, [5] in two, and [♭3] and [4] as single cases. The main caesura as well as the final tone of the third section, however, are generally placed on lower degrees: [4] in nine cases, [♭3] in five, [5] in two, [♭6] and [7] as single cases; [♭3] in eleven, [4] in three, and [1], [5], [8] as single cases. Nevertheless, the position of the third section in all the melodies, excepting Nos. 15 and 16, is in approximately the upper half of the range (apart from the final tone), frequently even touching the highest tones of

17. This accounts for the complete disappearance of small villages in central Hungary—a rather characteristic feature of the area.

18. The situation in the Balkan territories was quite different: these areas were conquered permanently. Turkish settlements emerged, such as the ones in Bulgaria (still in existence) and Macedonia. A considerable part of the inhabitants (for example, in Hercegovina) were converted to the Mohammedan faith by force or persuasion. Friendly or not, there was much social interaction whose traces can still be observed in the language, civilization, and even to a lesser degree in the folk music of these countries (see more details in *Serbo-Croatian Folk Songs*, pp. 55–56).

the scale. Melody Nos. 10, 11, 14, 20, 22, and 23 even have a range of a whole octave in their last section. In other words, there is a tendency to maintain the higher degrees as long as possible throughout the melodies.

(4) The melismatic groups, excepting melody Nos. 10a., 12, 15, 16, 22, and 23, present much more elaborate ornaments than those of Class 1. This circumstance perhaps may be the sign of Arabic influence, particularly as regards complicated melismatic arrangements (melody No. 21b.: last three measures of each stanza), cascadelike groups (melody No. 20: fifth measure of each stanza), and peculiar clucking sounds (melody Nos. 20, 21a.).

Traits common to Class 2 and 1 are the *parlando* rhythm, the scale, the position of section final tones almost exclusively on the pentatonic degrees, and the "descending" structure which, however, approaches its resolution later in Class 2 than in Class 1. These common characteristics link the two classes decidedly, so to say, into a twin class.

The melodies of Class 2 are from the Yürük and neighboring areas, excepting melody Nos. 15 and 16 (see below).

The features described under (1)–(4) do not occur in the Old Hungarian melodies with eleven-syllable sections; moreover, the metrical articulation of the latter is exclusively ♫♫ ♫♫ | ♪♩. 𝅗𝅥 ‖ or some other variation of this schema. Therefore, despite the related structure, no Hungarian variants of Class 2 melodies exist. Incidentally, it can be stated that some of the eighteen melodies of this class have texts of seemingly urban origin, and that the complicated aspect of the melodies somehow gives them a more artificial character in comparison with the simpler melodies of Class 1.

Melody Nos. 15 and 16 do not stem from the Yürük area but from the rather distant Çorum *vilayet* (that is, county), and they are the only Class 2 melodies which lack the distinguishing characteristics listed under (2), (3), and (4). Indeed, except for the syllabic number of the lines, their structure and character are absolutely identical with those of Class 1. As a matter of fact, they are variants of Old Hungarian melodies, regardless of the above-mentioned slight difference in the metrical articulation.

Classes 13 and 14 are next in importance—about ten percent of the collected vocal material. These are, particularly with regard to their "dotted" rhythm, related to the corresponding Hungarian classes of "dotted" rhythm melodies. Melody No. 42 even has Hungarian variants, and Nos. 40, 41, and 42 are very nearly related to Hungarian melodies not only in rhythm but also in melodic structure.

The "dotted" rhythms ♩. ♪ , ♪♩. (in faster tempo ♫ , ♫ ; in flattened rhythm ♩ ♪ , ♪♩) in Hungarian *tempo giusto* melodies with such characteristics result from the positional or natural quantity of the syllables. In the Turkish material only positional quantity occurs, since the Turkish language uses only short vowels.[19]

A very interesting peculiarity can be observed in these rhythms which occurs also in Hungarian and Rumanian melodies, and probably also in those of other peoples, which I call "rhythmic compensation." It consists of the following procedure: if for any reason a certain value is very slightly shortened or lengthened, some of the following values will be lengthened or shortened by exactly the same value in order to obtain equal measures of, let us say, 2/4 or 4/4. For example, in the second and fourth measures of melody No. 40 ♪♩⁝♩.. stands for ♪♩⁝♩. , in the third measure ♬♩⁝♩ ♪. for ♪♩⁝♩ ♪ , and so forth. No. 40 is a very good example of the consistent and frequent use of this device. In other pieces (melody Nos. 42, 45) it occurs only occasionally.

"Dotted" rhythm is extremely characteristic of certain classes of Hungarian folk melodies; it appears in some classes of Rumanian and Slovakian material, too, probably as a Hungarian influence. Our very scanty Turkish material shows not more than eight such melodies, and we do not know precisely whether "dotted"

19. Except in borrowed Arabic and Persian words which, however, occur less frequently in the rural than in the urban language, and in which the vowel lengths are more or less neglected when used in rural songs.

rhythm occurs elsewhere.[20] Therefore, this common feature in the Hungarian and Turkish material, however striking the similarity may be, cannot be taken as a convincing proof of the common origin of these rhythms.

The melodies representing the remaining classes are so few in number that no description of their type can be given and no conclusions drawn. Some of these melodies seem to be incomplete or in some way altered forms of Class 2 pieces (melody Nos. 27, 30, 35, 36, 37, 38, 39). In addition, others differ from Class 2 because of their major scale (Nos. 24, 28). Certain melodies are perhaps of urban, even European origin (Nos. 31, 32, 34, 47, 48, 52, 53, 57). And not even a guess can be made with regard to the origin of melodies such as Nos. 25, 26, 29, 33, 46, 50, 51, 54, 55, and 56. Melody No. 58, a hit song,[21] can be traced back to the Canzonetta "Halte-là! qui va là?" from Bizet's opera *Carmen*. The composer of the hit was obviously not too concerned with originality of ideas. *Habent sua fata—melodiae*!

A special account of Class 18, the Rain-begging songs (melody No. 49 and its variants), should be given. These songs have melodies with undetermined structure, consisting of repetitions of a 2/4 two-bar motif in rhythm which appears sometimes slightly transformed. They are very similar to the Children's song melodies of the Hungarians, Slovakians, and some Western European peoples, and are probably of a similar character throughout the entire Turkish territory, since the specimens in our collection stem from areas distant from one another (Ankara, Urfa, Seyhan *vilayet*) and show no essential differences. As to the ceremonies connected with the performance of these songs, investigation in that direction was unfortunately omitted. Rain-begging songs occur in the Rumanian and Serbo-Croatian material, yet are unknown in Hungarian and Slovakian territory. The Rumanian Rain-begging songs, however, generally have a de-

20. It seems that the so-called Scotch rhythm belongs to this type of rhythm.
21. See the Note to melody No. 58, p. 190.

termined four-section structure. We cannot form any decided opinion about those of the Serbo-Croatians,. since only a few specimens are known from published collections.

Whether the similarity between the above-mentioned Children's song melodies and the Turkish Rain-begging song melodies is a pure coincidence, or whether a mysterious connection exists between them, cannot be established for the moment.

Among the few instrumental pieces (Class 20), one deserves special mention: melody No. 62. Its designation "*Uzun Hava*" means "long [-drawn] air." As a matter of fact, this melody is a variant of the Rumanian *Cântec lung*[22] and the Ukraïnian *Dumy* melodies,[23] and originates from certain Persian[24] and Arabic[25] melody types. Melody No. 62 is one of the few specimens[26] of this kind known till now from Turkish territory. Its infiltration from Persian-Arabic territories can be easily explained but not its further spread into Rumanian and Ukraïnian areas, because of the missing links in the Bulgarian and Serbo-Croatian material.[27] As for the other instrumental or sung dance melodies, I had only one occasion to witness a dance performance of melody Nos. 61 and 63–66 in Çardak. A description of this event is given as follows:

One of the musicians played on an instrument something like an oboe, the *zurna*, the other on a big drum tied in front of him, a *davul*

22. See melody Nos. 643a.–g. in Vol. I (Instrumental Melodies) and Nos. 613a.–h. in Vol. II (Vocal Melodies) in B. Bartók, *Rumanian Folk Music*, and also melody Nos. 23a.–m. in Vol. V (Maramureş County) of the same publication series [previously published as *Volkmusik der Rumänen von Maramureş* (Munich: Drei Masken Verlag, 1923)].

23. Philaret Kolessa, *Melodien der ukraïnischen rezierenden Gesänge (Dumy)*, Beiträge zur ukraïnischen Ethnologie, XIII. XIV. Band, Lwow, 1910, 1913.

24. One specimen is on the Persian disc in the album "Musik des Orients" edited by E. v. Hornbostel.

25. Some of the discs commissioned by and issued for the "Institut de la Musique Orientale" of Cairo in 1932–1933 contain specimens, for example No. H.C. 26.

26. Another one was recorded by Mr. Constantin Brăiloiu in Istanbul a few years ago; the record is in the Archives of the Societatea Compozitorilor Români, Bucharest.

27. For further details, see *Serbo-Croatian Folk Songs*, p. 59.

(bass drum). He beat that drum with terrific energy with a wooden drumstick, and I really thought at times that either his big drum or my eardrum would break. Even the flames of the three flickering kerosene lamps jumped at every beat. And the dance! Four men danced, that is to say, one danced alone and the others, linked hand in hand, accompanied him with slow measured movements. Queerly enough, at times even the two musicians took part in the dance, with a few steps and gestures. After a few moments, however, the music and dancing came to an abrupt end, and one of the three dancers burst into a song. He had such a faraway, dreamy expression on his face that I can hardly find words to describe it. He began the song in a very high tenor and slowly descended at the end of his song to a more normal pitch.

After he had sung seven or eight verses, the players tuned up again for another kind of dance music. Later, a vocal solo followed in the same way as before.[28]

The alternating of dancing to instrumental accompaniment and of solo singing went on and on (see further details in the Notes to melody Nos. 43d. and 61).

SOME PECULIARITIES OF PERFORMANCE

The Turkish rural folk music is devoid of proper upbeats; in fact, structurally essential upbeats are also unknown in the folk music of the Czechs, Slovaks, Ukraïnians, Hungarians, Rumanians, Serbo-Croatians, and Bulgarians. Pseudo-upbeats, however, on syllables such as *ə*,[29] *hñ*, *ạy*, *hiy*, and so forth, are frequently used, and in a similar way as in the material of the above-listed peoples. These syllables do not belong to the proper text and must not be taken into account when determining syllabic structure. They are

28. Quoted from my article "Collecting Folksongs in Anatolia," *The Hungarian Quarterly* (Budapest), Summer, 1937. The author's revised form of this essay appears in *Béla Bartók Essays*, ed. Benjamin Suchoff (London: Faber & Faber, 1976).

29. Inverted *e*, meaning a blurred vowel similar to the Rumanian *ă*.

Zurna player

Dau̯ul player

Wedding Dance in southern Turkey

underscored with a wavy line (∿∿) in the music notations. A different kind of added syllables (*hiy* or *ah*) is to be found in melody Nos. 32, 42, and 45, which are neither pseudo-upbeats nor part of the proper text. These syllables appear, however, on the first downbeat of the measure, and they have the function of altering its original rhythm; for example, ♩♩ is changed into ♩ ♫ by adding *Ah* in melody No. 32. These added downbeat syllables are marked by ⏑ and they are also well known (in the form of *ej*, *hej*, *oj*, *hoj*) in the material of the above-mentioned peoples.

On the whole, the proper text lines form isometric text-stanza structures. In heterometric melody structures some portions of these isometric text lines are repeated, or refrain text lines of a different syllabic number are added in order to obtain heterometry.

There is a tendency to change the color of vowels or consonants,[30] to interpolate some syllables of different color during long-drawn tones, or to suppress entirely the syllable-closing consonant at the end of a section. A most peculiar *vibrato* is produced in the Yürük area, observed nowhere else. This *vibrato* generally appears on the last prolonged tone of the second and the last melody section. It is not possible to determine exactly what happens in the singer's mouth on the basis of direct observation. Judging from the emitted sound, it seems that the singer, by slight up and down vibration of his tongue, produces *y* semivowels which interrupt the continuous flow of the respective vowel. The result is a vibration in color, not in pitch. In most of the cases I tried to determine the exact number of vibrations, and to transcribe them as can be seen in melody Nos. 5 (fourth and eighth measures), 8c. (last measure), 17b. (sixth and twelfth measures), and so forth. All these interpolations and changed vowels

30. Change of vowel color during singing occurs in the music of other peoples, too.

are also underscored with a wavy line in the music notations.[31]

Another peculiarity is an emphatic performance of the successive single tones of certain melismatic groups, for example, melody No. 16 (sixth and ninth measures). Sometimes the emphasis is enhanced by the interpolation of certain peculiar "clucking" sounds, as in melody No. 20 (third and seventh measures, and so forth). Similar emphatic performance of melismatic tones occurs in the Serbo-Croatian material.[32] This phenomenon probably can be ascribed to the influence of Arabic urban music.

The pitch of the second degree (a^1 or $a^1\flat$) frequently shows a certain instability, being either slightly lower than $a^1\natural$, slightly higher than $a^1\flat$, or sometimes neutral. The deviations, marked by $\downarrow$ and $\uparrow$ signs,[31] occur also on the sixth degree (e^2 or $e^2\flat$) but less frequently.

Between an open last syllable of a word and the word-beginning vowel of the following word, generally a hiatus-filling consonant is inserted. For the most part *ñ* serves this purpose (melody Nos. 6, 8c., 9, 11, 12, 14, 15, 17a.b., 21a., 23, 25, 28, 34, 36, 43d., 45, 51, 52, 54, 58, 59), *y* less frequently (Nos. 1b., 8d., 14, 17c., 22, 41), and *m* only once (No. 47). The Hungarians use *j*, the Rumanians *d* and *i̯*, and the Serbo-Croatians *j* but rather rarely (at least, in the Milman Parry Collection).[33] In two cases, instead of insertion of a consonant, crasis originates: melting of two vowels (melody No. 7a.: *Ince‿elekten*; 8a.: *Gĭrĭldĭ‿elimin*). In the vast Hungarian material only one such case is known (*Hung. Folk Music* No. 10: *viseli-az isten*); similar examples occur to some extent in the Serbo-Croatian material. The Rumanian material (like the Italian), however, shows frequent use of crasis.

The emphatic pronunciation of syllable-closing consonants can

31. See Explanation of the Signs Used in the Music Notations, p. 60 (below).
32. See *Serbo-Croatian Folk Songs*, p. 77.
33. *Ibid.*, p. 81.

result in the "syllabification"[34] of the consonant, and is achieved by adding the sound ə after the consonant; the so-called liquids do not generally need this addition. The new syllable thus created is not a proper one and is to be disregarded when counting the syllables of the melody sections.

There is a tendency, at least in the Yürük and adjoining area, to sing in as high a pitch as possible, that is in the uppermost *tessitura* of the voice. This circumstance sometimes leads to certain inconveniences during research work (see the Notes to melody Nos. 3 and 12). It is a pity that I was unable to obtain any women singers (other than the old woman from Ankara and the little girl from Hüyük), all my efforts notwithstanding, because of the still prevalent religious superstition of the Mohammedans. This is a serious handicap in collecting Turkish folk songs. For instance, we do not know whether women also sing in their upper *tessitura* or whether they prefer lower ones. Do they use similar ornaments and clucking sounds in melodies with eleven-syllable sections or not? Do they sing such melodies at all or do they have some others in their repertory, never sung by men? Is it not awkward to have cradle songs recorded by men's rough-sounding voices when they evidently never sing them?! If this situation does not change, then half the Turkish population will be artificially excluded from making any contribution to folk music collections!

Terminology.—There is a very distinct demarcation between rural and urban folk songs, even to the extent of their designation, not observed elsewhere. The former are called *Türkü*, the latter *Şarkĭ*. As Kúnos has indicated in his collection of Osmanli-Turkish folk poems:

> . . . the *türkü* differs from the *şarkĭ* also in the metrical structure. . . . The metrical structure of the latter is based on quantity [of syllables], borrowed from the Arabs; that of the former is based on syllable counting

34. This word is used here in the sense of "making a syllable out of" a consonant.

[accentuated meter]. The latter has been written in a language intermixed with Arabic and Persian elements; the former arose in a rural, that is, pure Turkish language. . . . in the poetry of no other people is there such a difference between folk and art poetry. . . . For between the two categories there is a difference not only in the subject but also in the language, and what is more, the difference in their melodic style increases the discriminating features. The *türkü*-s have certain tunes and the *şarkĭ*-s others. The latter's tunes as well as their metrical structure are of Arabic origin, whereas the tunes of the former are national ones, born on Turkish soil.[35]

The expression "born on Turkish soil," of course, must be taken *cum grano salis*. Where folk melodies are born is a rather intricate question which cannot be answered in such a simple way.—As I would put it, *Türkü*-s are the melodies sung or played by Turkish rural people, wherever they may have been born; and *Şarkĭ*-s are those of the urban cultivated classes, exhibiting Arabic influence in their meter and language.[36] In the Yürük area I was informed that *Türkü* refers only to the texts; melody there is called *gayda* (*hava* being generally the known word for air = melody).

35. Ignác Kúnos, *Oszmán-török népköltési gyűtemény*, Hungarian Academy of Sciences, Budapest, 1889. [Hereafter cited as *O-t.n.g.* The reader will note that Bartók uses the breve as a diacritic above the letter *i* (*ĭ*), which changes the pronunciation to *ə* (as in *sir*). Present Turkish orthography employs this letter without dot (*ı*).]

36. It was probably the *Şarkĭ* whose performance was suddenly prohibited by Kemal Atatürk some years ago. Whether this decree was directed toward favoring the *Türkü* or the European music is not clear. Later on this decree was revoked.

COUNTIES, VILLAGES, PERFORMERS, AND OTHER DATA

Remarks: (1) During or just before 1936 a Turkish decree made it mandatory for everyone to adopt a permanent family name. Therefore, there is considerable confusion in this list: some of the singers had not yet chosen a family name and had indicated their names according to the old usage;[37] others already used their new family name preceded by the given name. The patronymic (or its substitute) or the family name is italicized in this list.

(2) All the performers are illiterate, except when indicated otherwise.

(3) The name of the *vilayet* (county) and town of Adana had just been changed to Seyhan; the latter name, therefore, appears in this list.

County	Village and Date of Recording (1936)	Name and Age of Performer	Melody Nos. Performed	Number of Melodies by:		
				Per-former	Vil-lage	County
Ankara	Ankara, 16 Nov.	Emine *Muktat*, 62	32, 33, 48b., 49a.b., 50, 51	7	**7**	*7*
Çorum	Hüyük, 16 Nov.[38]	Hatice *Deklioğlu*, 13	15, 16, 47, 48a., 52, 57	6	**6**	*6*
Kadirli	Avlik, 20 Nov.[39]	*Cinli* Ali, 32	5, 19	2		
		Ahmed *Torun*, 42 (literate)	6, 7a., 22, 25, 36, 44, 46	7	**9**	*9*

37. That is, a patronymic: father's given name + *oğlu* (son of), followed by the given name. In rare cases an attribute is substituted for the patronymic.
38. The recording took place in Ankara.
39. The recording took place in Seyhan, to which place the singers had been summoned from their village.

County	Village and Date of Recording (1936)	Name and Age of Performer	Melody Nos. Performed	Number of Melodies by: Performer	Village	County
Mersin	Dadal, 21 Nov.[40]	*Halil oğlu* Ali, 37	45, 56	2	**2**	*2*
Osmaniye	Çardak, 23 Nov.	Kâmil *Çenet*, 32 (literate)	55a.	1		
		Osman *Çenet*, 34	43d.	1		
		Yusuf *Çenet*, 27 (literate)	37	1		
		Basri *Demir*, 37 (literate)	55c.	1		
		Ibiş Mehmedin[41] Abdullah, 14	4, 27, 34, 58, 59	5		
		Mehmed oğlu Pir Sabit, 20 (literate)	26, 54, 55d.	3		
		Ömer oğlu Ali, 15 (literate)	24	1		
		Kâmil *Özgan*, 42 (literate)	8b., 55b.	2		
		? Ali, 24 / *Cuma* Ali, 38	61–66	6	**21**	
	Gebeli, 22 Nov.[42]	*Mustafa oğlu* Mehmet, 29 (literate)	43a.	1	**1**	
	Osmaniye, 22 Nov.	*Ali Bekir oğlu* Bekir, 70	7b., 8a., 10a.b., 42	5		
		Bekir oğlu Mahmud, 34 (literate)	43b.c., 60	3	**8**	*30*

Seyhan	Kara Isalĭ, 20 Nov.[43].	Zekeriye *Culha*, 23	1a.b., 17a.b., 21b., 38, 39, 41	8	**8**	
	Kelköy, 20 Nov.[43]	Abdullah *Karakuş*, 22	2, 8e., 13a., 29, 40, 49d.	6	**6**	
	Seyhan, 20, 25 Nov.	*Koca* Mehmet, 45	17c., 30, 35	3	**3**	
	Tabaklar, 22 Nov.[44]	*Kĭr* Ismail, 51	18, 23	2	**2**	
	Tüysüz,[45] 24 Nov.	*Memik Mustafa oğlu* Osman, 11	14	1		
	Tüysüz,[46] 24 Nov.	*Ahmed oğlu* Mehmet, 36	12	1		
		Ali oğlu Haci, 40–35[47]	9, 13b., 20	3		
		Bekir oğlu Mustafa, 15	3, 11	2		
		Hacĭ oğlu Ismail, 15	8c., 21a., 28	3		
		Ömer oğlu Hökkes, 35	8d.	1	**11**	*30*
Sivas	Vartan, 17 Nov.[48]	*Divrikli* Ali, 37	31, 53	2	**2**	*2*
Urfa	? 21 Nov.[49]	Abdul Kadir, 44	49c.	1	**1**	*1*

Eighty-seven melodies by twenty-seven performers from fourteen villages in eight counties.

40. The recording took place in the town of Mersin, where the singer happened to be at that time.
41. Or *Ibiş Mehmed oğlu*.
42. The recording took place in Osmaniye, where the singer happened to be at that time.
43. The recording took place in Seyhan. Both young men were summoned and led to Seyhan by gendarmes who did not even let them know the purpose for this forced journey. One can easily imagine how frightened both men were not knowing whether they were being led to prison, perhaps, for some unknown delinquency!
44. Recorded in Osmaniye.
45. Settlement of the Kumazlĭ tribe.
46. Settlement of the Tecirli tribe.
47. He did not know his exact age!
48. Recorded in Ankara.
49. Recorded in Mersin. The name of the village is somehow missing.

CHARACTERISTICS OF CERTAIN PERFORMERS

Emine Muktat is one of the inhabitants of Old Ankara, and she was born and lived the greater part of her life there when it was still a village. She exhibits all the characteristics of a village singer.

Hatice Deklioğlu went to Ankara for three months in 1933 to earn her livelihood as a servant. Her parents were village farmers at Hüyük. She returned to Ankara in 1936, and she sang her songs for me at the home of her employer, Dr. Hamid Zübeyr.

Basri Demir is a native of Çardak and a former member of the Turkish Parliament. He was the initiator of the gathering of singers, players, and dancers at Çardak who supplied all the material of that village, except the song contributed by the boy Ibiş Mehmedin Abdullah.

Ibiş Mehmedin Abdullah had a repertory whose greater part consisted of songs of doubtful (urban) origin, such as, for instance, melody Nos. 58 and 59.

? *and Cuma Ali* are from the Abdal tribe which provides professional musicians as the gypsies provide for the gypsy bands in Hungary and elsewhere. The first man, whose name is somehow missing, plays the *zurna*, the second plays the *daỵul*. Their tribe does not have a very well-established reputation, does not seem to be of Turkish origin, and is more or less despised by the Turks for several reasons, just as the gypsies are by Hungarians in many places.

Ali Bekir oğlu Bekir, as well as all the other inhabitants of Osmaniye, is a member of the Ulaş tribe. Originally nomadic, the tribe was compelled by the government to settle down about seventy years ago. *Bekir oğlu Mahmud* is his son.

Koca Mehmet is a native of Seyhan and a lumberman who conveys forest timber on rafts; he looked at least ten years older than his given age of forty-five. He spent a certain amount of time in Karsantĭ (Taurus area) and in Kara Isalĭ.

Kır Ismail, who recorded melody Nos. 18 and 23, performing with his *cura ırızva*

Kĭr Ismail is a native of the village of Tabaklar (or Tabaklarköy?) in the Düziçi-Peçeneg area, Harunie district, who happened to be in Osmaniye at that time. He looked more like a wandering professional troubador than a simple village singer, not only because of his instrument but also by reason of the complicated structure of the two melodies he contributed (although they are evidently related to the eleven-syllable melodic structure of Nos. 10–22). He cannot be regarded as reliable a source for rural songs as the other performers of the eleven-syllable melodies.

Memik Mustafa oğlu Osman, a boy, was the only singer available at the tent settlement, since all the men were away and the women refused to sing. This settlement is rather distant—perhaps fifteen miles—from the settlement of the Tecirli tribe.

Bekir oğlu Mustafa was the first singer to sing into the phonograph in his tribal settlement, and he could only be persuaded with great difficulty to do so; he was afraid he would "lose his voice" permanently if the machine should "take it." It is a joy for the student of folk music to find that as late as 1936 there were still people quite unfamiliar with talking machines, though it is quite natural that nomad tribes neither possess nor transport gramaphones on the backs of their camels to and fro between their summer and winter settlements!

Hacĭ oğlu Ismail is the son of Ali oğlu Hacĭ.

Divrikli Ali was a kind of doorman at an official building in Ankara, and he had more an urban than a rural aspect as a singer. His repertory consisted of melodies of doubtful origin.

EXPLANATION OF THE SIGNS USED IN THE MUSIC NOTATIONS

(1) At the end of each section in the first stanza (sometimes in one of the following stanzas) over the final tone or the tone considered as structurally the final tone, appear the figures in ⊐, □, or ⊏.

(2) Above the first staff at the right side appear, if necessary, the figure symbols indicating the range of the melody and the syllabic number of the melody sections. In certain melodies bracketed figures appear after the syllabic number to indicate the metrical articulation of the section; parenthetical figures appearing before it indicate the syllabic number of the text line from which the syllabic number of the melody section is derived by addition or repetition. Other symbols used in this connection are < which means: this derivation from < this source; and > which means: from this source > this derivation.

(3) If, because of the length of the melody sections, it was not possible to notate each section on a separate staff, the two staves representing a single melody section are connected by a brace (}) at the right side. The melody stanzas are distinguished by punctulated Arabic figures (1., 2., 3., and so forth).

(4) After each piece are listed the data concerning the record number in the possession of the Department of Anthropology of the National Museum at Budapest; the name of the village; the name of the *vilayet* (county) in parentheses; the name of the performer; his or her age; the indication "illiterate" if the performer could not read or write; and the date of the recording. When no record number is given, the piece was not recorded by phonograph.

(5) Asterisks, such as *, **, and so forth, refer to the Notes to the Melodies on pp. 181–192.

(6) Before the first bar of the piece is its pitch indication, a black note without stem (in treble clef for voices of women singers, or boys with yet unchanged voices; in bass clef for men singers) which always refers to g^1.

(7) When no time signatures are used, the performance is *parlando-rubato*. Parenthetical time signatures are also *parlando-rubato*, with the extension that the parenthetical values were originally intended in the respective measures, but that in some (or all) of the measures certain deviations from the indicated time values appear.

Time signatures without parentheses indicate *tempo giusto* (more or less rigid rhythm).

(8) Key signatures are used only when the respective degrees are affected throughout the entire piece. Exception: small-head notes.

(9) The sign or means a gliding (*portamento*) in which single degrees are not discernible. The same sign above or under a melismatic group indicates a blur of the group by gliding.

(10) The arrow above a note, pointing upward, means slightly higher pitch than notated; pointing downward, slightly lower pitch. Arrows are used above accidentals—even above natural signs!—as well as note heads; in the former case they are valid as long as are the respective accidentals; if they are in parentheses it means that their validity may sometimes be interrupted.

(11) Brackets ([ ]) above the staff line means that the respective portion of the melody is an addition from the structural point of view and, therefore, is not considered when determining melodic structure.

(12) Melismatic groups always have a slur. Each single note in groups connected with a beam, yet without slur, is sung to a separate syllable. A dotted slur means that what appears to be two (or more) syllables belonging to a group is regarded as structurally one syllable.

(13) The values of small-head notes connected with a large-head note by a slur, but not by a beam, have to be substituted from the value of the large-head note; for example:  equals  ; when connected with a beam:  , no subtraction will be made. The use of small-head notes in transcription means that the respective tones are sung with less intensity.

(14) Notations such as mean that the bracketed notes represent a value equal to that of the small-head note appearing just above the bracket (instead of the usual ♩).

(15) The vibration of some long-drawn tones, described on p. 49, is transcribed:  (or in some other val-

ues), each note representing one vibration of connected with *yi*, or half a vibration if connected alternatingly with *y* and *i*.

(16) Letters or syllables underlined with ⁓ are additional particles, not belonging structurally to the proper text (see pp. 46–49); those underlined with ⌣ are downbeat additions (p. 49) which are not taken into consideration when determining the syllabic number of the section.

(17) Special symbols are used for "clucking sounds" (see p. 50); ♪ for definite pitch, ♪ for indefinite (approximate) pitch. The symbol ♪ instead of a note, means indefinite (approximate) pitch.

(18) Refrains are marked with ⏞r. (or ⏞1.r., ⏞2.r.); longer ones occupying one entire staff with r. { (or 1.r. {, 2.r. {, and so forth) at the left side of the staves.[50]

(19) For unintelligible syllables, - - - - are substituted, each dash for one syllable; for unpublishable, indecent words, ... , each dot for one letter.

(20) A tie underneath two vowels connected by hyphen (e‿e, ĭ‿e) means that they constitute only one syllable.[51]

50. Or with the abbreviation *refr.*

51. Editorial addition, derived from the author's explanation on p. 50, above.

Music Examples

I

1a. Nenni *

1-7, 8(>8,8,8,6,)

♪=276

1. Da- -uul- cu-lar da-ma dol-du,
Dam ba-şı-ma zın-dan ol-du.
Ba-ban duy-du, Şam-dan gel-di,
Nen-ni yau-rum, nen-ni;
Ye-di yıl-da bir bul-du-ğum
Nen-ni gu-zum, nen-ni.

2. Nen-ni çal-dım sa-de-si-ne---iy,
At-lım in-miş o-da-sı-na.
Çıg-rın dyar-cın ba-ba-sı-na,
Nen-ni gör-pen, nen-ni,
Ye-di yıl-da bir bul-du-ğu--m
Nen-ni yau-rum,

M.F. 3156 b), Kara Isalı (Seyhan), Zekeriye Culha (23), ill., 20. XI. 1936.

2

1b.
Agıt *
♪=270
1-7, < 8,
1. Gap- - lan gel- di ________ ba-ğır-ma-ya, _
Ya-şı değ- di ____________ yir-mi-ye,
Her _____ an-ne-nin _______ kâ-rı de-ğil _____
Böy-le ye-ğit ________ do-ğur-ma-ya. _
Of, ________________________ of. _
2. Yü- ce dağ-da, _______ çam yı-kıl-dı, ______
Da-lı, bu-da-ğı ____ ye-re dö-kül-dü.
Halk - sa-na- - - ya ____ Sar'A-ho-me-dim, _____
Ho-ca ba-ba-yın __________ be-li bü-kül-dü.
Of, _________________________ of! _
3. Ü-züm ga- ra, _______ dü-züm ga-ra, ______

3

Sal-kım-cığ-mı yü-züm ga-ra,
O Şim-di yem-mim, da-yım du-yar,
Ağ-la-ma-ya yü-züm ga-ra.
Of, Sar Ah-me-dim, of!

M. F. 3157 b), 3158 a), Kara Isalı (Seyhan), Zekeriye Culha (23), 20. XI. 1936.

2.
♪=368
1–8, 8,
1. Ev-le-ri-nin ö-nü ga-ya-ya,
Ga-ya-dan ba- - - - -xar-lar a-ya, yey.
Hav-li-da-ki, de du-ru ta-ya
Bin gi-de-lim, em-mim oğ-lu, yey.
♪=300
2. Ev-lek kes-tim, bi-ber saç-tı-yı-m,

4

Al_ ö- kü- zü-yü- m çif- te goş- tum,___
hm Ben bir ha-la- ya-l ma-la düş- tüm:___
Ben gi-de-mem,______em-mim gi-zi---yey.

M. F. 3158 b), Kelköy (Seyhan), Abdullah Karakus (22), ill., 20.XI.1936.

3.

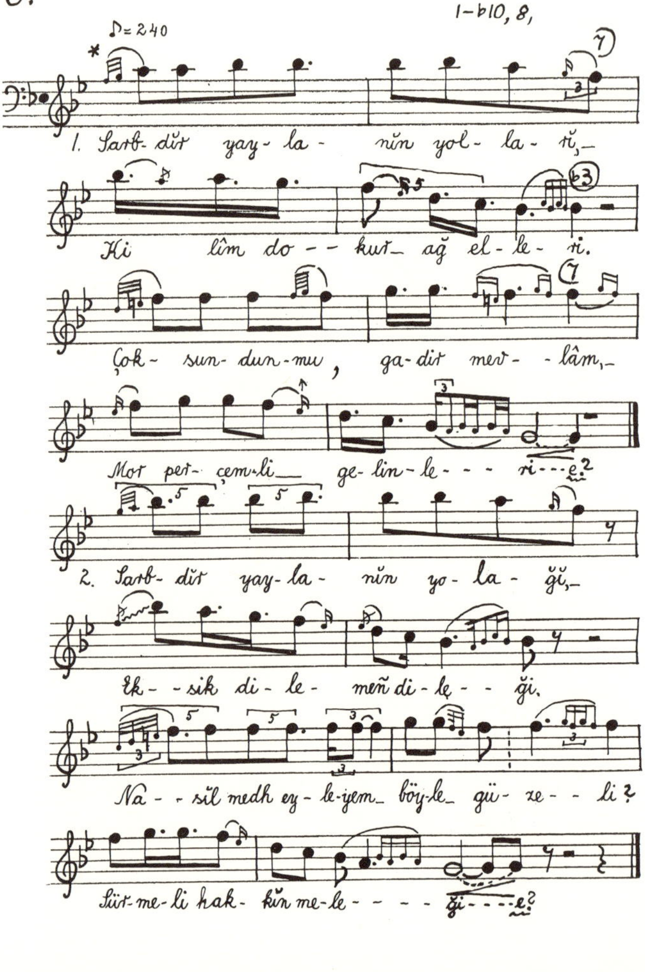

1–♭10, 8,

♪=240

1. Sarb- dır yay- la- nın yol- la- rı,_
Ki lîm do-- kur_ ağ el- le- ri.
Çok- sun- dun- mu, ga- dır mev- - lâm,_
Mor pet- çem-li__ ge- lin- le- - - ri---e?

2. Sarb- dır yay- la- nın yo- la- ğı,_
Ek- - sik di- le- meñ di- lę- - ği.
Na- - sil medh ey- le-yem_ böy-le_ gü- ze- - li?
Sür-me-li hak- kın me-le- - - - ği---e?

M. F. 3191 a), Tüysüz (Seyhan), Bekir oğlu Mustafa (15), ill., of the Tecirli tribe, 24.XI.1936.

4.

1–b6, 8,

M. F. 3175 c), Çardak (Osmaniye), İbiş Mehmedin Abdullah (14), ill., 23. XI. 1936.

M.F. 3161a), Avlik (Kadirli), Cinli Ali (32), ill., 20.XI.1936.

M. F. 3157 a), Avlık (Kadirli), Ahmed Torun (42), 20. XI. 1936.

7a. Nenni*

3. st. = 2., ma:

M. F. 3156 a), Avlik (Kadirli), Ahmed Torun (42), 20. XI. 1936.

7b.
Oyun havası*
♪=256
1–9, < 8,
1. De-ve-yi de- ve-ye,- çat-tım, be-beg oy— oy oy,
Yu-la-rın boy- nu-ma dak- tım,
(2.r.) Nen-ni-de,— nen-ni-de, nen-ni-de,- ne-yi-yen.
2. Ga-yın ba-bam-dan hi-cap et-tim, be-beg oy oy oy,
m Be-bek gal-dı, di-ye-me-dim,
(2.r.) Nen-ni-de,— nen-ni-de, nen-ni-de, ne-yi-yen.
3. Ha-va-da du-man ye-li-şir, be-be-ği oy oy oy oy,
Ça-dır-da düş-man gü-lü-şür,—
♪=100
(2.r.) Nen-ni-de, nen-ni-de, nen-ni-de, ne-yi-yen.

M. F. 3166 a) Osmaniye (Osmaniye), Ali Bekir oğlu Bekir (70), ill., 22.XI.1936.

II

8 a.

♪=264
*Kemençe:
1–8, 8,
♪=264
1. Hiy, Kurt pa-şa çık-tı Go-za-na-yiyiyi yiyiyi yiyiyi yiyiyiyiy,
A-kıl yet-mez bu dü-ze-ne;
♪=240
Öl-dür-müş-ler Gu-zan oğ-lu, yiy,
Ya-sak me-ze-rin ya-za-ña-na, yiy.
(Kemençe)

12

♪=320
2. Is-tan-bu-lun â-lim-le-
Ne_ zor_ o- lur ta-lim-le-ri-yi yi,—
Kör o-la-sı Der-viş pa-şa,_ ya,-
Hep dul goz- du_ gê-lin-le-ri,_ yi._
(Kemençe)
♪=320
poco acc.
3. Hn Göy-yü-zün-de dö-nen guş-la-
Bu guş-lar në-re-de giş- - la- - - yır?
hn_ Za-bit-lar sün- - ğü so-kun- ca,_ yi-
A-ğam o-ku-ma-ya_ baş-la--yı._

13

M. F. 3164, 3165, Osmaniye (Osmaniye). Ali Bekir oğlu Bekir (70), ill., 22. XI. 1936.

M. F. 3181a), Çardak (Osmaniye), Kâmil Özgan (42), 23. XI. 1936.

15

1–♭10,<8,

♪=368

1. Şi- çan__ do- lap- ta ñ-o- - - tu- - rır,

Guz- ru- ğun ba- la_ ba- - tü- l- - - - rır;

Hız- met- kâ- ra söz ye- - - ti- rır, de

1)

Söş- çü ba- şı_ gü- cü- cük şı- ça- yı- yı- yı- yı- yı- yı- yı- yı- yın.

2. volta

1)

yı- yı- yın.

2. Gap- la- ma gi- liç be- - he- he- lin- - - de,

Sün- gü dag mar- tin e- - - - - lin - - - - de,

Dün ge- ce ñ Ha- lep yo- - - - - - lun- - da, da

Kev- ran al- mış gü- cü- cük ___ şı- ça- yı- yı- yı- yı- yı- yı- yın.

3. Şi- çan ge- lir zırt- ba- - - ya- - - - nayn

Beş- yüz at- lı gırt- be- - - yi- - - - - neyn.

16

Ek-meğn' al ga- çat tot-ba- - -ye- nan, da
Cen-darm ol-muş- gü-cü-cük sı-ça-yi-yi-yi-yi-yin.

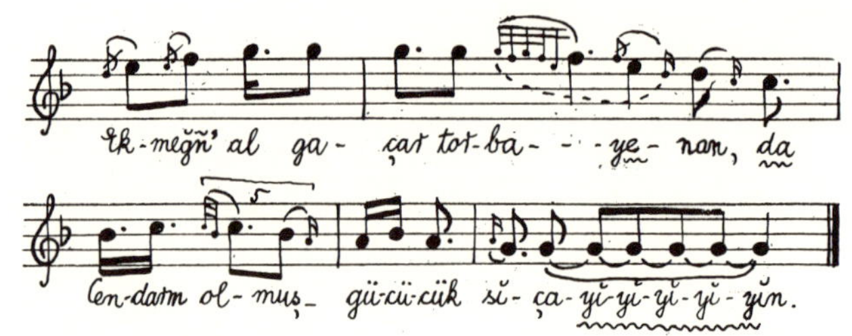

M.F. 3190 a), Tüysüz (Seyhan), Hacı oğlu İsmail (15), ill., of the Tecirli tribe, 24.XI.1

8 d.

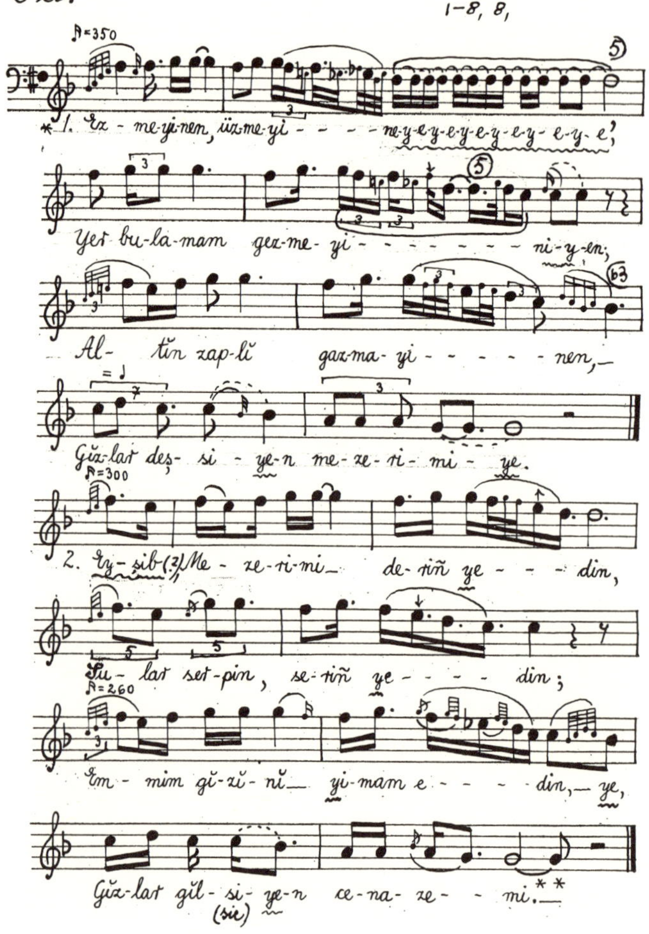

1-8, 8,
♪=350
*1. Ez - me-yi-nen, üz-me-yi - - - - ne-y-e-y-e-y-e-y-e-y-e-y-e,
Yer bu-la-mam gez-me-yi - - - - - - - - ni-y-en;
Al- tın zap-lı gaz-ma-yi - - - - - nen,-
Gız-lar deş- si - ye-n me-ze-ri- mi - ye.
♪=300
2. Ez-sib(?) Me - ze-ri-mi de-rin ye - - - din,
Su- lar ser-pin, se-rin ye - - - - din;
♪=260
Em - mim gı-zı-nı yi-mam e - - - - din, ye,
Gız-lar gil- si- ye-n ce-na-ze- - mi.**
(sic)

M.F. 3192 a) Tüysüz (Seyhan), Ömer oğlu Hökkeş (35), ill., of the Tecirli tribe, 24.XI.1936.

17

M. F. 3149 a), Kelköy (Seyhan), Abdullah Karakuṣ (22), ill., 19. XI. 1936.

9.
1–11, 8,
♪=400
1. Bu al- ma - - yı kim di-eş- le - - - - di? __
Çev- re_ ya- nın gü- müş- - - le- di? __
Bu- nu __ ba - - ña __ ba - ğış - - la-dı?
(*) Bu al- ma bi-r dost al - - - - ma - - sı, __ yi- ye.
♪=300
2. Bu al- - ma - - yı __ ben diş- le - - dim, __
Çev- re_ ya-nın gü-müş - - - le- dim, __
Bu- nu dos- - ta __ ba - - ğış - la-dım; __
(*) Bu al- ma bi-r dost al - - - - ma - - sı, __ yi-
3. Bu al- ma __ bir __ dal-da bit - - ti, __
Dal_ dal ol- du, ko- lun __ at- tı. __

19

M. F. 3194, Tüysüz (Seyhan), Ali oğlu Hacı (40-35), ill., of the Tecirli tribe, 24.XI.1936.

20

10a.
Karaca oğlan*
♪=264
1–11, <11[6+4+1],
1. A - - - la göz- le-ri-ni sev-di-ğim dil-be-ye-r,
o Se-nin ba-χış- la-rın ba-na_ yar ge-li-yi-r.
Bu dün-ye-de yaχ-ru gü-zel sev-me-yen, sev-me-yi-yi-ye-n
Ah-re-te hay-van gel-miş bün gi-de-yi-ye-r, bün gi-de-yi-yi-ye-r.
♪=192
2. Hn Til-li mah-ra-ma-sın at-mış_ ba-şı-na-yı,_
Gu-di-ret-ten ga-lem çek-miş ga-şı- na-yı,_
m Bir yi-ğit-te düş-me- - yin-ce e-şi-ne,_ e-şi-ne-yi-ye_
♪=168
Ah de-dik-çe yü-re-ğin-den gan ge-li-yi-yi yi-r, gan ge-li-ri-yi-yi-ye.

M. F. 3167 a), Osmaniye (Osmaniye), Ali Bekir oğlu Bekir (70), ill., 22. XI. 1936.

Ob.

M. F. 3167 b), Osmaniye (Osmaniye), Ali Bekir oğlu Bekir (70), ill., 22. XI. 1936.

II.
1–b10, 11[6+3+2]
♪=400
1. Av-şar beğ-le- rin-de___ gör-düm bir gü-zel,
♪=480
Gu-zan a-ra- - - sï-na - - ye__ çek-miş gö- - çü-nü;__
ah, Na-sïl med-hey - - le-yim___ böy-le gö- - ze-li- ğin:
Sït-may-ñañ__ ga- rï- ye-ş- dïr-miş sa- - çï- nï - - - ye.
2. Her sa-bah, sa- - bah da___ gen-di-ñi n-ö- ğer,
Al-tïn saç ba- - ğï da- - - ye__ to-pu-ğun dö- ğer.
Sa-de ga-şïy- - na- - - ye-n gir-pi-ği___ dë- ğe- ğer
A-cem öl-ke- - - si-nin_ tah- tïn, ta- cï- nï.__
♪=464
3. Mis go-xuyor_ zü- lü- - - - fü-nün u-cun-dan,
Ö- pe-yi-dim__ al ya- - - ña-ğïn pur- - cun-dan!

♪=400
Yeğ-le-nip gal- - - di-ğim___ se-nin___ yü-zün-de-ğe-n,
Üç beş se- ne- ye bek-lë- - - - ye-lim Ha- - ci-ni._
♪=464
4. Ga- - ra- - ca Oğ-lan_ der_ de:___ yeğ-len-dim, gal-dim,
Mu-hab-bet ne- - - - yi-miş___ ye-ni- ce___ bil-dim,
♪=380
Kim-se dah-let- me- sin:___ mi-ri-den___ al-di-ye-m
Üç beş se-ne___ gü-zel- - le- rin pa- ci-ni- - - -e.

M. F. 3188, Tüysüz (Seyhan), Bekir oğlu Mustafa (15), ill., of the Tecirli tribe, 24. XI. 1936.

2.

1-9, 11[6+4+1],

♪=260
1. Din-le-yin a-ğa-la-yat be-nim sö-zü-mü,
Has bah-ça-ñ-i-çin-de_ gül em-mim oğ-luñ;
Em- mim oğ-lu ñ-a-ra-ba-sin çek-miş gi-di-yor,
Bu ga-za-ya ñ-al-lahdan bi-le- mem, oğ- lum.

24

M. F. 3191 c), Tüysüz (Seyhan), Ahmed oğlu Mehmet (36), ill., of the Tecirli tribe, 24. XI. 1936.

3a.

M. F. 3147 b), Kelköy (Seyhan), Abdullah Karakuş (22), ill., 19. XI. 1936.

M.F. 3192b), Türysüz (Seyhan), Ali oğlu Hacı (40-35***?), ill., of the Tecirli tribe, 24. XI. 1936.

M.F. 3187a), Tüysüz (Seyhan), Memik Mustafa oğlu Osman (11), ill., of the Kumazli tribe, 24. XI. 1936.

28
15.
1–8, 11[6+3+2],
♪=370
♪=276
1. İs-tan-bul-dan çık-tım dır-ya_ yü-zü-ñü-ñü-üü-ne,
i Mey-lim düş-tü et-me-ni-ñiñ gı-zı-ñı-ñı--na.
Y-ye-me, iç-me, bax yav-rı-nın_ gö-zü-ñü--ne,
(+.) Al_ be-ni ter-ki-ñe, gi-dek, kürd o-ño-lu!
2. İ Çan-lı çer-kes sa-fah-la-yın u-ya-ña-ña-n-dı,
kiñ Ağ goy-na-ğı al ğan-la-ra be-le-ñe-ñe-n-di.
hiy Bu-na çer-kes ğı-zı-na-sıl_ da-ya-ñan-dı?
(+.) Al be-ni ter-ki-ñe, gi-dek,_ kürd o--ño-lu!
3. Hiy U-fa-cık ta-şı-nan ka-le_ ya-pı-ñı-ñı-l-maz,
hiy Cı-ğıp cı-ğıp yar yo-lu-na ba-xı-xı--l-maz;

M.F. 3136, Hüyük (Çorum), Hatice Deklioğlu (13), ill., 16. XI. 1936.

16.

1-9, 11 [6+3+2]

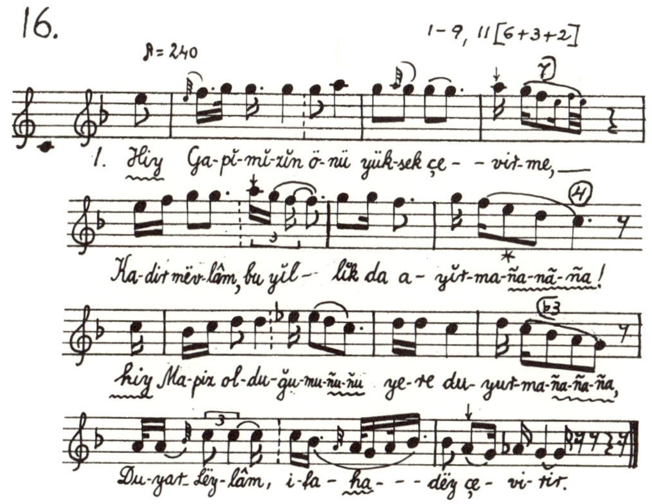

2. Lëy-lâm, ğalk, gi-de-lim, yo-lu-muz ï-ra-ña,**
Ï-ra-ğa da-yan-ma-ña-z, derd-li-dir yü-re-ñe-ñe-k,
Ha-cï-lar kö-yü-nü-ñü-ñü bir kim-den so-ra-ña-ña-ña.
Iş-te ğa-rip ğa-ri-ñi - - - pr ge-di-yor, Lëy-lâm,
Ga-rış-tï kürt-le-re-he, ge-di-yor Lëy-lâm.
3. Lëy-lâm, ğalk, gi-de-lim Ha-cï-kö-yü-ne-ñe,
A-ce-mi-sin, gü-ve-ne-me-me-m hu-yu-na-ña-ña;
6 Lëy-lâm, gur-ban o-la-ña-ña-m u-sul bo-yu-na-ña-ña-ña!
Iş-te ğa-rip ğa-ri-ñi - - - pr ge-di-yor Lëy-lâm.
4. Ëy Ma-vi ço-rap- gey-miş lap-çin i-çin-de-he-he,
Dö-kün-müş lâ-van-ta-ña, go-xar sa-çin-da-ña-ña.

31

M.F.3142, Hüyük (Çorum), Hatice Dekkioğlu (13), ill., 16. XI. 1936.

17a.

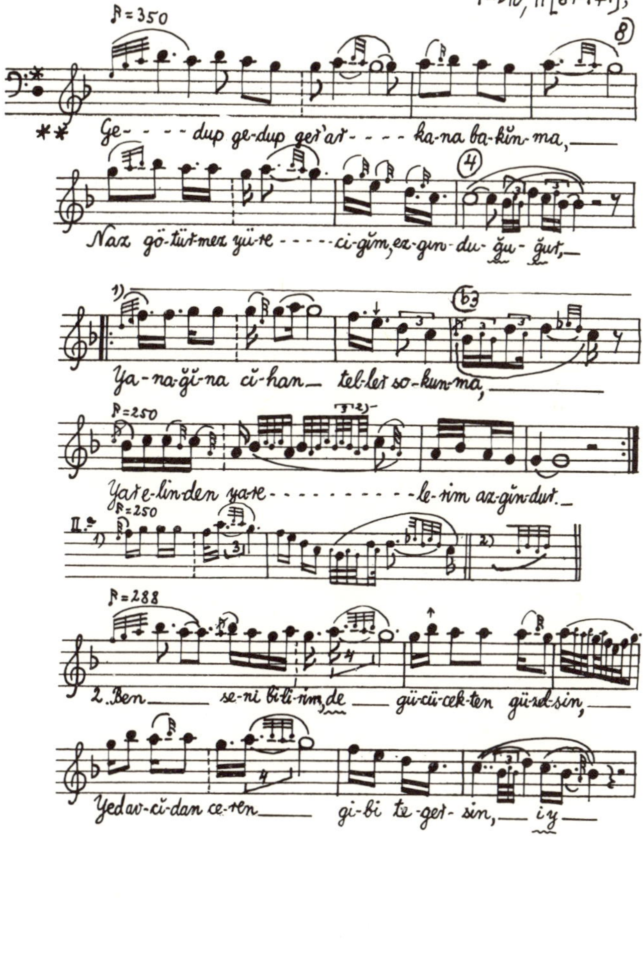

1-♭10, 11[6+4+1],

♪=350

Ge- - - - dup ge-dup get'ar- - - - ka-na ba-kın-ma,___

Naz gö-tür-mez yü-re - - - - ci-ğim, ez-gin-du-ğu-ğut,_

Ya-na-ğı-na ci-han_ tel-ler so-kun-ma,___

♪=250

Yar e-lin-den yare- - - - - - - - - - le-rim az-gın-dır._

II. ♪=250

♪=288

2. Ben___ se-ni bi-li-rim, de___ gü-cü-cek-ten gü-zel-sin,___

Yedav-cı-dan ce-ren___ gi-bi te-ger-sin,__ iy__

Dos-tum ne-den me-lül mah-zun ge-zer-sin?
Baş bir yan-na zi-lif- le-rin ey-gin-dir.
♪=288
3. Der Ka-ra-ca-ñ-Oğ-lan: de-dim, o-tur-dum,
O- tur-dum, da lâ-le, süm-bül bi-tir-dim;
Gen-dim İs-tan-bul-dan fer-man ge-tir-dim:
Her ke-sin sev- di-ği vë-ril-sin dë-yi.

M.F. 3154 b), 3155 a), Kara Isalı (Seyhan), Zekeriye Culha (23), ill., 20.XI.1936.

M. F. 3159 b), 3160 a), Kara Isalı (Seyhan), Zekeriye Culha (23), ill., 20. XI. 1936.

34

17c.
1. Zey- tün be- li-
gürle-ye-re-
Ben gi- zi- mi
ge-lin et-ti
Ben gi-zi-mi
ge-lin et- tim
Ü- zen- gi-si- yey
pat- la- ya- ta-
2. Hı Gi-zin gız- la
i- çin- de- he
Ye-men gi-na
si sa-çın-da
Tor- lak ma- ya
lar gi-bi sal-la-nır
Zey-tin be- li- nin
i- çin-de-
3. Hı At- ka- sın- da
çay öt- gü- sü,
Bu-da let-ve
rin göt- gü- sü-

35

Gü- na-ma-yı̆ - - - ye-ye-ye-ye-ye- [n], yem-mi,_ da- yı̆,
poco acc
Gö- zel-lik Al - - - lah ver-gi-si-ye-ye-ye-ye-ye-ye-ye-yo-ye-ye-ye-ye-ye-ye-ye-ye-ye-ye.
M.F. 3197, 3198, Seyhan (Seyhan), Koca Mehmed (45), ill., 20. and 25. XI. 1936.
18.
♪=236
1~11,
Cura irizva*
1. o Ey
Göy
yü-zün-de de bö-lük bö-lük dut-na-
lat, yü-zün-de bö-lük bö-lük dut-na-la- ha-t, Et-ken ey-le, şu ha-li-me
bak be-nim, o - ho ho- hoy oy.
hn Dey

(4)
(sic)
hi - hi-ho-hi-hi Şa-hin pen-çe vur-du ga-nat-la-rım ya-re-li, ya-ra-lı ñe,
Şu si-na-me bir ok değ-di berk be-ni - hi - hi - m, oy, berk be - ni - - - - - ye.
2. Hn De - - - - - ha-ha-ha-hi-hi
Şa-hin pen-çe vur-du, ga-nat-la-rım ya-re-li, n-a-man, ya-re - li,
Ay** ? ? Şu si-na-me bir ok değ-di berk be-nim, o - ho ho yu - yu,
berk be-ni - - yi.

M. F. 3173 a), Tabaklar (Seyhan), Kır Ismail (51), ill., 22. XI. 1936.

19.

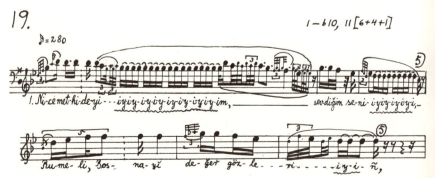

1 – 610, 11 [6+4+1]

♪ = 280

1. Ni-ce-met-hi-de-yi - - - iy-i-y-i-y-iy-iy-i-y-i-y-im, sev-diğim se-ni- i-y-i-y-i-y-i-y-i, –

(5)

Ru-me-li, Bos- na-yı de-ğer göz-le - - - ri - - - - iy-i - ñ,

(5)

Â-lem-de bu-lun-ma-y-i-y-i-y-i-y-i - - - - - - - - - - - ro-nuh u-ta-va-nı - - - - - - ñin,
İz-mi-ri, Go-nya-yi-ye de-ğer göz-le- - rin.
2. Al-nı-na çe-kil-mi-i-y-i-y-i-y-i-y-i-y-i-y-i - - - - - - yi - - - - gü-zel ni-şa-nı - - i-y-i-y-i-yi-yi-yiy,
Se-ni se-ven - - - le-rin ar-tar fu-ğa - - - nı - - - - yiy,
Har-si, Ahış-ka-yı-yi-y-i-y-i-y-i-y-i - - - - - - yi-yi-yi-yiy, Er-zu-rum Va-nı-yi - - - - y,
Bal-hi, Pu-ha - - ra-nyı-yi de-ğer göz-le-ri - - - - yi-n.
3. Him-se-de gör-me-di-yi-y-i-y-i-y-i-yi - - - - - - - - - - m sen-de-ki na-zı-y-i-y-i-y-i-yi-yi-yiy,
Ye-me-ni, Bağ-da-di-yın, A-cem, Şi-ra-zı-yın,
Bü-tün Gür-cüs-ta-nı - - iy-i-y-iy-i-y-i-y - yi - yi, Mı-sır, Hi-ca-zı-yı - - - - yi-yiy,
Hin-di, Hin-dis-ta-nı-yı de-ğer göz-le-ri - - yi-yin.

38

4. Güzel gözlügöç yiyiyiyiyiyi - - - - - yi-yi-yi- yi, - - ği-te naz o- lu- - uyuyuyuyuyur,
Vak- - ti ge-lir, gül a-ğa- çi-lir, yaz o- lu- uur,
Mi-si-rin haz-na-si yiyiyiyiyi - - - yi-yi-yi-yin_ ver-sem a zo-lu-yu - - - - -,
Bü- tün İs- tam-bu- lu- yi de-ğer göz-le- ri - - - yi-yin.

M. F. 3149 b), 3150, Avlik (Kadirli), Cinli Ali (32), ill., 19. XI. 1936.

20.

1–♭10, II [6+4+1],

♪=250
1. Pen- ce- re- den___ ma- yil ________ ma-yil ba-ka-en yar,
Ci- ğe- ri- mi ________ işk ö- t- - - - - - - - dü-ne ya-ka-en yar,
♪=208
Ben ö-lür-sem,_ sen kim - - - - - - - - le-re ba-yi- kan yar?
Ba-na sen-de-he-he-he-yan ol-du- yu- yu, ki-me ne__ di-yim?

39

♪=195
2. Pen-ce-re-den ma-yil ___ ma-yil ba-ka-ğï- rïm,
♪=168
Ci-ğe-ri-ni-hi-hi işkö-hö- hör- - dü-ne ya-ka-ğï-rïm.
Sen_ ö-lür-se- ğe-ñ, ak-su** - - - - - - - - - - - ta yï-ka-ğï- rï- - yï-m,
Öl-dür-me-yin Mah- - mu-du- yu,___ ben de- he ___ ö-lü-rü-yüm.
♪=192
3. Yük-sek pen- ce- - - re- den ___ ye- re ba-kïl- ma-yï-z,
Yü-ce mer- di- - - - - - - ven-de- he-n, ___ a-man, çï-kïl-maz.—
*** - - - - bir ben öl- me- yi-nen ___ â-lem yï-kïl ___ ma-yï-z,
Ba- na sen-de- - - ye-n ol-du-yu- yu- ki- me ne ___ di- yim?

F. 3193, Tüysüz (Seyhan), Ali oğlu Hacï (40-35), ill., of the Tecirli tribe, 24. XI. 1936.

40

21a.

1–b10, 11[6+4+1]
♪=256
1. Bir e- mir gel - se, de ___ kâh-ya-lar a-sil-sa,-
Şu dün-ya - dan yü - ri - - - - ye-ti ke - sil-se, ___
Av - ra-di dul gal-sa, da ___ gi-zi-yi - yi-yi ba-sil-sa - yi - yi - - - e!
♪=175
Ga-çak-la-rin baş- dü - yü-ş- ma-ni kâh - ya - la-yi-yi-yi-yi-yi-yi-yi-yi-yi[-r],
♪=256 ♪=150
Kâh-ya-lar oy, ___ de-yus-lar oy, ___ ket-ha-ne-ci-ler oy _ oy oy oy oy oy oy oy!
♪=256
2. I - ma-min e - vin-de ___ tü-tün tüt-me - si-en, ___
♪=188
Kâh-ya-nin e-vin-de ___ n-oğ-lan yet-me - - - si- yo yo yo yo yo yo yo yo yoy[-
♪=216
Ho-ran-ta-cak sa-bah - - - - la-ta ___ çik-ma- - - sin!
♪=180
Ga- çak- la- rin baş dü- yü-ş- ma-ni kâh- ya - la-yi-yi-yi-yi-yi-yi-yi-yi-yi[-r],
♪=216 ♪=150
Kâhya-lar oy, ___ de-yus-lar oy, ___ düm-bik-ler oy, ___ el-li se-kiz-ler oy-oy-oy-oy-oy-oy

♪=212
3. Čan- dar- ma gel miş, de bi- r ge- çi du- tar,
Kâh- ya der ki- ne dört te- - - - ne yë - te- ë- er,
Buğ- - da- yï, bul- gu- ru da hep u- yu - na ğa- ta- yë - - - er.
♪=180
(r.) Ga- çak- la- rïn baş dü- - yüş ma- ni kâh- ya- la- yï- yï- yï- yï- yï- yï- yï- yï [-r],
Kâh- ya- lar, oy düm- bük- ler, oy el- li se- kiz- ler, oy her- ha- ne- ci- ler- oy- oy- oy.

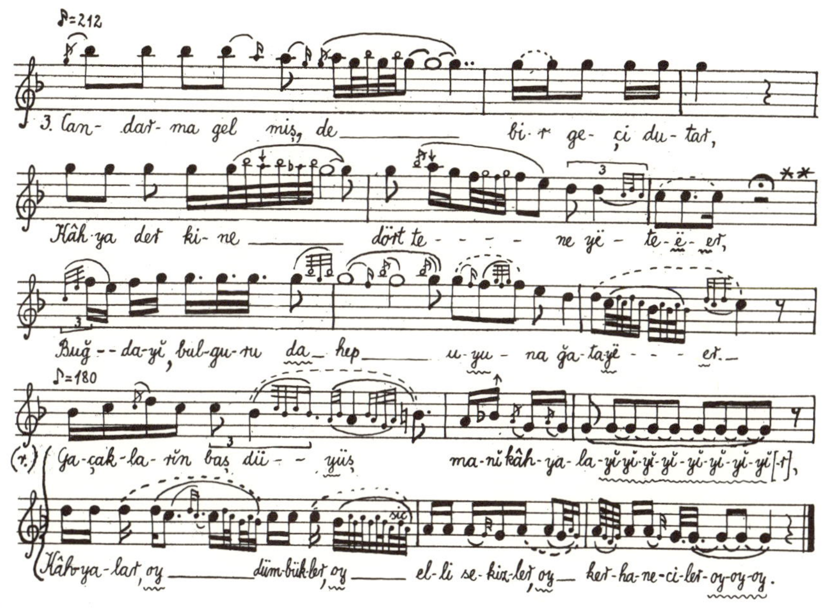

M. F. 3195, Tüysüz (Seyhan), Hacï oğlu Ismail (15), ill., of the Tecirli tribe, 24. XI. 1936.

21b.

Bozlak (?)*

1– 11, < 11 [6+3+2],

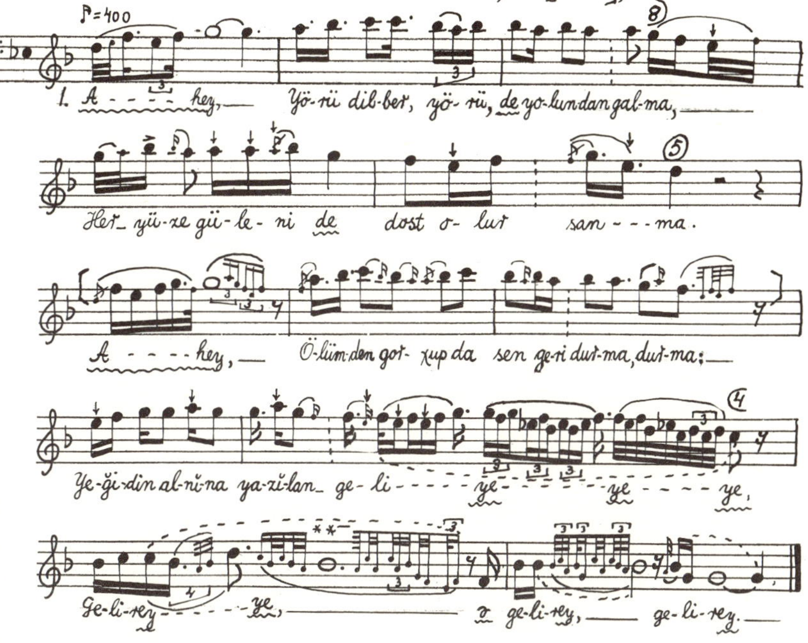

♪=400
1. A - - - hey, Yö- rü dil- ber, yö- rü, de yo- lun- dan gal- ma,
Her yü- ze gü- le- ni de dost o- lur san- - - ma.
A - - - - hey, Ö- lüm- den gor- xup da sen ge- ri dur- ma, dur- ma;
Ye- ği- din al- nï- na ya- zï- lan ge- li - - - - ye - - - - ye - - - - ye,
Ge- li- rey- - - - - - ye, ž ge- li- rey, ge- li- rey.

M. F. 3146 b), 3147 a), Kara Isalı (Seyhan), Zekeriye Culha (23), ill., 19. XI. 1936.

43

2. Hñ ay, Ni-çin düş-tüm şu gö- - -ze-lin ar-dı-na, a-man, ar-dı-na?
Hen-di göç-sün, bir go-na-lım yur-du-na, of,
hñ ey, Yı-kı-la-sı gar-lı da-ğın ar-dı-na.
(r.) Ya-şıp gi-der bir göz-le-ri- - - -ye sür-me-li-yim uy-ie n-ah, sür-me-li-iy-iy-iy-iy-iy-iy-iy.
3. Hñ ay-ay-ay-ay-ay-ay-ay-ay-ay-ay, A-yağı-na gey-i-miş da gır-mı-zı ye-me-ni, a-man, ye-me-ni,
Gel dos-tum, gal-dı-ra-lım a- - ra-da-ki gü-ma-nı.
hñ a-y-ay-a-y-ay-a-y-ay-ay, Ağ to-puk üs-tün-de da san-dal tü-ma-nı.
(r.) Dö-küp gi-der, bir göz-le-ri- - - - ye, sür-me-lim u-y-uy-u-y-uy-uy, ñ-ah sür-me-li-iy-iy-iy-iy-yi-yim.

M. F. 3151, Avlık (Kadirli), Ahmed Torun (42), 19. XI. 1936.

23.

♪=220
♪=194
1–610,
* 2. Hey_ n-Axış-ka-nın at-dı_ cı-ğı dağ i-dı-e,_ n-Axış-ka-nın at-dı_
cı-ğı dağ i-dı,_ Ba-bam pa-şa, gar- da- şım bey i-di hı hı hı.
Cura ırızva
♪=220
♪=184
hey,_ Böy-le ol-ma-dan bi-ze- yë ö-lüm yeğ
di,_ Böy-le ol-ma-dan bi-ze-yi_ ö-lüm yeğ i-di._ ye-
♪=220
Gü-zel-le-ri-ye-
sir- ge de ñ A-xış-ka-ña--hı hı- ni- yi- n, Axış-ka-nın!_

45

hın, Böy-le ol-ma-dan bi-ze-yi — ö-lüm
yeğ i-di - - ye Gü-zel-le-ri ye-sir-ge-sin Ah-ış-ka - nin!
♪=208
3. ı İy — A-dı-mı so-rat-san, da-ye: — ben-li-ñ-ı-mi-ne, — hey — A-dı-mı so-
♪=186
rat-san, da-ye: — ben-li ñ-ı-mi-ne - ye, Al-tın bur-ma da-ha-hoe- ki-nıt-dım go-lu-ma,
of.

M. F. 3172, Tabaklar (Seyhan), Kır Ismail (51), ill., 22. XI. 1936.

24.
Aşiret gaydası*
1–9, 11 [4+4+3 or 6+4+1]
♪=ca 400
1. E-de-he-m, Buce-re-nin __ su-la-hak la-rı __ ga-ya- lı,
E-dem, Buce- re-nin __ su-la-hak- - - la-rı __ ga-ya-- lı,
Ga-ya-sın-da __ le-le-he-hye __ süm-bül da- ya- lı.
2. E-dem, __ Şe-ker yi- miş __ du-dak- - la-rı __ bo-ya- - lı,
E-dem, Şe-ker yi-miş __ du-dak- - la-rı __ bo- ya- - lı,
Şe -her-de ga-har- şı-ma __ geç- ti bir ce-ren.
M. F. 3180 a), Çardak (Osmaniye), Ömer oğlu Ali (15), 23. XI. 1936.
25.
Ağıt*
VII–4, 8,
♪=300
1. Hñ De-de-ni- ye-n de dö-şü ñen---li, ** __
hñ Nen-ni Boy-taz __ oğ-lum, nen---ni! __

48

M. F. 3161 b), Avlik (Kadirli), Ahmed Torun (42), 20. XI. 1936.

49

M. F. 3184 a), Çardak (Osmaniye), Mehmed oğlu Pir Sabit (20), 23. XI. 1936.

27.

1–7, 11 [6+2+3],
♪ = 240
1. Her kës sev-di- ği-ni ya-nı-na gë-tir-di-yi- - ye,
Sal-lan, geç gat- - şı-ma, na-zı-yı - - - ye me-nek-şem,
2. An-na-cın-dan ge-len gü-cü - - cük ge-li-yi-yen,
Bir sa-at gat-şım-da du-ra- - yı - - bi-lin-mi-ye?
3. Di-va-ne göy- - nü-mün ta-li-bi, -bi sen-si-ye-n,
Gi-rül-dü ga- - na-dım, sa-ra-yı - - - bi-lin-mi-ye?

M. F. 3175 a), Çardak (Osmaniye), Ibiş Mehmedin Abdullah (14), ill., 23. XI. 1936.

28.

M.F.3189, Tüysüz (Seyhan), Hacı oğlu Ismail(15), ill., of the Tecirli tribe, 24.XI.1936.

9.

M. F. 3160 b), Kelköy (Seyhan), Abdullah Karakuş (22), ill., 20. XI. 1936.

30.

M. F. 3196, Seyhan (Seyhan), Koca Mehmed (45), ill., 20 and 25. XI. 1936.

M. F. 3144 a), Vartan (Sivas), Divrikli Ali (37), ill., 17. XI. 1936.

32.

1–8, (r) 9,

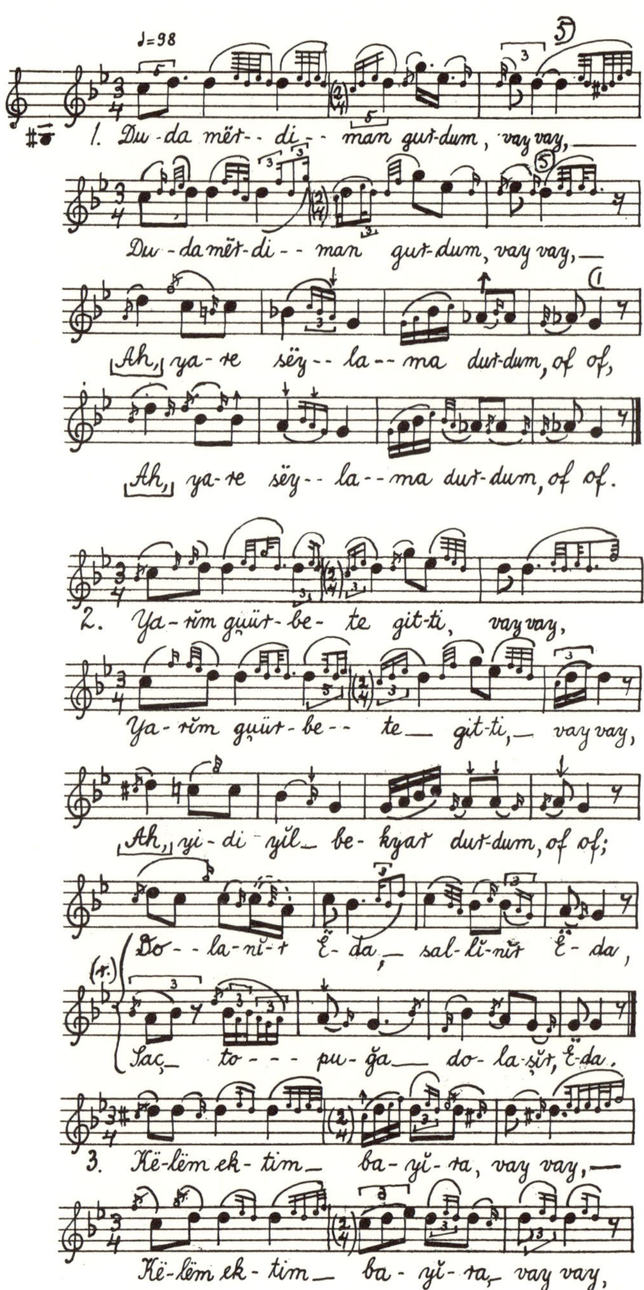
♩=98
1. Du-da mër-- di-- man gur-dum, vay vay,
Du-da mër-di-- man gur-dum, vay vay,
Ah, ya-re sëy--la--ma dur-dum, of of,
Ah, ya-re sëy--la--ma dur-dum, of of.
2. Ya-rim guür-be- te git-ti, vay vay,
Ya-rim guür-be-- te git-ti, vay vay,
Ah, yi-di yil be-kyar dur-dum, of of;
(r.) Do--la-ni-r Ë-da, sal-li-nir Ë-da,
Saç to--- pu-ğa do-la-şir, Ë-da.
3. Kë-lëm ek-tim ba-yi-ra, vay vay,
Kë-lëm ek-tim ba-yi-ra, vay vay,

M. F. 3138 b), Ankara (Ankara), Emine Muktat (62), ill., 16·XI·1936.

33. Kĭna türküsü *

56

Yar, ë- - lin, gi-nañ 6 gut-lu ol-sun,
Bun-da dir- - - - li- ği- n dat-lu ol-sun!
3. Hat-la- - dï, çïg-dï ë- ṣi- ği,
Hat- la- - dï, çïg-dï ë- - ṣi - ği,
Suf- ra- - da gal- - dï ga-ṣï- ği.
4. 6 Gïz a- - na- - sï-nïñ da- nï- sï,
Gïz a- - - na- - sï-nïñ da-nï - sï,
Yar ë - li- - - n, gi- nañ al ol- - sun,
Bun- da dir- - li- - ğin bal ol-sun!
5. Mër-ci-mek e-kb-dim, bit-ti-mi?
Mër-ci- mek eg-dim, 6 bit- ti- mi?
Dâ-lin-de bül-bül öt-tü-mü?

M.F. 3140, Ankara (Ankara), Emine Muktat (62), ill., 16. XI. 1936.

34.

1–b6, 10[5+5],

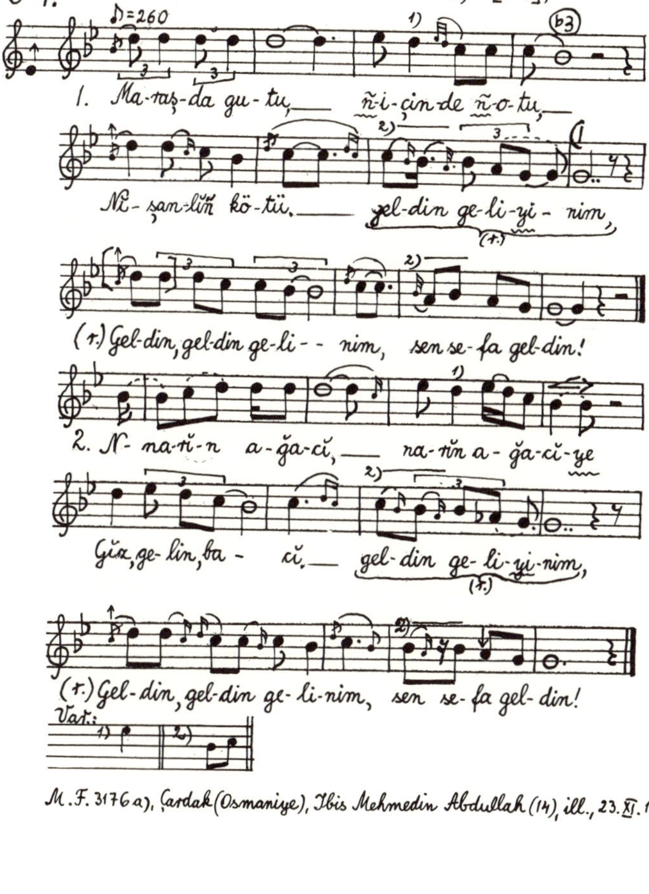

♪=260

1. Ma-raş-da gu-tu, ___ ñ-i-çin-de ñ-o-tu, ___

Ni-şan-lïñ kö-tü. ___ gel-din ge-li-yi - nim, (r.)

(r.) Gel-din, gel-din ge-li - - nim, sen se-fa gel-din!

2. N- na-rï-n a-ğa-cï, ___ na-rïn a - ğa-cï-ye

Gïz, ge-lin, ba - cï. ___ gel-din ge-li-yi-nim, (r.)

(r.) Gel-din, gel-din ge-li-nim, sen se-fa gel-din!

Var.: 1) 2)

M.F. 3176a), Çardak (Osmaniye), Ibis Mehmedin Abdullah (14), ill., 23. XI. 1936.

35.
a) 1–8
b) 1–5 } (11 [4+4+3]) 8, 6, 8, 6,
♪=300
a) 1. Hñ Za - bah - dan oğ - ra - dım da ben bir
Ge-li-ne - yeyeyeye yeyeyeye yeyeyeye, ye ye ye, ge-li-ne - yeyeyeyeye,
♪=400
Bal bu - la-mış da do - da - ğı - - na,
♪=350
♪=330
Di-li-ney - ye-ye-ye - - ye, di-li-ne
2. Hñ Hayı - ce-de-yim de bun-ca ma-lı
Yo-lu-na - - - yayayayayayayayayayayaya - - - - ya - ya-ya, yolu-na ya-yayaya,
hñ Az ge - lir - se da, dat - lı ca - nı
Vėr-me-li-yi - - yi - - - yi, vėr-me - li-yi yiyiyi yiyiyi yiyi yiyi yi yi yi yi yi, dost.
♪=280
b) 1. Hñ Za - bah - dan oğ - ra - dım da ben bir
♪=326
acc.
Ge-li - ne - - yeyeyeyeyeyeyeyeyeyeyeyeye ye ye, ge-li-ne - yeyeyeye,

M.F. 3200, Seyhan (Seyhan), Koca Mehmed (45), ill., 20. and 25. XI. 1936

36. Il bey oğlu*

1–11, (11 [6+3+2, or 6+4+1, or 4+4+3]) 11, 8, 6,

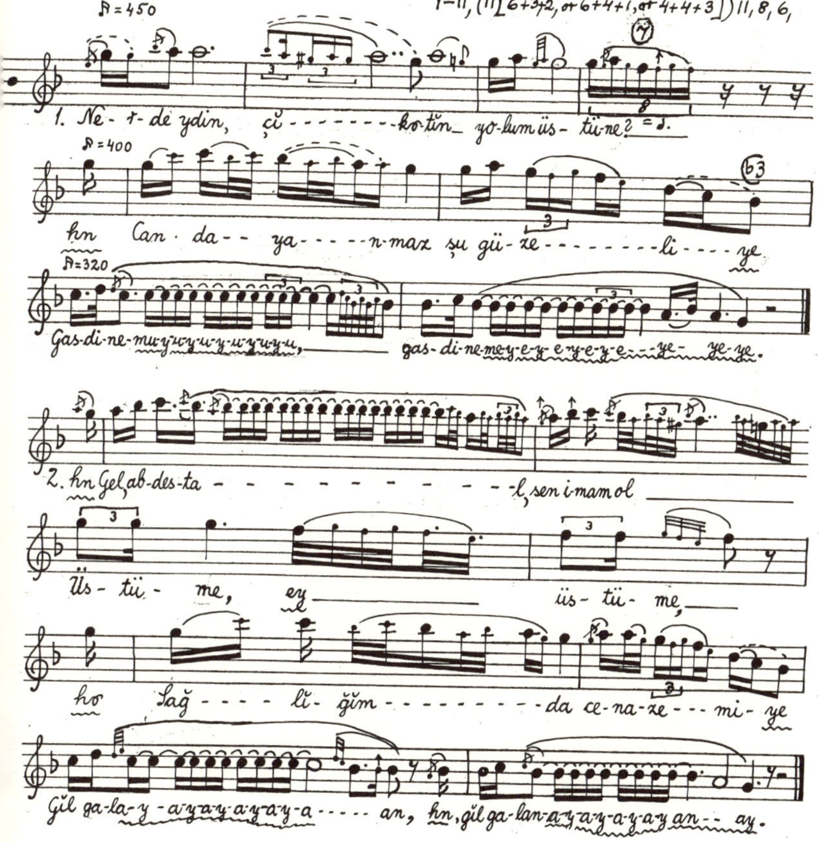

♪ = 450

1. Ne- r- de ydin, çi - - - - - - - - ko-tin yo-lum üs- tü-ne? = ♩.

♪ = 400

hn Can - da - - ya - - - - n-maz şu gü- ze - - - - - - - - - li - - - ye

♪ = 320

Gas-di-ne-mu-y-u-y-u-y-u-y-u-y-u, gas-di-ne-me-y-e-y-e-y-e-y-e - - - ye- ye-ye.

2. hn Gel, ab-des-ta - - - - - - - - - - - - - - l, sen i-mam ol

Üs - tü - me, ey üs - tü - me,

ho Sağ - - - - lı- ğım - - - - - - - - - - da ce-na-ze - - - mi - ye

Gül ga-la-y-a-y-a-y-a-y-a-y-a - - - - an, hn, gül ga-lan-a-y-a-y-a-y-a-y-an - - ay.

M. F. 3154 a) Avlik (Kadirli), Ahmed Torun (42), 20. XI. 1936.

37. Uzun hava*

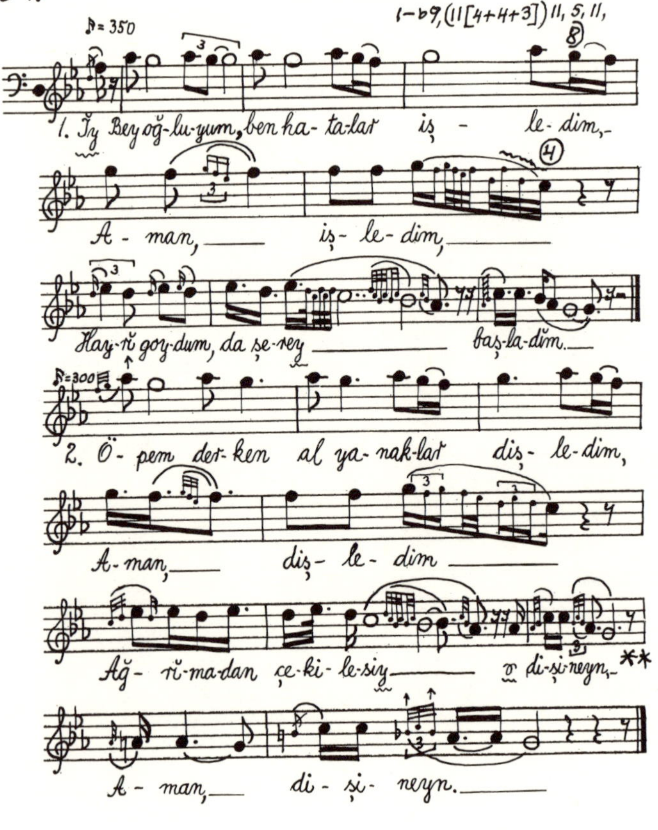

♪= 350 1–b9, (11[4+4+3]) 11, 5, 11, (8)

1. Iy Bey oğ-lu-yum, ben ha-ta-lar iş - le-dim,-

A - man, iş- le-dim, (4)

Hay-ri goy-dum, da şe-rey baş-la-dim.

♪=300

2. Ö-pem der-ken al ya-nak-lar diş- le-dim,

A-man, diş- le- dim

Ağ- ri-ma-dan çe-ki-le-siy o di-şi-neyn,- **

A - man, di - şi- neyn.

61

M. F. 3179, Çardak (Osmaniye), Yusuf Çenet (27), 23. XI. 1936.

38.

Çafak ağzı*

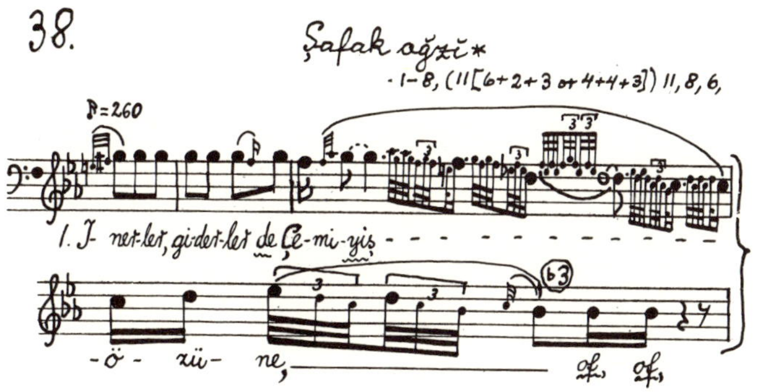

62

M. F. 3159 a), Kara Isalı (Seyhan), Zekeriye Culha (23), ill., 20.XI.1936.

63

39.
Senir ağzı *
1–7, (11 [4+4+3]) 11, 11, 6,
♪ = ca 350
1. Ya-zın gel-di-ği de ne-re-sin-de - - - - ğen bel-lü-dü - - - - ğen?
ya Gon- ca gü-lün yap-ra-cı-ğı dür-gün-dü - - - ğen,
Dür-gün-dü - - ğen, dür-gün-dü-ğe-ye-ye-ye-ye-ye-ye-ye-ye - - - - ğen.
2. So - - ğuk fur-muş da ör-se-le-mi - - yen yü-zü-nü - - - - ğen
Be-nim gön-lüm bir Ley-la-ya fur-gun-dur - - ğur,
Fur-gun-dur, ğur fur-gun-du-ğu-yu-yu - - - - - - - - r, yet of.
3. Ya - - zın gel-di-ği de ne-re sin-de - - ğen bel-lü-dü - - - ğen?
Ne ded' o-la boz bu-la-nık de-re-le - - - ğen, e
De-re-le - - - - - - - ğen e, de-re-le-ye-ye - - - - - r, yet of?

♪=ca 228
4. Her kes sev-di-ği-ni a-li - - - yen ya-tın-ca - - - - - ğen
Art-ti der-dim, ye-ni-le-di ya-re-ler yen,
yer Ya-re-ler yen yer, ya-re-le-ye-ye - - - - yer of.
M. F. 3146 a), Kara İsalı (Seyhan), Zekeriye Culha (23), ill., 19. XI. 1936.

40.
Oyun havası*
T. giusto, ♩. = 94
1–4, 7,
1. Ça-la- - dan e- ni-yor- dum,
**
(sempre sim.)
Ça-ğır- - san dö- - - nü-yor- - du- - - m.
Yar cim-dal-lı, cim- - dal- - lı,
Sar cim-dal-lı, cim- - dal- - lı. Şi

65

M.F. 3148 a), Kelköy (Seyhan), Abdullah Karakuş (22), ill., 19.XI.1936.

66
41.
Oyun havası*
1-5, 7,
♩=98
1. Köp - - - rü-nün al - - - tı ti - - ken,
(1.t.) Yë - şil - lim, yë - şil - lim, a - - man, a - ma - ğan, of,
Yax - dın be - ni gül i - ken,
(2.t.) E - fen - dim, e - fen - - - dim eğ - lën, eğ - lën.
2. Al - lah da se - - - - - - - - ni yax - sın,
(1.t.) Yë - şil - lim, yë - şil - lim, a - - - man, a - ma - ğan, of,
Üç gün - lük ge - - - lin i - ken,
(3.t.) Sür - - - me - lim, sür - - - me - lim eğ - lën, eğ - lën.
3. Al - lah da se - - - - ni yax - sın,
(1.t.) Yë - şil - lim, yë - şil - lim eğ - lën, eğ - lë - yën, of;
Üç gün - lük ge - - - lin i - ken,
(3.t.) Sür - - - me - lim, sür - - me - lim eğ - lën, eğ - lën.

M.F. 3148 b), Kara Isali (Seyhan), Zekeriye Çulha (23), ill., 19.XI.1936.

68

M. F. 3166 b), Osmaniye (Osmaniye), Ali Bekir oğlu Bekir (70), ill., 22. XI. 1936.

43 a. Oyun havasĭ*

M. F. 3173 b), Gebeli (Osmaniye), Mustafa oğlu Mehmet (29), 22. XI. 1936.

43b. Halay havasi*

1–9, (7)14,
♪=232
**1. Hay- di!– Ga-le-den in-dim i- - - -niş, men-di-lim do- lu yi - - - - miş;
Ya-ta sal-dim, yi- me - miş, de____ yat gen- di gel- - - -sin di-miş.
♪=280
♪=200
A-man, a-man, pu- sa- rik, baş-ta da dut-maz bu sa- - rik,
♪=220
Dol-dur sev-di-ğim ga-de- - - hi,____ bel-ki yol-da____ su-sa-rik.
♪=220
2. Hay- di! In-dim gu-yu di-bi - - - - - - ne,– gu-yu di-bi sa-zi - - miş,–
Ya-lan de-ğil,– sev-di-ğim, da-ye– gö-mür göz-lü____ gi-zi-mi-yeş,–
Ah– çin-çi-nim,– çin-çi-nim, ö-pem ağ-zin– i-çi-ni;
Ö-per-ken i-sit-mi- -şim, da-ye,– sen ba-ğaş-la____ su-çu-mu-ye!

M. F. 3168 b), Osmaniye (Osmaniye), Bekir oğlu Mahmud (34), 22. XI. 1936.

43c.
Kemençe: 1a volta
poco a poco acc.
al ♩=290
sic
2a volta
M. F. 3168 a), Osmaniye (Osmaniye), Bekir oğlu Mahmud (34), 22. XI. 1936.
43d.
Halay havasĭ*
1–8, (γ) 14,
1. Ur-fa-nĭn bo-zo gĭ-ra- cĭ,_ çift gë-zer-i- ki ba- - cĭ;
Ṣa-han ol-sam, av- lan-sam da goy-nun-da-kĭ tu- ra-cĭ._
Ur- fa, ñ-Ur-fa, ñ-uc o- - - lur, ** dyom-la-le-ri_ tuc o- - - lur;

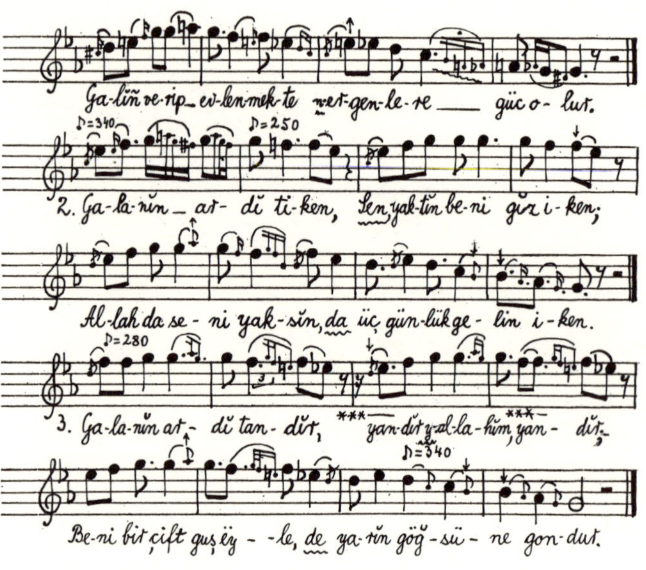
Ga-lîñ ve-rip ev-len-mek-te ver-gen-le-re güc o-lur.
2. Ga-la-nın at- dı ti-ken, Sen yak-tın be-ni gız i-ken;
Al-lah da se-ni yak-sın, da üç gün-lük ge-lin i-ken.
3. Ga-la-nın at- dı tan-dır, yan-dır yal-la-hım, yan- dır;
Be-ni bir çift guş ey- -le, de ya-rin göğ-sü-ne gon-dur.

M. F. 3177 a), Çardak (Osmaniye), Osman Çenet (34), ill., 23. XI. 1936.

44. Oyun havası *

1-7, (7) 14,
1. Hey, Dud a- ğa- cı dut ve rir, yap-ra-ğı-nı git ve-rir,
Er-gen oğ-lan, bü-yük gız, sa-rıl-dık-ca dat ve-rir.
sic.
Şu yan- - na dön-der be-ni, bu yan-na dön der be-ni;
Sağ ya-nım-da ya-rem va- - - r, ya-rı-me gön-der be-ni

M. F. 3153 b), Avlik (Kadirli), Ahmed Torun (42), 19. XI. 1936.

45.
Uçkur havası*
♩=102
1-8, (11[4+4+3]), 11, 11, 15, 7+7,
1. Gu-ta gut-muş yol üs-tü-ne çık-tı-ğı,
Ah, gu-ta gut-muş yol üs-tü-ne çık-tı-ğı,
Ay-dın ha-va-sı-na bü-ker ip-li-ği, ñ-el-ler, el-ler,
(r.)
(1. r.)
A-ma-nın dër-ler, dër-ler, ho-ta-zım nen-ni, nen-ni,
Ke-le-şim nen-ni, nen-ni, bir da-nem nen-ni, nen-ni.
♩=108
2. Ev-le-ri-nin ö-nü de, ñ-a-man, id-ri-sah,
ev-le-ri-nin ö-nü de ñ-a-man, id-ri-sah,
Ah, bo-yu-ñu-zun, gen-di şah, el-ler, el-ler, el-ler, el-ler,
(r.)
(2. r.)
A-ma-nın dër-ler, dër-ler, ho-ta-zım nen-ni, nen-ni,
Bir da-nem nen-ni, nen-ni, ke-le-şim nen-ni, nen-ni.

75

M. F. 3163 a), Dadal (Mersin), Halil oğlu Ali (37), 21. XI. 1936.

76

1)
Dil-be-r, dil-be-r,_ ca-nım dil-be-r,
(r.) Ca-nı-mın yay- - - - la-sı dil-be-r,
Gön-lü-mün eğ- - - - le-si dil-ber.
3. Ga- - - ra ça-na- - - ğın yap- ra- ğı,
Ga- - -ra_ ça-na- - - ğın_yap- - ra- ğı,
Di- -bin-den al- - - - - dım top- ra- ğı,
Di-bin-den al- - - - - dım top- ra- ğı.
4. o Di-l-be-r gü-zel- ler_ap- - la- ğı,
Di- l- be-r gü-zel- - - ler ap- la- - ğı.

77

M. F. 3153 a), Avlik (Kadirli), Ahmed Torun (42), 19. XI. 1936.

47.

1–4, (8) 10,

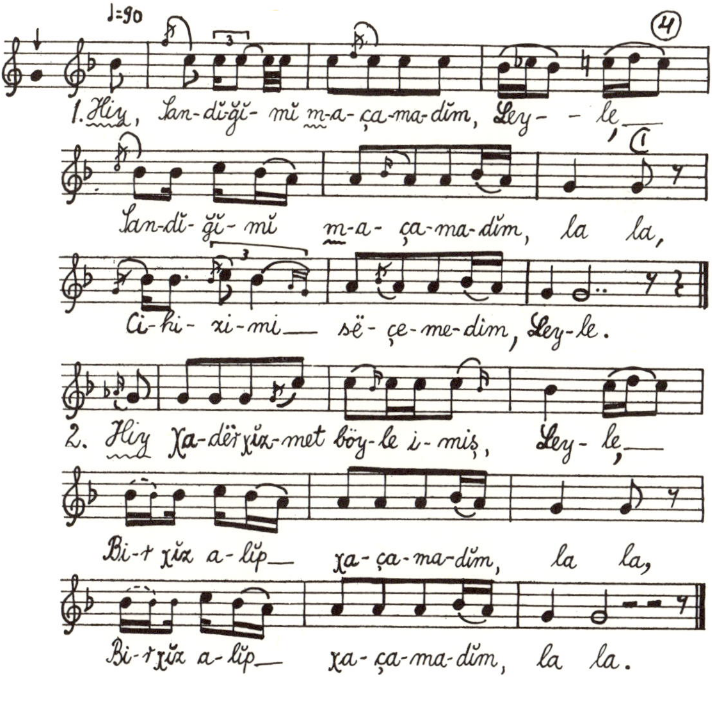

♩=90

1. Hıy, San-dı-ğı- mı m-a-ça-ma-dım, Ley- - le,__

San-dı- ğı- mı m-a- ça-ma-dım, la la,

Ci-hi- zi-mi__ së- çe-me-dim, Ley-le.

2. Hıy Ka-dër kız-met böy-le i-miş, Ley- le,__

Bi-r kız a-lıp__ ka-ça-ma-dım, la la,

Bi-r kız a-lıp__ ka-ça-ma-dım, la la.

78

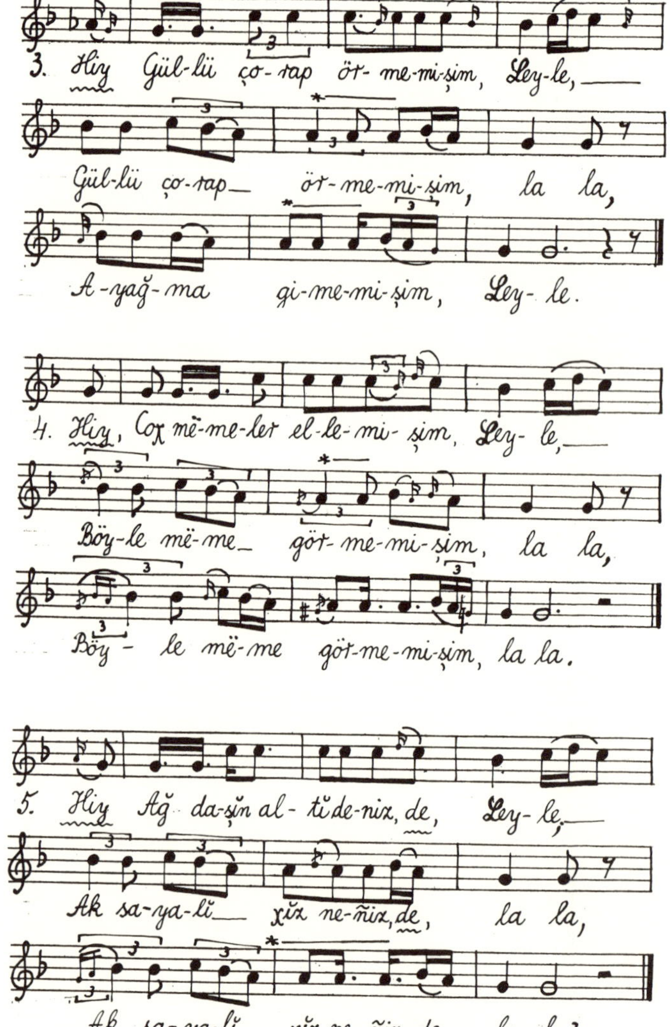
3. Hiy Gül-lü ço-rap ör-me-mi-şim, Ley-le,
Gül-lü ço-rap ör-me-mi-şim, la la,
A-yağ-ma gi-me-mi-şim, Ley-le.
4. Hiy, Cox më-me-ler el-le-mi-şim, Ley-le,
Böy-le më-me göt-me-mi-şim, la la,
Böy - le më-me göt-me-mi-şim, la la.
5. Hiy Ağ da-şin al-tï de-niz, de, Ley-le,
Ak sa-ya-lï xïz ne-ñiz, de, la la,
Ak sa-ya-lï xïz ne-ñiz, de, la la.

M. F. 3137 a), Hüyük (Çorum), Hatice Deklioğlu (13), ill., 16. XI. 1936.

79

48 a.
1-5, (7) 7, 7, 10, 10,
♪=91
1. Hiy Ma-vi-lim Daş-ba-şın-da,
Ma-vi-lim Daş-ba-şın-da
In-ci-li-ñ fes ba-şın-da, ma-vi-lim,
In-ci-li-ñ fes ba-şın-da, ma-vi-lim.
2. Hiy Kız, ni-yeñ ağ-la-mı-yon?
Kız,— ni-yeñ ağ-la-mı-yon?
Ni-şan-lıñ gıth ya-şın-da, ma-vi-lim,
Ni-şan-lıñ gıth ya-şın-da, ma-vi-lim,
3. M-ma---vi-lim, ğak, gi-de-lim,
Ma--vi-lim, ğak, gi-de-lim,

M.F. 3137 b), Hüyük (Çorum). Hatice Deklioğlu (13), ill., 16.XI.1936.

48b.

1–5, (7) 7, 7, 10, 10,

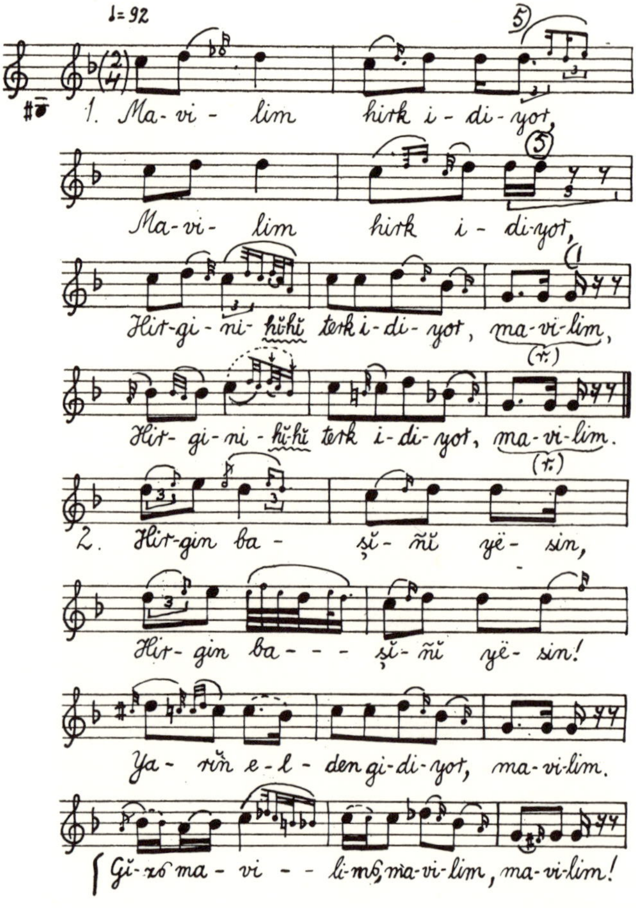

♩= 92

1. Ma-vi-lim hirk i-di-yot,
Ma-vi-lim hirk i-di-yot,
Hir-gi-ni-hi-hi terk i-di-yot, ma-vi-lim,
(r.)
Hir-gi-ni-hi-hi terk i-di-yot, ma-vi-lim.
(r.)

2. Hir-gin ba-şĭ-ñĭ yë-sin,
Hir-gin ba---şĭ-ñĭ yë-sin!
Ya-rĭn e-l-den gi-di-yot, ma-vi-lim.
Gi-zo ma-vi--li-mo, ma-vi-lim, ma-vi-lim!

(r.?) Çal da-u̯ŭl- - - cŭ da-u̯ŭ- lŭ, da-u̯ŭ-lŭ,
Çal zu-rr-na - cŭ zur-na-yŭ,__ zur-na-yŭ!
3. Ma-vi-lim,____ kalk, gi- de- li- m,
Ma-- vi- - lim,__ kalk, gi- de- lim,
Fë- ne- ri___ yak, gi-de-lim, ma-vi-lim,
Fë- ne- ri___ yak, gi-de-lim, ma-vi-lim.
(r.)
4. Gö- - zë- le____ doy-mag ol- maz,
Gö- - zë - le____ doy-mag ol- maz,
Bir ça- la bak, gi-de-lim, ma-vi-lim,
Bir ça-la bak, gi- de- lim, ma-vi-lim.
(r.)

M. F. 3138 a), Ankara (Ankara), Emine Muktat (62), ill., (r.) 16. XI. 1936.

49a. Yağmur duası *
♩= 88
Yağ-mur-cu-ğum ya-ğı vir,
Be-ni_ yo-la sal-dı-lar,
acc. - - - - - al
Ku-yu-cu-ğum do-lu vir!
Yol-da bir yu- mak bul-dum,
♩= 96
Ek-mek ge-tir, yi-ye-lim,
Yu-ma-ğı e-be- me vir-dim.
acc. - - - - al
Gay-ta-n ge-tir, gi- - ye-lim,
E-be-m ba-ña da-rı vir-di,
♩= 100
Al-lah, al-lah di-ye-lim!
Ben da- rı-yı guş-la-ra vir-dim,
♩= 96
Ü-şü-düm, ü-şü-düm, üş ol-dum,
Guş-lar_ ba-ña ga-nat vir-di,
Bir to-pa-cık kış ol- dum.
Ga- nat-lan-dım, gö- - ye uc-dum.
Ki-şi-mi_ e-lim-den al-dı-lar,
Göy ba-ña yağ - mır vir - di,

83

M. F. 3141 a), Ankara (Ankara), Emine Muktat (62), ill., 16. XI. 1936.

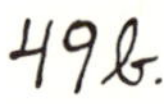
49b.

Yağmur duasĭ*

♩= 125
Te- kö- ne- de ha- mut,
A- ta- ba- da ça- mut,
Vir al-la-hi-m su- lu su- lu yağ-mur,

Topal gizin giçina yağmur!**

M. F. 3139 b), Ankara (Ankara), Emine Muktat (62), ill., 16. XI. 1936.

49c.
Yağmur duasĭ*
♪= ca 126
Bo-di, bo-di
Ne-den ō- di.
Bir ga-şi-cak su- dan ō- di.
Yağ- mur gi- zi yağ is- ter,
Pal- ta, kü- rek bal is- ter,
Goç, go- yun gur- ban is- ter,
Gö- bek- li hat- man is- ter.
**Ver allahim, ver bir sulu sulu yağmur!

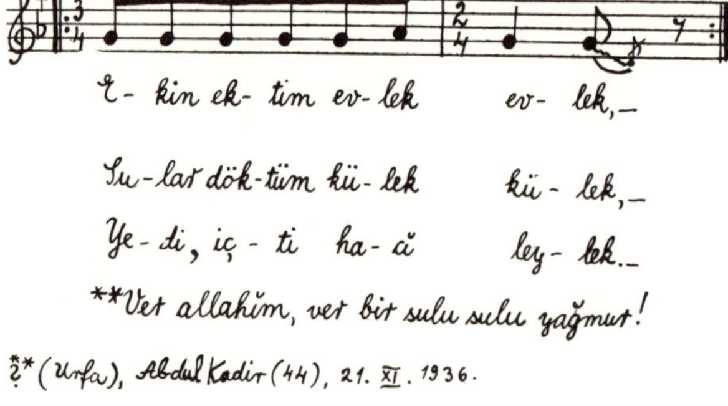
E- kin ek- tim ev- lek ev- lek,
Su- lar dök- tüm kü- lek kü- lek,
Ye- di, iç- ti ha- cĭ ley- lek.
**Ver allahim, ver bir sulu sulu yağmur!

?* (Urfa), Abdul Kadir (44), 21. XI. 1936.

49d. Yağmur duası *
** ♪=200
Bo- du, bo- du, a-nan në-den öl- dü?
Bir ga- şı- cak su- dan öl - dü.
A - yağ'm ça- mır yis - ter,
Bo- ga- zım ha- mır yis - ter.

***Gastı, yer yarıldı,
Saban girildi.
Ver, allahım, veeeeeeeer
Sulu sulu yağmur,
Ver, allahım, ver!

****
Bo- du, bo- du,— a-nan në-den öl-dü?
Bir ga- şı- cak su- dan öl- dü,—
A- yağ'm ça- mır yis- ter,—
Bo- ğa- zım ha - mır yis - ter.—

M.F. 3155 b), Kelköy (Seyhan), Abdullah Karakuş (22), ill., 20.XI.1936.

50. Nenni*

♪=230
1. Nen-ni yau-rŭm, nen-ni,
Nen-ni di- - - yi- be-le-dim,
Al ba-ğĭt-da- - - - - xĭ do-la-dĭm,
Yau-rum nen-ni, nen-ni!
hiz Sĕ-nye hak-dan di-le-dim,
Gu-zum nen-ni, nen-ni, hu!
2. Nen-ni di-dim bë-şi-ği-ne,
Yau-rum nen-ni, nen-ni!
Dev-let kon-sun e-şi-ği-ne,
Yau-rum nen- ni, nen-ni, hu!

87

M. F. 3139 a), Ankara (Ankara), Emine Muktat (62), ill., 16. XI. 1936.

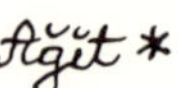

51.

Ağıt *

♪ = 260
sic
Hiy Ya-tır-mış-ler de ya-zı-mı, ___ i gu-zum oy ___ oy ___ oy, ___
Hi-cin gi-bi yaŋ-rım yaŋ---- rım, da ___ y-a-y-a-y-a-y oy oy ___ oy, ___
hñ Sa-rı sa-çı da gu-zum, ___ si-cim-gi-bi ___ yaŋ-rım oy ___ oy. ___
Hñ Ge-lin gar-daş-la-rım ___ yaŋ-rı-ma, ñ-oy ___ oy ___ oy,
Ağ-lı-ya-lı-m da ba-cım gi-bi, ___ yaŋ-rım oy ___ oy! ___
M-me-ze-rin de yol üs-- tü-ne gaz-sın-lat, ___ oy----- yo-yo-yo-yo-yoy oy ___ oy,
Yol üs-tü-ne goy-sun-lat, yaŋ-rım oy, ___ oy, ___ oy! ___

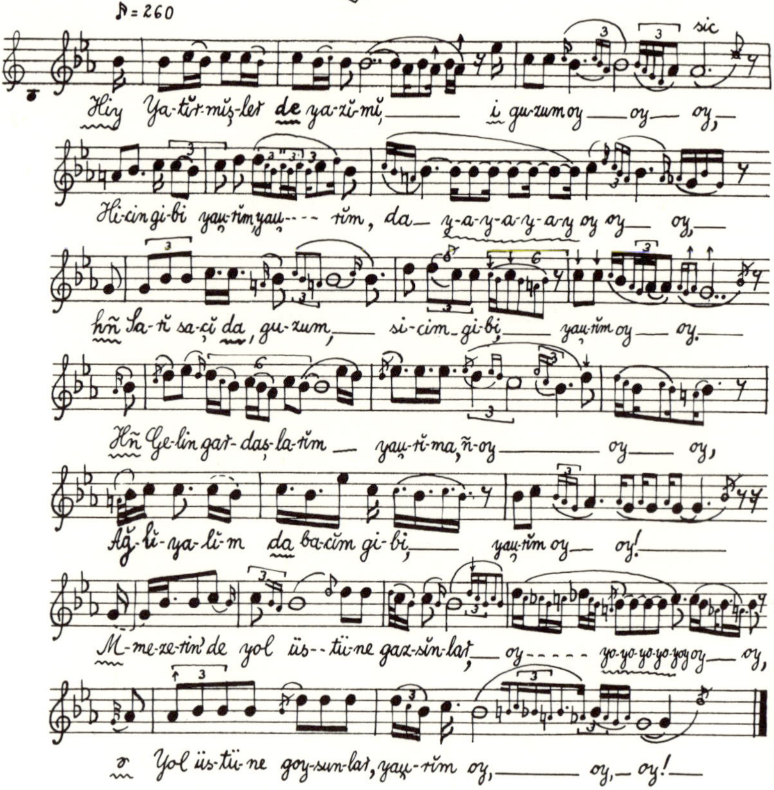

M.F. 3141 b), Ankara (Ankara), Emine Muktat (62), ill., 16. XI. 1936.

52.

♩ = 123
* 1. Sir-ri-sa-- rı-- ñıñ ___ al----- tı, ___
Ge-lin-ler yë- sir ___ al----- dı. (sic!)

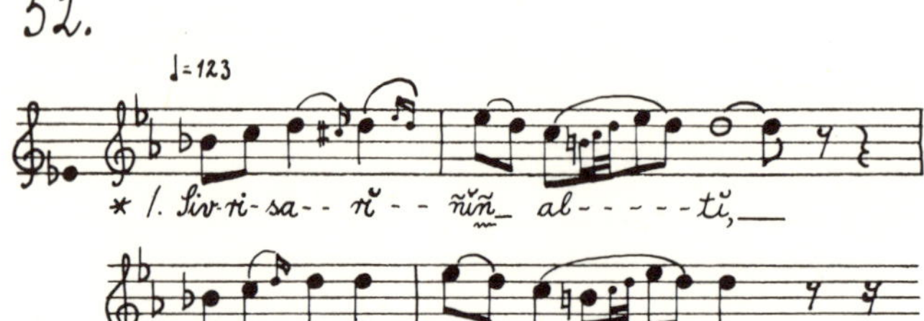

89

M.F. 3143 b), Hüyük (Çorum), Hatice Deklioğlu (13), ill., 16. XI. 1936.

53.

♪=212
Yü-ce dağ ba- şı-nın_ dört ya- nı- - hı yol-dur,
dört ya - - - nı - - - hı yol - dur,
hiy Dol-dur Su-nam,_ dol-dur, su-yu-nun_ dol-du-hur,
su- yu- nu - - - n dol- du- hu- hur, oy.—
♪=224
Yo-lu-nun üs- tü- ne_ ya-tam, u - - hu-yu-yam,
ya- - tam, ___ u - - - hu-yu-yam,
Mev-lâ-yı sye- vet-syen, gel, be- - ni gal-dı- hır,
gel, be - - ni ___ gal-dı-hır, — oy. —
(r.) Du-man- lı dağ - - - lar, bo-ran-lı dağ-lar, gül yüz-lüm ağ-lar.—

M.F. 3145 b), Vartan (Sivas), Divrikli Ali (37), ill., 17. XI. 1936.

M. F. 3184 B), Çardak (Osmaniye), Mehmed oğlu Pir Sabit (20), 23. XI. 1936.

55a.
Halay havası*
♪=350
1. Ha-san da-ğı, Ha-san da - - - - - - ğı,
Sen-den yü-ce dağ ol - - - - - - ma-mı?
Se-ni yay-lı- yan gü- - ze - - - - lin
♪=320
Al ya-na-ğı bal ol- - - - - - ma-mı?
2. A-man, gü-ley- me-me- - le- - rim,
Ca-nım, gü-ley me-me-le - - - - rim!
♪=244
Kör o-la-sı ter-zi ba- şı,
Ne sık dik-miş düğ-mey - - - - - - le-rim!

M. F. 3177 b), Çardak (Osmaniye), Kâmil Çenet (32), 23. XI. 1936.

55 b.
♪=264
Halay havasĭ *
1. Ha-san da-ğĭ, Ha- san da - - ğĭ,
Sen-den yü-ce dağ ol- ma - - mĭ?
2. Se-ni yay-lĭ - - - yan gö- - - ze - - - lin,
Se- ni yay- lĭ - - - yan gö - - - ze - - lin
Al ya- na-ğĭ bal ol- - - ma- mĭ?
3. A-man, gü-ley me- me- le - - - ri,
A-man, gü-ley me - me - - le - - - ri,
Çe-şil-me-yor düğ-me- - le- - - ri!

M. F. 3178 a), Çardak (Osmaniye), Kâmil Özgan (42), 23. XI. 1936.

55c.
Halay havası*
♪=220
1. Ha-san da-ğı, Ha-san da-ğı,
Sen-den yü-ce dağ ol-ma-mı?
2. Se-ni yay- lı- - - yan gö- - ze- - - lin,
Se-ni yay- lı- - yan gö- - - ze- - - lin
Al ya-na-ğı bal ol- - - ma-mı?
3. I - yau-rım gü-ley me-me- le- - ri,
x Gü-züm gü- ley me-me- le- - ri,
Çe- zil-mi-yot düğ-me- - le- - ri.

M. F. 3178 b), Çardak (Osmaniye), Basri Demir (37),** 23. XI. 1936.

55d. Halay havası*

M. F. 3181 b), Çardak (Osmaniye), Mehmed oğlu Pir Sabit (20), 23. XI. 1936.

56. Oyun havası*

♩= 108
1. Ga-ta-man-dan ge-lir_ i-ken,___
Yan-dım, Ga-ta-man-dan ge-lir__ i-ken
A-ya- - - ğı-ma___ bat - tı_ da ti-ken.
2. Ay-rı-lık tır___ be- li-mi bü-ken.___
Ağ-la-ma ci-va-nım çer- - kes__ gi-zi.
Sen al___ ge-yin,_ ben___ gır- mı-zı,
Çı-ka-lım da dağ-la- rın__ ba- şı-na,
Se-n gül top-la,__ ben__ ner- gi-zi.

97

3. Ga-ta-ma-nın alt ya-nı gu-yu,
Yan-dım, Ga-ta-ma- nın- alt- ya-nı gu-yu,
Gu-yu- - - - -dan çe- ker- - ler- su-yu,
Gu- yu- - -dan çe- - - ker- - ler- su-yu.
4. O ya-rı-mın es- ki de hu-yu.
Oy- na-ma cı-va-nım çer- - kes- gı-zı.
(r.) Sen al ge-yin, ben gır- mı-zı,
Çı- ka-lım da dağ- la- rın ba- şı-na,
***

M.F. 3163 b), Dadal (Mersin), Halil oğlu Ali (37), 21. XI. 1936.

57.
Keklik halayı *
♪=330
1. Hıñ Gar-şı-da kürd ev-le-ri, ğoy ver el-le-rim, ğoy ver,
Gar-şı-da kürd ev-le-ri, ğoy ver el-le-rim, ğoy ver,
Ya-yı-lır de-ve-le-ri, de, ge-lin, el-le-rim, ğoy ver.
2. Sâ-li-nır, su-ya i--ner, ğoy ver el-le-rim, ğoy ver,
Sâ-li-nır, su-ya i--ner, ğoy ver el-le-rim ğoy ve--r,
Türk-me-nin ma-ha-la-rı, da, ge-lin, el-le-rim, ğoy ver,
Türk-me-nin ma-ha-la-rı, da, kek-lik, el-le-rim, ğoy ver.
3. Mı Gar-şı-da ğa**--yın yer-ler, ğoy ver el-le-rim, ğoy ver,
Gar-şı-da ğa**-yın yer-ler, ğoy ver el-le-rim, ğoy ver,
Biz de var-sax ne der-ler? Ge-lin, el-le-rim, ğoy ver.

M. F. 3143 a), Hüyük (Çorum), Hatice Deklioğlu (13), ill., 16. XI. 1936.

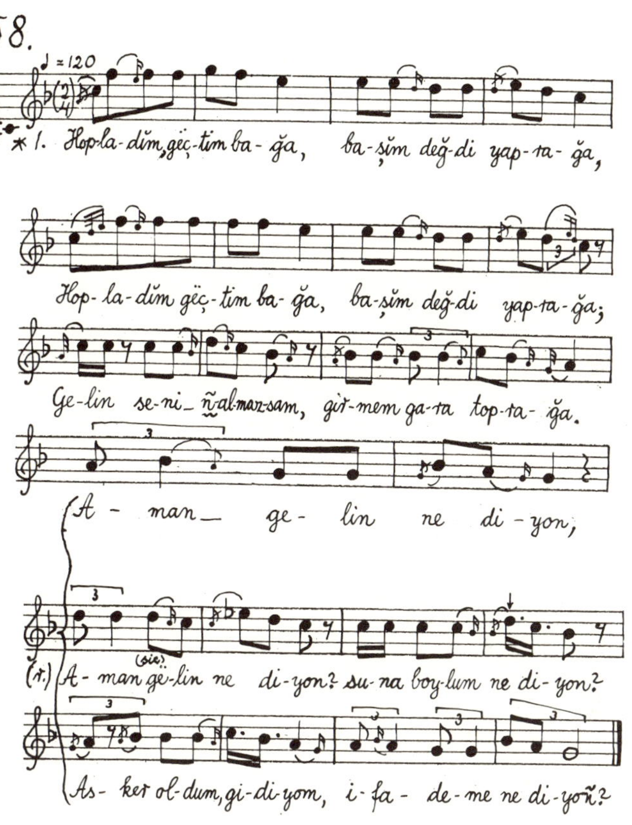
58.
♩ = 120
*1. Hop-la-dım, geç-tim ba-ğa, ba-şım değ-di yap-ta-ğa,
Hop-la-dım geç-tim ba-ğa, ba-şım değ-di yap-ta-ğa;
Ge-lin se-ni_ñ_al-mar-sam, gir-mem ga-ra top-ta-ğa.
A - man_ ge- lin ne di-yon,
(r.) A-man ge-lin ne di-yon? su-na boy-lum ne di-yon?
(sic)
As- ker ol-dum, gi-di-yom, i-fa- de-me ne di-yoñ?

M. F. 3175 b), Çardak (Osmaniye), Ibiş Mehmedin Abdullah (17), ill., 23. XI. 1936.

M. F. 3176 B), Çardak (Osmaniye), Ibiş Mehmedin Abdullah (14), ill., 23. XI. 1936.

101

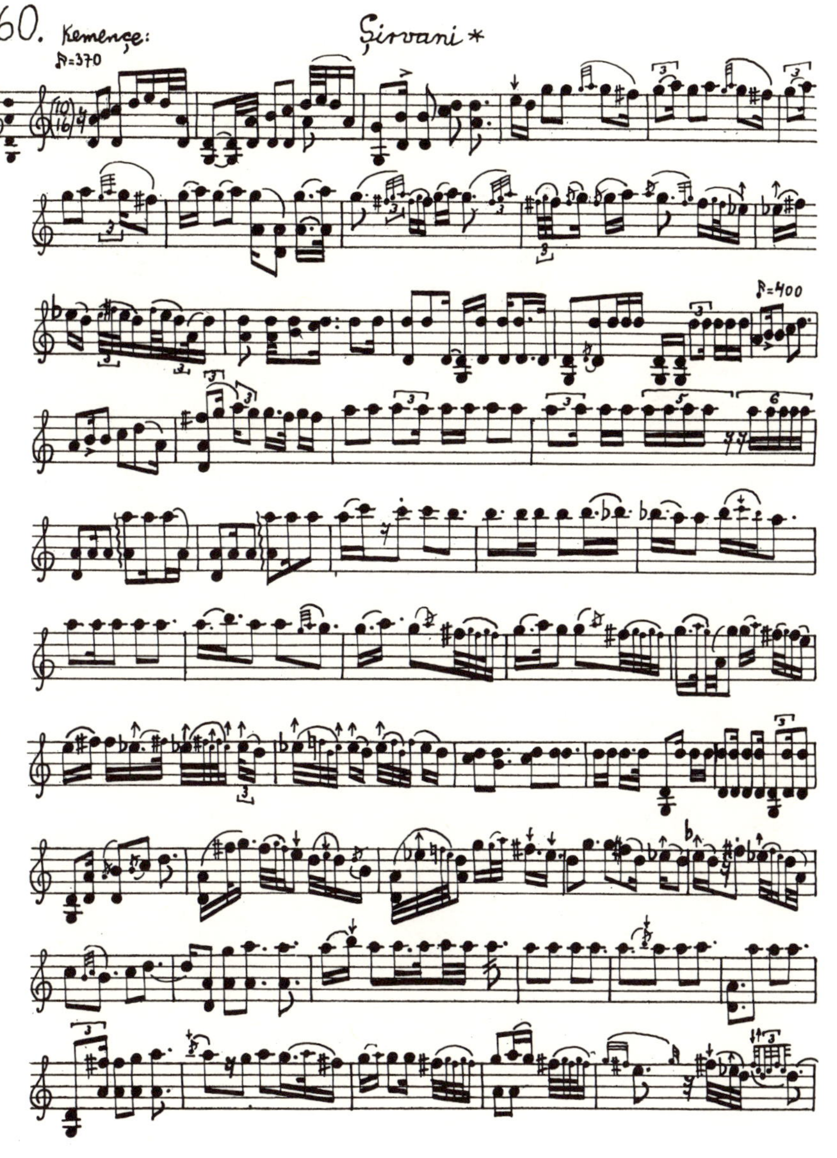
60. Kemençe:
Şirvani *
♪=370
♪=400

102

M. F. 3170, Osmaniye (Osmaniye), Bekir oğlu Mahmud (34), 22. XI. 1936.

61. Halay havasi*

3a volta

***

M. F. 3183, Çardak (Osmaniye), zurna: ? Ali (24) / davul: Cuma Ali (38) } ill., of the Abdal tribe, 23. XI. 1937.

105

F. 3182, Cardak (Osmaniye), zurna: ? Ali (24), davul: Cuma Ali (38) } ill., of the Abdal tribe, 23. XI. 1936.

63.
Maraş*
♩=115
Zurna
**
m.d.
Davul
m.s

. F. 3185 a), Çardak (Osmaniye), zurna: ? Ali (24) / davul: Cuma Ali (38) } ill., of the Abdal tribe, 23. XI. 1936.

4.

Garip*

109

M. F. 3185 b), Çardak (Osmaniye), zurna: ? Ali (24) / davul: Cuma Ali (38) } ill., of the Abdal tribe, 23. XI. 1936.

65.

Kaba*

111

M. F. 3186 b), Çardak (Osmaniye), zurna: ? Ali (24), davul: Cuma Ali (38) } ill., of the Abdal tribe, 23. XI. 1936.

66.

113

h. F. 3186 a), Çardak (Osmaniye), zurna: ? Ali (24) / davul: Cuma Ali (38) } ill., of the Abdal tribe, 23. XI. 1936.

Appendix

I. Var. of № 2.*

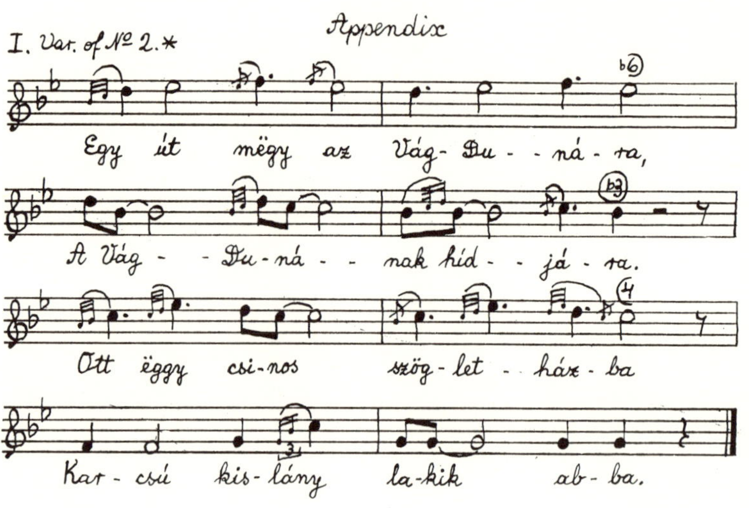
Egy út mëgy az Vág-Du--ná-ra,
A Vág--Du-ná--nak híd--já-ra.
Ott ëggy csi-nos szög-let--ház-ba
Kar-csú kis-lány la-kik ab-ba.

II. Var. of № 5.*

Fe-hér Lász-ló lo-vat lo--pott
A Fe-ke--te-ha-lom a--ló;
Pej pa-ri-pát kan-tá-ros-tól,
Cif-ra nyer-gës-szër-szá--mos--tól.

III. Var. of № 8 a.*

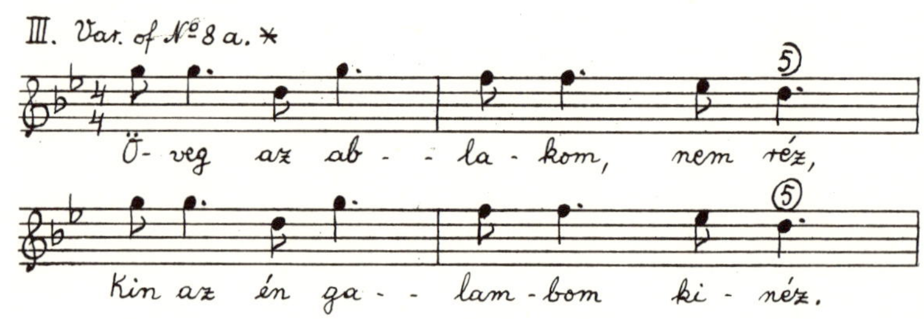
Ö-veg az ab--la-kom, nem réz,
Kin az én ga--lam-bom ki-néz.

115

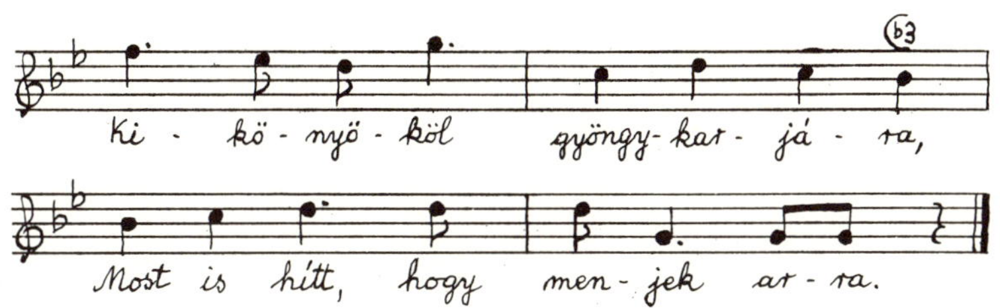

Ki - kö - nyö - köl gyöngy - kat - já - ra,
Most is hítt, hogy men - jek ar - ra.

IV. Var. of № 8 *
Á - tal is ment a Kö - - rö - zsön,
Be - le is fúlt ö - rö - kö - sön.
Nyár - fa - le - vél, fűz - fa - le - vél,
Hej, de min-dent is el - so - dor a szél.

V. Var. of the 2nd half of № 17. *
Knji - gu pi - še Muk - tar pa - ša, haj haj haj haj,
Knji - gu - pi - še Muk - tar pa - ša, pa - ?
[sic!]

Notes to the Melodies

1a. *Cradle song (Lullaby).
**According to the transcription of the text on the spot: *bunum.*
***The cylinder ended before the missing portion of the stanza could be recorded. N.B.—The pitch was $c\sharp$ (!) before the recording.

1b. *Mourning song.

2. *The pitch was *g* before the recording. Hungarian variant: Appendix, No. I.

3. *The performer sang the melody at least eight to ten times for the transcription on the spot, before the recording took place. Because of the extremely high pitch these singers always chose, his voice was so tired when the time came for recording, that he could not produce the highest tone $g^1\flat$ (in the transposition $b^2\flat$) at the beginning. The correct form of the beginning appears in the second and third stanzas.

4. *Although the text is a mourning one, over someone who died, the song does not seem to be a Mourning song nor was it even so called.

5. *Mourning song. Hungarian variant: Appendix, No. II.
**This skeleton form of the melody, transcribed on the spot before the recording took place, seems to give the more usual main tones of the melody. The first two measures of the recording are, in any case, wrong. The singer said that the texts of this melody generally are improvised. The actual text he used was improvised fifty years ago by a woman when her son died.

6. *Mourning song.
**Faulty beginning; the correct form is to be found in st. 2.

7a. *Cradle song (Lullaby). The singer said it is the cradle song of a childless woman, craving for a child. This remark obviously applies only to the text.

**The second section was omitted in this stanza. Such omissions generally do not occur in the performance of this melody.

7b. *Dance song.

8a. *The *kemençe* part had to be transposed in the transcription according to the vocal part. The singer played the melody continuously on the instrument even when singing. His voice, however, overwhelmed the sound of the instrument in the record to the extent that it was impossible to transcribe the latter. There are numerous Hungarian variants of this melody. Two of them appear in the Appendix as Nos. III and IV. N.B.—The *kemençe* is an instrument quite similar to the violin, tuned $g\ d^1\ a^1\ d^2$ (!), and played in the oriental manner: the neck of the instrument upward, the body downward (that is, like a violoncello).

8b. *The gathered singers were asked whether they knew song No. 8a. It appeared that many of them knew it except the words which they had forgotten. With our help they managed to sing two stanzas of the text.

8d. *This facetious text is said to have been made by a man just before he died!

**The singer changed *-mi* to something like *-ri*.

8e. *The designation of this song is said to be *Hacĭ bey* which, however, seems to refer only to the text. Not more than two stanzas of the latter are transcribed; the continuation is missing. N.B.—The pitch was *g* before the recording.

9. *These two additional (improvised) syllables, not belonging to the text proper, are unintelligible from the record.

10a. *The meaning of this designation could not be determined, nor whether it refers to the text or to something else.

**The transcription on the spot of the third and fourth text stanzas was omitted; they are unintelligible from the record. Even the melody of the fourth stanza could not be transcribed without due understanding of the words.

10b. *This piece is melody No. 10a. performed on the *kemençe*.

**The cylinder ended, and the recording had to be interrupted.

12. *This version is the skeleton form of the melody, as transcribed before the recording took place. The singer repeated the melody at least eight to ten times for this purpose, so that his voice tired because of the extremely high pitch which these singers customarily employ. When the time came for the recording, therefore, he could not produce the highest tones in the required pitch as seen in the skeleton form. Thus the tones of the skeleton form must be regarded as the authentic ones, at least so far as the pitch is concerned.

**The following three tones, marked with a brace, are off-pitch.

13a. *This word sounds as *nasĭp* in the record.

**A *vibrato* of the same character as the one described on pp. 49 and 60, transcribed in detailed values in other pieces, was sung on this tone. Here, however, the rhythm of the pulsation is rather unclear. N.B.—The singer said the text is of his own making, that he invented it on the occasion of the death of one of his relatives who was struck by a thunderbolt the previous summer (such information is not always reliable!).

13b. *This designation is the name of a tribal head. According to some people he lived 100 years ago, to others 200 years ago. The designation of the song, that is, probably of the text, is in his honor, and it is generally sung when the tribe moves from the lower country to the mountains in the springtime.

**The missing syllables (probably seven in st. 2, eleven in st. 3, and five in st. 4) are unintelligible from the record and were not transcribed on the spot.

***The singer did not know exactly when he was born.

15. *These interpolations of *ñ* consonants and the following ones (measures 6, 9, 12, and so forth) sound rather emphatic and give the impression of being separate, new syllables. The pitch was *a* before the recording of the piece. Hungarian variant: No. 62 in *Hung. Folk Music* (*op. cit.*).

16. *Same remark as to No. 15*.

** = *ĭrak.*

17a. *The pitch was *c*♯ before the recording.

**Serbo-Croatian variant: Appendix No. V.

17b. *The meaning of this designation is not clear, nor if it refers only to the text.

**Cylinder 3,159 ended before the repetition of the fourth melody section could be recorded. The following stanza contains the repetition.

17c. *St. 4–6 are recorded on M.F. 3,198 but were not transcribed in order to preserve the cylinder.

18. *See the Notes to No. 23.

**Two syllables are not transcribed on the spot and unintelligible from the recording.

19. *The pitch was c♯ before the recording.

20. *These extraordinary *appoggiature* (marked with white-head notes) sound like very short metallic clangs. Their usage possibly originates from Arabic sources.

**This word sounds like *aksura* in the record; the transcription on the spot has *aksurumu*.

***These five missing syllables were not transcribed on the spot and are unintelligible from the record.

21a. *Same remark as to No. 20*. N.B.—The singer is the son of the performer of melody No. 20.

**A sudden stop: the singer probably did not recollect the continuation of the text.

21b. *The meaning of this frequently recurring designation could not be established. The singer said that a hundred-year-old man taught him the song (probably only the text) in order that the former should remember him, and that no one else knows the piece. In Seyhan the melody is known with the designation *Türkmeni*.

**Uncertain (that is, unsteady) vibration.

22. *This value contains eleven equal parts as a succession of vibrations. Each of the first six vibrations is sung to *iy*, the remainder shows no difference in vowel color.

**Eight vibrations of equal value, each sung to *iy*.

***Nine vibrations of equal value, all sung to *iy* except the last one which shows no difference in vowel color.

***Eight vibrations of equal value, each sung to *iy*.

(*) Ten vibrations of equal value, each of the first four sung to *iy*, the remainder shows no difference in vowel color. N.B.—The pitch was the same before the recording.

23. *St. 1 is recorded on M.F. 3,171 but was not transcribed, however, in order to preserve the cylinder without deterioration. The performer played continuously on his instrument even when he was singing, and with just the same result as in melody Nos. 8a., 18, and 42; the accompaniments doubling the vocal form are too indistinct to be transcribed. Melodies such as Nos. 23 and 18 are, in fact, very large extensions of the eleven-syllable isometric descending type (melody Nos. 10–17, 19–22). The extension causes the increase of text syllables as a result of the repetition of the eleven-syllable line or (rarely) part of it, or of the placement of two eleven-syllable lines under one melody section. Sometimes both procedures are combined.

**It is rather startling to see that the singer never descends to the final tone in the vocal form, which is reached only by the instrument in the postlude to each stanza. Before the recording took place, however, he came down to the final tone in this piece but not in the following one (published here as melody No. 18). N.B.—The *cura ĭrizva* is a three-stringed, plucked instrument with frets. The open strings are tuned I II III

(in the transposed transcription appearing as ).
The scale of the III string created by the placement of the frets is as follows:

Original sound:

Transposed:

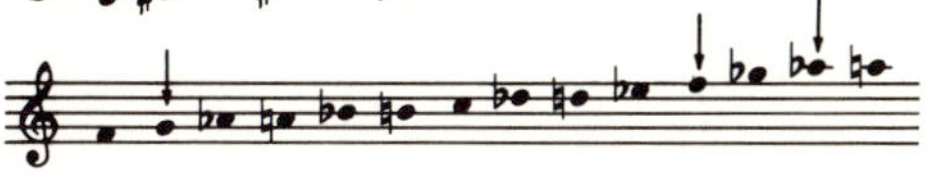

The arrow means almost a quarter-tone difference in pitch.

24. *Melody of the *Aşiret* (name of a nomadic tribe).

25. *Mourning song.

**These *vibrato* g^1-s are sung to *yi yi yi* interpolated syllables similar to those in melody No. 22.

26. **Maraş* is the designation of a dance. This melody, however,

was sung, and was said to be sung only as an "entre-dance" item between the performance of the *Maraş* dance by dancers and instruments (without any singing) as given in melody No. 63, and a following different dance.

29. *This designation seems to refer to the portion of the piece, given as the first and second stanzas, which is a sung invitation to the dance. The dance proper appears in the *Tempo giusto* part which, however, is never sung, only played on the *zurna*, probably with *daṷul* accompaniment (see the Notes to melody Nos. 60–66 for remarks about these instruments). The performer sang it for me to meaningless loose syllables, since no *zurna* player was available.

**These variants—transcriptions made on the spot by ear—seem to have a more correct form, or are in any case more frequent.

30. *This tone is sung with a *vibrato* similar to the one in the first measure.

**No more essential changes in the third and fourth stanzas.

31. *The refrain was not considered when establishing the structure of the melody.

32. *Unfinished record: the cylinder ended before a fourth and fifth section, similar to those of st. 2 (with the same refrain) could be recorded.

33. *Henna song: probably sung when henna—a red paint made from a certain plant and used for coloring women's face and nails—is put on the future bride for the last time prior to the wedding ceremony. It therefore belongs to the category of Wedding songs.

35. *The singer chose a too-high pitch for version b). This choice accounts for the change in the melody. The correct form of the piece appears in version a).

**The cylinder ended before the last measure of the melody (the repeat of *diline*) could be recorded.

36. *The meaning of this designation could not be established. *Il bey* seems to be a certain area.

37. *This designation means Long[-drawn] song. The piece, how-

ever, has nothing in common with the *Cântec Lung* mentioned on p. 45 (above) and with melody No. 62 of this volume. The singer learned the piece from one of his fellow soldiers, a native of İslahiye, Antep *vilayet*, and, according to him, it is unknown to anyone else in Çardak.

38. *The literal meaning of this designation is The Mouth of Dawn. *Ağiz* (mouth), however, may have another meaning which is perhaps the designation of a certain kind of melodies. It could not be ascertained whether the designation refers to a certain melody, to a certain genre, or to the text of this piece.

39. *This designation seems to be that of a certain genre of songs; it could not be established whether the reference is to the melody or to the text. The piece is sung only by men in a state of solitude.
Same remark as to No. 13a..

39. *This designation seem to be that of a certain genre of songs; it could not be established whether the reference is to the melody or to the text. The piece is sung only by men in a state of solitude.
Same remark as to No. 13a..

40. *The designation means Dance song.
**The piece is generally performed by women with accompaniment played on a tin pan which is struck by the inner wrist and the fingertips of the right hand. As the Milman Parry Collection of Serbo-Croatian folk songs (contained in the Widener Library of Harvard University) shows, Yugoslav women also occasionally use a tin pan ("*tepsije*") in the guise of a percussion instrument for song accompaniment, probably as a result of Turkish influence.
***This repeat of the first section is exceptional.

41. *The designation means Dance song.

42. *Same remark as to No. 8a.*.

43a. *Dance song.

43b.c. *Same designation as to No. 29. Variant c., however, contains only a *tempo giusto* part, so that it becomes doubtful what "*Halay Havasi*" means.

**The performer alternated *kemençe* playing and his singing of the piece. After the *1ª volta* of variant c., the first stanza of variant b. is sung; then the *2ª volta* of c. is played, followed by st. 2 of b. His singing was a fourth lower than the pitch of his instrumental performance, because the pitch of the *kemençe* did not tally with the range of his voice.

43d. *These kinds of melodies are said to be sung during the intervals between dance performances. One might term them "entre-dances." See the description of the dancing in Çardak on pp. 45–46 (above).

**This word was *dökme-*, according to the on-the-spot transcription.

***This word was *ban-*, according to the on-the-spot transcription.

44. *Dance song. Men dance it in a way similar to that described in the Note to No. 46*.

**The cylinder ended before the last measure of the stanza could be recorded.

45. **Uçkur* means shoelace, an unclear designation. According to some people, the designation refers to the indecency of the text. The piece is a Dance song, said to be "making the whores dance." Men perform it with dancelike ventral motions and with a snap by both hands on each (2/4) beat.

46. *The designation apparently originates from the text. The piece is a Dance song performed at wedding festivities as follows: four women, standing in pairs at both ends of a row of participants, each of the four holding a handkerchief in each hand, sing the stanzas alternately and by pairs. The women standing between the paired singers never sing. If *zurna* and *daul* players are present, no singing occurs, the *zurna* player alone performs the melody. The singer was unable to describe what rhythm the *zurna* player uses in this piece. N.B.—Before the recording, the pitch was *a*, and the tempo was fixed at ♪ = 160.

47. *The pitch of these a^1-s is slightly lower.

48a. *The transcription of this portion of the text was omitted on the spot; the words are unintelligible from the record.

49a. *Rain-begging song.
**Spoken.
***Recited with speech sound.

49b. *Rain-begging song.
**This line is recited.

49c. *Rain-begging song.
**Spoken. N.B.—The singer did not remember his birthplace, only the *vilayet* (Urfa). He learned the song in Tarsus where he migrated when he was still a child.

49d. *Rain-begging song.
**This version was sung for the phonograph recording.
***Spoken.
****The performer sang this entirely different version before the recording took place. without being conscious of the difference!

50. *Cradle song (Lullaby).

51. *Mourning song

52. *The text refers to the last war with the Greeks.

54. *Same remark as to No. 26* (substituting *Garip* for *Maraş*, and melody No. 64 for No. 63). There seems to be some relation between this melody and that of No. 64.

55a. *Same remark as to No. 43d.*. Instrumental variant: melody No. 61.
**Vibration in intensity of tone (not in pitch), somehow similar to those produced with *yi-yi* sounds (described on p. 49, above).

55b. *See the Note to No. 43d.*.

55c. *See the Note to No. 43d.*.
**The singer is a former member of parliament!

55d. *See the Note to No. 43d.*.

56. *Dance song. This piece seems to be of doubtful origin. For instance, the last melismatic group of the second measure in st. 1, 2, 4 is a characteristic pattern of Arabic art music.
**The pitch of $e^2\flat$ is variable.
***The cylinder ended and thus could not hold the last (fifth) section as seen in st. 2.

57. *This is a Dance song. The dancers are young people of both

sexes who sing it when dancing on festival days or at wedding festivities.

58. *Obviously a melody of urban origin, now diffused everywhere. The structure is unstabilized: other singers omit some of the repetitions or add more of them. Such inconstancy can occur even in the performance by the same singer.

59. *According to Mr. Ahmed Adnan Saygun, this melody is derived from the following urban melody, a "hit" song which is very well known, especially by soldiers:

The composer of this version was evidently "inspired" by the famous *Canzonetta* "Halte-là! Qui va là" in Bizet's opera *Carmen*. After the recording of this piece the singer says: "*Çardak köyündĕn—Ibíş Mehméd óğlu Abdullăh—ónbeş yaşĭndă*" (*ónbeş* is a slip of the tongue; the word should be *ondört*): "In the village of Çardak—Ibis Mehmed's son Abdullah—fifteen years old." (The double prime indicates main accents, the single prime lesser ones.)

60. *An instrumental dance melody. The piece is also recorded on M.F. 3,169.

61. *See the Note to No. 55a.* (that is, to No. 43d.*) which is the vocal variant of this piece. It is, however, uncertain whether these kinds of melodies are ever performed customarily on instruments or whether the actual performance was only an exceptional one.

**The *zurna* is a kind of rather loud and rough-sounding oboe, known everywhere in Arab territories in North Africa as *γeiṭa*. Its scale could not be examined and established. It is an instrument used to provide dance music par excellence for dance recreations, with the accompaniment of the *Daụul*, a kind of bass drum with two heads, identical with the *Ṭábăl* of the Arabs. A regular (unfelted) wooden drumstick is used in the right hand, a flexible wooden rod in the left. The instrument is attached to the waist of the performer who sometimes walks to and fro in dance steps during the performance. The *zurna* player, by the way, also moves in similar fashion as he plays.

***The record contains some other repetitions of the melody, which were not transcribed.

62. *Concerning *Bozlak* see the Note to No. 21b.*, about *Uzun Hava* (Long[-drawn] song) see the Note to No. 37*. This melody, however, is unrelated to either piece; on the contrary, it is obviously the real Long-drawn Melody, the *Cântec Lung* of the Rumanians (see the explanations on p. 45, above). The only puzzling circumstance in this piece is the constant 13/16 time, since the Long-drawn Melody could have no regular measures. On the other hand, if we look at and listen to the *zurna* part, independently from the percussion accompaniment, it appears to be a real *rubato* melody. Evidently the 13/16 measure is only due to the percussion player. We have here the interesting case, not uncommon in Arab rural music, too, of the matching of two heterogeneous kinds of rhythms: one is a *rubato* rhythm, the other is in regular measures.

About the instruments, see the Note to No. 61.

Same remark as to No. 61.

63. *See the Note to No. 26*.

About the instruments, see the Note to No. 61.

***At this point there was an involuntary, short interruption in the recording, after which the performance continued in a way similar to the previous part of the record.

64. *See the Notes to Nos. 54* and 26*.

About the instruments, see the Note to No. 61.

***The cylinder ended and the recording had to be halted.

65. *Designation of a dance.

About the instruments, see the Note to No. 61.

66. *Designation of a dance.

About the instruments, see the Note to No. 61.

APPENDIX

I., II. *The data, unfortunately, are not at hand.

III. *From Hontfüzesgyarmat, collected by Zoltán Kodály in 1912.

IV. *From the neighborhood of Enrőd, collected by Dr. Eugen Krüger about forty years ago. The leap into the higher octave at the end of the melody, as well as the increase in syllabic number in the last melody section, are exceptional features. The text is the second stanza of a well-known Hungarian folk text. Dr. Krüger sent me the piece from Nagyvárad after I had delivered a lecture over Budapest Radio in January, 1937, on the results of my collecting work in Turkey. As he stated in his accompanying letter, this variant is almost identical with the respective Turkish melody (No. 8a.); in any case it is more similar than the melody given as Appendix No. III (which was quoted as a Hungarian parallel during my lecture).

V. *Quoted from Ludvík Kuba, *Slovanstvo ve svých zpevech* (Pardubice, Poděbrady, Praha, 1884–1929), Vol. XII, No. 18 (from Šabac, pre–World War I Serbia).

PART TWO

Introduction to Part Two

TEXTS

ORTHOGRAPHY

About twelve years ago, when the Latin alphabet was adopted with certain modifications by the Turks, the same mistake was made as happened one hundred years ago in Hungary: linguists of both countries neglected to provide for a discrimination between open and closed *e*. Although most of the *e* vowels are open in the Turkish language, closed *e* vowels also occur. For the latter, therefore, I decided to use *ë* in this publication—the same letter which is used for this sound by Hungarians in scientific publications. Other additional letters used in this book are as follows:

u̯ for bilabial *u*;

x for a gutteral sound like the Spanish *j*;

– on long vowels when the length is a result of the disappearance of a *ğ*.

N.B.—It was in many cases difficult to establish the difference between *ğ* and *y* when they appear as a softened form of *g*. The rule states that: the softening of *g* will result in *ğ* between low (velar) vowels and in *y* between high (palatal) vowels. In this publication, however, there are many deviations from this rule.

TEXT LINE METRICS

As it has been pointed to above, the text lines of the Turkish rural folk poems are based on a syllable-counting metrical structure; that is, each meter has a fixed number of syllables, generally unchanged during the entire poem, with the main accent on the first syllable whether or not it coincides with the spoken accent.[52] In this collection are text lines whose structure is indicated in the following tabulation (|| means a main caesura appears between the meters, | a secondary one):

No. of Syllables	Metric Structure	Remarks
8	4 || 4	Typical of Class 1
8	3 | 2 || 3	In melody No. 33 only
11	{ 6 || 4 | 1 6 || 3 | 2 }	Typical of Class 2
11	6 || 2 | 3	In No. 27 only
11	4 | 4 || 3	In Nos. 24, 35–39, 45
7	4 || 3	Typical of Class 13 (in some pieces: 7+7)
7	3 || 4	In Nos. 31, 48
10	5 || 5	In No. 34 only
6	4 || 2	In some melodies of Class 18 (interchanged with lines extended to eight syllables, such as 6 || 2)

TEXT-STANZA STRUCTURE

The Turkish rural folk texts have rigorous stanza structure with fixed rhymes, similar to the Hungarian, Czech, Slovakian, and Ukraïnian folk texts; and at variance with the Bulgarian and

52. Contrary to the accentuation rules of the Turkish language in which the last syllable of words (with certain exceptions) is accented.

Serbo-Croatian ones in which no text-stanza structures or rhymes occur, and the Rumanian which have rhymes but no stanza structure. The texts of the most characteristic Turkish folk melodies, that is, Classes 1, 2, and 13, have text stanzas consisting of four separate proper text lines for each melody stanza; in other words, there are no repeats and no refrains.[53] Text-line repetition and refrains are observed in some of the remaining classes, except Class 18 (Rain-begging songs) which, by the way, has no stanza structure at all in its texts. Melody stanzas made up of three melody sections may have the same text line repeated for the first and second melody sections (melody Nos. 24, 33, 37). In this case the text stanzas do not tally with the melody stanzas, since two of the latter are apportioned to one text stanza. In view of the fact that text stanzas always consist of four text lines, the result will be as follows:

Melody-stanza 1	1st text line 1st text line	> 1st text line	Text-stanza 1
	2nd text line	→ 2nd text line	
Melody-stanza 2	3rd text line 3rd text line	> 3rd text line	
	4th text line	→ 4th text line	

The same phenomenon appears in two-section melodies, with no text-line repeats (melody Nos. 25, 26, 28, and so forth), and also in four-section melodies, if refrain text lines are used as a substitute for some of the proper text-line repeats:

53. Some exceptions are observed: melody Nos. 9, 15, 21a., 22, 40, 41, 44 have a refrain with the same metrical structure as the proper text lines (in No. 22 the same syllabic number but with 4 | 4 || 3 as meters; and in Nos. 1a., 7a.b. a refrain with a different metrical structure). The rather free extensions of the melody sections in Nos. 18 and 23, both sung by the same man, involve text-line repetitions.

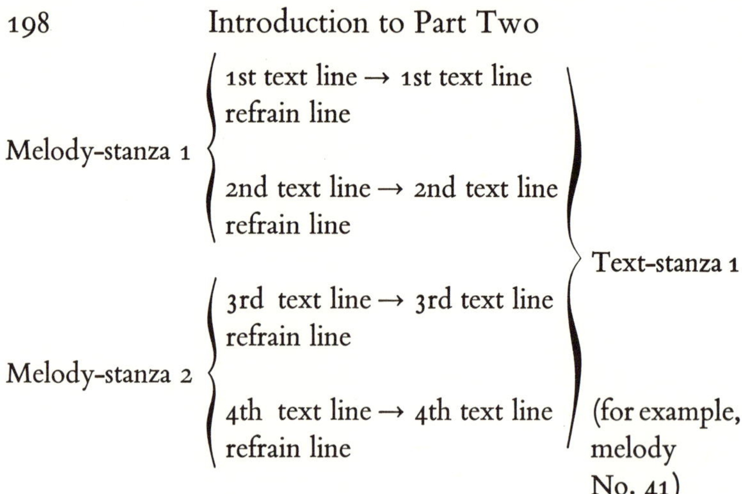

Text-line repeats occur in more than fourteen vocal melodies of the seventy-eight in our collection (melody Nos. 24, 31, 32, 33, 40, 45–47, 48a.b., 56–59), that is, other than Nos. 40 and 45, exclusively in those which belong to the characteristic Old Turkish stock.

REFRAINS

Refrains, too, are less frequent in this material than they are supposed to be in the folk texts (such as those collected by Kúnos: see below). Before going into details, we must establish the limits of what is or what is not to be regarded as a refrain. Recurring additions of one or two syllables, by which the syllabic number of a section is extended, are not considered as refrains (for example, melody No. 24: *Edem*; No. 32: *vay vay* or *of of*; these two-syllable extensions transform the seven-syllable text line to a nine-syllable one). All other additions, however, are considered as refrains if (1) they exceed two but are less than seven syllables, or are single or multiple text lines; (2) they stand for proper text lines; (3) they are generally in rather loose contextual connection with the main text parts; and (4) they recur in each stanza.[54]

54. Except melody Nos. 32 and 46, in which they reappear in every other stanza.

The complete list of refrains and their metrical structure is as follows:[55]

Mel. No. 1a. : 6(4||2), 8(4||4), 6(4||2),
7a. : 9(4|2||3),
7b. : *1.r.* = 3, *2.r.* = 10(3|3||4),
9 : 8(4||4),
15 : 11(6||3|2),
21a. : 11(6||4|1),
22 : 11(4|4||3),
30 : 4,
31 : *1.r.*, *2.r.* = 4,
32 : 12(6||6), 9(4||3|2),
34 : 10(5||5),
40 : 7(4||3), 7(4||3),
41 : 7(4||3), 7(4||3),
44 : 7+7, 7+7, (4×4||3)
45 : *1.r.*, *2.r.* = 4+7, 7, 7, (7, = 4||3)
46 : 3×8, (8, = 4||4)
48a.b. : 3,
52 : 8(2|4|2),
53 : 15(5|5||5),
56 : 10, 8, 10, 8, (10, = 6||4; 8, = 4||4)
57 : 7(4||3).
58 : 5×7, (7 = 4||3)
59 : 10(5||5),

The first seven of these twenty-three refrains, occurring in Classes 1 and 2, have been mentioned above (fn. 53). The remainder show that independent refrains, not standing as a substitute for a proper text line, occur exclusively in classes which are less characteristic of or entirely disassociated from genuine Turkish

55. See the editorial commentary concerning this tabulation on p. 26.

rural melodies. But even there, they are less frequently found than, for instance, in the texts of the mentioned Kúnos collection.[56]

SOME ADDITIONAL PECULIARITIES IN THE TEXTS

(1) When the metrical structures of eleven-syllable lines are examined apart from their melodies, the articulation seems to be 4|4||3. When they are sung to their respective melodies, however, the melodic articulation will divide them as previously listed (p. 196), that is, into 6||4|1 or 6||3|2 for Class 2. The exceptions are the eleven-syllable lines in melodies of other classes or, in other words, less typical melodies where the articulation will be 4|4||3. In some of these cases the structure of the melody stanza will even require one or more repeats of the last three syllables. This diversity and particularly its interdependence with the melodic style is a rather puzzling phenomenon.

(2) Another phenomenon is connected with the cutting of words by the metrical caesuras. In the metrical structure of the folk poems of the Slav peoples appears a very rigidly adhered-to rule that the main caesura and in many cases the secondary caesura must not divide words.[57] In the Hungarian material there are so many exceptions that we cannot assume the existence of established rules. This irregularity is still more prevalent in the Turkish texts. In a considerable portion of the text lines in this publication —twenty-four percent—the main caesura divides words. The fre-

56. Refrains are found in 120 of 151 of its texts (the so-called *mani* and *bekçi* songs excluded). It is evident that Kúnos must have collected his texts in areas where the characteristic Old Turkish stock of melodies have not been preserved. A later Kúnos publication, *Ada-Kálei török népdalok* [Turkish folk songs from Ada Kale], published by the Hungarian Academy of Sciences in Budapest, 1906, shows approximately the same proportion: 72 of 82 texts have refrains. Incidentally, some of these texts consist of lines with more complicated metrical structure (thirteen, fourteen, or fifteen syllables in the line) which apparently are unknown in the Yürük area.

57. For further details, see *Serbo-Croatian Folk Songs*, pp. 38–41.

quency of word splitting in the Hungarian material occurs less often but is nevertheless not negligible.

It would be a most interesting task to determine the reasons for the essential difference in the metrical rules of the Turkish and Hungarian texts on the one hand, and of the Slav folk texts on the other hand. For the moment, one can only guess at several hypotheses without being in a position to prove them. One reason can be sought in the difference in grammatical system: the Slav languages which belong to the Indo-European family are inflecting languages; the Turkish and Hungarian languages are agglutinative ones. Agglutination can produce excessive extensions of words by accumulation of particles; the added particles melting into a unit with the main word, however, were previously independent words. A subconscious feeling of this independence may lessen the reluctance for dividing words by caesuras. Another explanation could be given in terms of the accentuation rules of the Turkish language (see p. 196).[58] The placement of the accent on the last syllable of words might have the power of making it suitable as the first syllable of the meter. A third guess would be to suppose in these peoples a general lack of sense for any wordcuts.

(3) The reader should bear in mind that deviations from the structural formulas (eight, eleven, seven, and so forth, syllables) in certain individual text lines are not rare; in any case they occur more frequently in the Turkish material than in the Hungarian and Slav texts. Generally, added proper text syllables are found in these deviating lines; since their appearance obviously is only casual, they have no structural meaning whatever (for example, melody No. 8d.: st. 2, third section; No. 13b.: first section; No. 44: st. 2, second section, and so forth). Other deviations result from the casual interpolation of syllables that do not belong to the proper text but are there for decorative purposes, such as *da* or *de*.

58. This rule does not apply to the Hungarian language which, contrarily, applies the accent to the first syllable of words.

Although the two syllables have the sense of "too" or "also," in this case they are used without meaning.[59] These interpolations are underscored with a wavy line (⁓) in the music notations, are omitted in the Texts and Translations, and should not be taken into account when the syllabic number of sections is established. Additions such as *aman* (mercy, grace) and similar words are found sometimes as proper syllables, at other times not. In the latter case they are also indicated by a wavy underline; although they have definite sense, they are not in contextual connection with the other words. Irregularity of the meters (metrical division) also occurs: 5||3 instead of 4||4 in melody No. 50 (st. 1, third section); 7||2|2 instead of 6||3|2 in No. 16 (st. 3, second section); and 3||5 instead of 4||4 in No. 3 (st. 1, second section).

(4) A certain difficulty is presented by the singular behavior of the consonant *ğ*. As Kúnos observed more than sixty years ago, it has a tendency to disappear completely in the pronunciation, thus changing the preceding short vowel into a long one when it is a syllable-closing consonant or when it is placed between two different vowels. This kind of occurrence is readily perceived by the transcriber of the melodies. The difficulties arise, however, when *ğ* flanked by two identical vowels disappears (for example, *iği* > *ī*), when the second vowel is eliminated, or when the remaining two different vowels melt into a diphthong. In these cases the musician is inclined to interpret the long vowel or the diphthong as one syllable, although it should be regarded metrically and structurally as one syllable—a contraction standing for two syllables. There are cases, however,—and these may be the result of a newer development—when such contracted long vowels function as one syllable. Some examples are as follows:

Melody No. 39 (st. 1, 3: first measure): *geldiği* sounds, so to say, as *geldī*. This circumstance accounts for the twelve syllables instead

59. Hungarian folk texts, seemingly of recent origin, use a similar interpolated one-syllable word—curious coincidence!—*de*. This word, however, has the sense of "but," and in these cases is also used without meaning.

of eleven—the singer evidently felt *geldī* as two syllables and not as three.[60]

No. 47 (st. 3, second section): *ayağma* stands for *ayağĭma* and is possibly pronounced *ayāma*.[60] In this case the elision of *ĭ* resulted in a shortening of the musical measure to 3/8.

No. 22 (st. 3, first section): *Ayağĭna* was pronounced something like *Ayayna*.

No. 36 (st. 3, second section): *aklĭcĭğmĭ* stands for *aklĭcĭğĭmĭ*. The elision of *ĭ* conforms the text line to the regular pattern of eleven-syllable structure.

No. 1b. (st. 3, second section): *Salkĭmcĭğmĭ* for *Salkĭmcĭğĭmĭ*—same remark as to the preceding example.

No. 49d. (third line): *Ayağ'm* for *ayağĭma*. This case differs from that of melody No. 47, since the result of the elision is the typical ♫♫ | ♩ ♩ musical rhythm.

RHYMES

The most characteristic rhyme schema is *a a b a*, appearing in twenty-eight texts of this collection. Next in importance is *a a a b* (in twenty-three texts) and its variation *a a a + refrain* (in nine texts). Exceptional schemata are to be found in three texts, and six texts have no regular rhyme formation.

The first scheme, *a a b a*, is known only from Turkish folk texts among Eastern European folk texts, and it must therefore be considered as a special feature of Turkish rural folk poems.[61]

The rhyming technique is extremely primitive and is contrary to the established rules for rhyme building in Western art poetry.

60. I was influenced too much by the written picture of the text transcriptions, made by Ahmed Adnan Saygun on the spot, and I felt a certain reluctance to eliminate these *ğ*s when transcribing the melodies.

61. Of the 401 "*mani*" texts in Kúnos' first publication (*O.-t.n.g.*, pp. 181–252), 376 have *a a b a* rhymes, the remainder mostly *a a a a*. "*Mani*" songs are short songs consisting of only one stanza, sung on certain occasions and with certain purposes. Their lines consist of seven (4 || 3) syllables.

The most primitive means of rhyme building consists of simply using the same words for *a* rhymes (text No. 1b., st. 2; No. 2, st. 2). A peculiar phenomenon appears in this connection, rarely observed in the Hungarian folk texts: the difference of vowel color in the suffixes or radicals is not taken into account, that is, identical suffixes or radicals with identical consonants that differ only in vowel color are considered as having rhyming qualities. This phenomenon is, of course, in connection with the so-called vowel harmony law.[62] Thus *oldu* and *geldi* (text No. 1a., st. 1) are considered to be rhyming words as well as *mezere* and *nazara* (No. 5, st. 1) or *yelişir* and *gülüşür* (No. 7b., st. 3), and so forth.[63]

The more complicated procedure of using rhyming words which belong to a different part of speech groups, or which have different grammatical form, very rarely occurs (text No. 17c., st. 4: *firez* and *biraz*).

TEXTS AS EXPRESSION OF IDEAS

In this field the stranger encounters great difficulties; indeed, when he looks at the translations in this publication, he will be at a loss how to make sense of them. Certainly some lines or parts of any Eastern European lyrical folk texts may be almost untranslatable into any other language or, when translated literally, may appear rather awkward. A rather efficacious example is this Hungarian one-stanza text (from Bartók, *Hung. Folk Music*, text No. 181):

62. "In virtue of this law one and the same word can only contain either palatal (high) or velar (low) vowels. *I* and closed *e* are neutral in this respect, that is, they may also enter into words of velar vowels. As a result practically all the suffixes and flexional affixes exist in two (sometimes three) forms. . . ." From *A Companion to Hungarian Studies*, Budapest, 1943, p. 280. An approximately similar law prevails in the Turkish language. The Ural-Altaï family of languages shows a similar vowel-harmony system.

63. There is one Hungarian example: *hajlandó* and *illendő*, in No. 133 (lines 7–8) in B. Bartók and Z. Kodály, *Transylvanian Hungarians. Folk-songs*, The Popular Literary Society, Budapest, 1921.

The rushes are in bloom,—
Your mother promised you to me.
The radish has rotted in the soil,—
It is somebody else whom I love.

The stranger who knows nothing of certain devices used in Hungarian lyrical folk texts, will be rather puzzled about the purpose of the first and third lines (see below for more details about such lines). He will certainly understand the sense of the second and fourth lines, which are the backbone of what the singer wants to say, but he will find even these lines rather stale and commonplace in tone. The original version of these four lines, however, has a humorous vigor that is the outcome not so much of the conveyed sense as of the rhythm of the metrical structure, the rhymes, and the choice and order of words.

Examples such as this particular text are infrequently found in the Hungarian material, and are almost completely lacking in the Slav. In the Turkish material, however, stanzas like these constitute the "mildest" specimens, the overwhelming majority being much more "abstract," sometimes reminding the reader of the symbolistic, surrealistic, and whatnot art poetry of the beginning of this century. A student in New York, originating from the Adana region, whose native language is Turkish and who knew many such texts from her childhood, asserted that the abstruseness is deliberate; in fact, that in Turkish rural folk poems the harmonious effects resulting from the succession and sound of the words, the rhymes, and so forth,—and not the meaning of the text lines or stanzas—are of primary importance. This theory is open to question, for it alone does not account for the abstract character of the texts. Certain devices in the stanza construction and other circumstances are also acceptable as reasons for the phenomenon. Let us examine some of them:

(1) The Turkish lyrical folk poem stanzas begin very frequently with one or two text lines whose content (a) has absolutely nothing in common with the content of the following lines; (b)

represents a more or less loose simile; or (c) is in contrast to the content of the following lines.[64] These lines, hovering above those of main content, generally give a short description of a natural picture or scene, or of a moment in the author's (?!) own life. Certainly, strangers unprepared for this phenomenon will be disconcerted when they read such lines.

(2) The reader should be aware that these lyrical poems are not conceived for strangers. They are intended for villagers by their fellows, all having the same common feelings and knowledge of the same facts, all being on the same level of civilization, and all forming a community which interprets the phenomena of the world in a similarly typical way. Therefore, description or even mention of facts, events, and circumstances known by everyone seems to be entirely superfluous to these people, the knowledge of which, however, is necessary for the full understanding of the text.

Concerning the device described under (1), additional explanations of some importance should be given. Only Turks and Hungarians use it, no other Eastern European peoples.[65] In fact, during the time when I was unfamiliar with Turkish folk texts I thought this device to be a new usage in Hungarian folk texts—an opinion based on the latter's more "modern" character.[66] But now that I know about its much more extended use in the Turkish lyrical folk texts, I am convinced that this device is also an Old Turkish

64. The same device is used in the Hungarian lyrical folk poems, perhaps less often. The translation quoted on p. 205 (above) is an excellent example of (a), excepting the change in order of the lines. Hungarian stanzas sometimes carry on the idea begun in the first line as far as the third line; the main idea appears as a flashlike surprise only in the fourth line (for example, Bartók, *Hung. Folk Music*, text Nos. 91, 116, 139).

65. Whether it is used by the Cheremiss, Kazan Turko-Tartars, or by some western or central Asiatic peoples is, for the moment, unknown to me. It appears very rarely in the Slovakian and Rumanian material, so that it may be then regarded as a Hungarian influence. The stereotyped beginnings in Rumanian folk texts, such as "*Frunză verde nucului*," and so forth, have a different character and seem to be in connection with an Old Italian usage.

66. Seemingly very old epic texts and other texts of similar age never use it.

inheritance, kept alive by the Hungarians for fifteen centuries up to the present day. This common usage, therefore, adds new proof of the near relation between the Old Hungarian and Old Turkish civilization, a proof which fortunately is in concordance with that offered by linguistics, music, and other sources (see pp. 39–40, above).

It already has been stated that some of the texts, particularly those with eleven-syllable lines (Class 2), have somehow an artificial aspect and are probably of urban origin.[67] I will only point to two texts of this kind. No. 19 is a dithyramb to feminine beauty—even the ecstatic spirit of the entire piece is somewhat artificial. And if we consider the geographical knowledge exhibited in the poem, it becomes evident that no person of the typical rural civilization could ever have conceived the piece. The second example is No. 21 which has an exceptionally artificial allusion to the figure 58! This figure is used to indicate a passive pederast, because of the use of the Arabic word "*ibné*" [= boy] which also has a numerical sense; that is, the numerical meaning of the word's single letters is 5, 50, 2, 1 or, by addition, 58! Quite obviously no rural person could have had recourse to such an artificial expression, even if he had known its meaning. A curious phenomenon: such artificial poems are easier to understand than the simpler rural pieces!

In connection with text No. 21 it will be interesting to note that of seventy-eight texts this is the one which contains an allusion to pederasty. The Milman Parry Collection of recorded Serbo-Croatian folk songs includes about 200 "women's" songs (that is, non-heroic poems); of these, one ballad, in absolutely rural style (*Serbo-Croatian Folk Songs*, No. 10b.), contains a similar though veiled allusion. Thus, it seems, one need only touch the surface of

67. I do not mean to imply any *şarkı* influence, of course! What is meant is that the originators of such texts must have been persons with some kind of urban education who tried to speak in the pure Turkish language and to use Turkish metrics, and not simple illiterate peasants.

folk poetry in the Balkans and Near Oriental countries to immediately find this kind of text matter. On the other hand, not a single piece of the more than 12,000 Hungarian folk texts in manuscripts in Budapest contains a similar reference.[68] The same circumstance applies to my Slovakian collection of about 2,500 folk texts in manuscripts[69] and to about the same amount of them in my Rumanian material.[70] If we regard lyrical folk texts as the truest mirror of the life and sentiments of peasants, then may we consider the given statistics as evidence that the Oriental custom of pederasty infiltrated even into the peasant classes of Turkey and the Balkans, whereas the peasantry of the countries situated more to the north apparently does not know pederasty even from hearsay?

Just as it is useful to issue literary works of older times in the form of annotated publications, so would it seem to be helpful to similarly produce these Turkish texts. In the former case the span of time makes it imperative; in the latter case the distance in space and civilization. In this publication, unfortunately, it cannot be accomplished for several reasons. I will therefore confine myself to

68. The Hungarian material, however, includes many highly "indecent," often indescribably "shocking" pieces (many of these, however, have an incredibly sparkling esprit and high literary value). This fact does not offer any evidence of the "immorality" of the people. Knowing or, to be more exact, subconsciously feeling that *Naturalia non sunt turpia*, they talk and sing about eating and drinking with as much ease and as naturally as about any other bodily functions. They know, of course, that "gentlemen" have, or at least pretend to have, a different opinion, and the former try to avoid "shocking" subjects in the presence of the latter. But if a gentleman succeeds in winning their confidence, and if he accidentally is in research of folk songs, then the floodgates open—from the youngest boy to the oldest man, from the oldest woman down to the youngest girl—and everyone contributes with his or her best gifts. Fortunately, 900 years of church effort could not destroy the natural-mindedness of these peasants!

69. Only manuscripts can be taken as authentic sources in this regard, because heaven alone knows what has been omitted in publications by editors, for the sake of "decency." At the present time, two of the three volumes of Bartók's *Slovak Folk Songs* (*Slovenské L'udové Piesne*, I: 1959; II: 1970) have been published by the Academia Scientiarum Slovaca, Bratislava.

70. See Class *L* (*Kryptadia*) in *Rumanian Folk Music* (*op. cit.*), Vol. III, 415–423.

the thorough explanation of at least a few of the texts, for even this minimal discussion may lead the reader to a better understanding of the other pieces.

EXPLANATION OF TEXT NOS. 1B., 2, 3, 7A.

Remarks: (1) read first the strict translation for each of the respective melodies;

(2) the italicized words (below) constitute the original translations;

(3) the order of the lines is exactly the same as in the original translations.

1b. St. 1. Just as a *tiger*, when he comes to full age, *reaches* his ability of *roaring* with full strength,
In the same way this youth, Sarĭ Ahmed, *reached the age of twenty*, when he met that terrible disaster you all know about.
He was such an extraordinary youth that *it is not possible for any* other *mother*
To give birth to such a brave one.

St. 2. He fell as *on the high mountains the fir tree falls* when rooted up by a hurricane,
And its boughs and twigs fall to earth.
Arise only once more, *my Sarĭ Ahmed*!
Don't you see that *the waist of your grandfather is bent* because of the sorrow he feels about your sudden death?

St. 3. This disaster creates a blackness around us, as black as *the grapes are black, the chain of sausages*[71] *is black,*
The locks of my face (that is, head) are black.
Now my uncles, too, *will hear of this* terrible event.

71. "Chain of sausages" is a rather unpoetic word in English. Possibly it has a different value in the Turkish language; or perhaps it is used here in a different sense which, however, could not be determined.

My face is mortified by the sentiment of guiltiness in this disaster, mortified to such a degree that it seems to be quite black, *black* to such a degree that I am unable even *to cry.*

2 (The first two lines in both stanzas are "decorative" lines such as the ones mentioned under (1a), p. 205, without any contextual connection with the main part of the text. Therefore, only the third and fourth lines require explanation):

St. 1. [Somebody's young wife tries to persuade her "cousin"—possibly her sweetheart[72]—to run away with her. She says:]

Get on the bay filly,

And let us go, my cousin.

St. 2. [The cousin refuses, saying:]

You are *the lawful property* of your husband. *I fell against* it when I fell in love with you:

I am not going, my cousin.

3 (The first two lines in all stanzas are the same type as those of text No. 2. The remainder is the complaint of a lover about the death of his sixteen-year-old sweetheart):

St. 1. [Remonstrances to God] How could you not have mercy? *Did you* perhaps *consider, my Almighty God, too many*

The young girls, that you this one away from life?

St. 2. She was such *a beauty that I cannot even praise* her adequately,

She was *a painted-eyed angel of God.*

St. 3. (No explanations needed.)

7a. (This is an imaginary Lullaby to an imaginary child.[73] The only necessary explanation is in regard to the use of sand: it

72. Perhaps "cousin" also means sweetheart, just as in Rumanian *bade* or *nene* (elder brother) and *lele* or *nana* (elder sister) also means sweetheart.

73. See the Note to the melody.

seems that babies are placed on sand instead of being swaddled in linen, and when the sand becomes "used" after a while, it is probably—and expectedly—changed.)

RELATION BETWEEN TEXT AND MELODY

The main question is whether each melody has its own text or whether texts and melodies are interchangeable within the limits of metrical circumstances. The number of melodies is too small to make a decisive answer possible. Rain-begging songs, of course, must have rain-begging texts. Regarding the other categories, however, the question remains open. We can see, for instance, that melody Nos. 8a. and 8b. have the same text; Nos. 55a., 55b., 55c., and 55d., too; and Nos. 48a. and 48b. have a similar one. On the other hand, Nos. 8c., 8d., and 8e. have different texts; Nos. 42 and 43d. have identical first text stanzas; and the same person sang a Lullaby text to melody No. 1a. and a Mourning song text to melody No. 1b.! On the whole, it seems more likely that in classes with abundant melodies of similar structure, the melodies will not have special texts for each of them; in other words, texts and melodies are evidently interchangeable.

CONCLUSIONS

The thorough study of this Turkish material disclosed the following facts:

(1) The seemingly oldest, most characteristic, and homogenous part (representing forty-three percent of the material) consists of isometric four-section melodies with eight- or eleven-syllable text lines; in *parlando* rhythm; in Dorian, Aeolian, or Phrygian mode; with descending structure; and in which traces of a pentatonic system appear, a system well known from Hungarian and Cheremiss folk melodies.

(2) A part of the material described in the preceding paragraph,

the one with eight-syllable melody sections, is identical with Old Hungarian eight-syllable material. The other part, with eleven-syllable melody sections, is in near relation to the Old Hungarian material. These kinships point to a common western-central Asiatic origin of both Turkish and Hungarian materials and determine their age as being at least fifteen centuries.

(3) The eight- or eleven-syllable text lines of the above-mentioned material form four-line stanzas, a text stanza for each melody stanza, without the occurrence of text-line repetitions. The rhymes represent *a a b a* or *a a a b* formulas.

(4) The beginning of the stanzas in Turkish as well as Hungarian lyrical folk texts frequently consists of so-called "decorative" lines which have no contextual connection with the main text part. This device seems to be an ancient usage common to both peoples and it is not known to any other neighboring peoples.

(5) The remainder of the material, that is the part not described under (1), is rather heterogeneous and seems to originate from various sources.

EXPLANATION OF SIGNS USED IN THE TEXTS

(1) The metrical articulation is marked by the addition of caesura signs (|) between the respective syllables.

(2) Rhyming formulas, in the form of italicized letters (*a* or *b*), are added at the right side of the texts. When such letters are underscored, it means that there is an inter-stanza rhyme schema. The addition of vertical braces (}) with the rhyming formulas is for the purpose of delineating schemata occurring when the text stanzas do not tally with the respective melody stanzas (see the discussion on text-stanza structure, pp. 197–198, above).

(3) Absolutely necessary additional words, which the original Turkish version does not contain, are placed in brackets ([ ]) in the translations.

(4) Repeats of lines, portions of lines, and words are indicated by |: :| or by 2^a *volta* {.

(5) Variants in text lines are marked *var.* {.

(6) Asterisks refer to the Notes to the Texts, p. 251.

(7) Dashes are used for unintelligible syllables (one dash for each syllable), dots for unprintable words (each dot for a letter).

(8) Dialect words are explained in the marginal notes. Unusual word forms or words of unknown meaning are indicated by *sic.*

(9) Syllables connected by an arc are to be pronounced as one syllable (for example, text No. 21b., st. 2, line two: Ne-ğadar).

(10) Special phonetic symbols used in the texts are fully explained on p. 195, above.

(11) The occurrence of refrains is marked by *refr.* (*1. refr.*, *2. refr.*, or *3. refr.*), with or without parentheses and horizontal or vertical braces.

Texts and Translations

The Turkish texts are given in this part without the added syllables which do not belong to the text proper (for example, omitting the pseudo-upbeat syllables, the *yi yi yi* and similar prolongations of long-drawn syllables). Swallowed consonants and all other changes involved in singing, however, are included.

As for the English translations, made by Mrs. G. Kresz—on the basis of a literal French and Hungarian translation—the guiding principle was to present as literal a translation as possible, even if the result seemed queer in some cases.

	Nenni		Lullaby
1a.			
	1. Daųulcular | dama doldu,	a	The drummers filled up the house-roof,[3]
(Nenni)	Dam başïma | zindan oldu.	a	The roof became a prison for my [poor] head.
	Baban duydu, | Şamdan geldi,	a	Thy father heard of it, he came from Damascu
(refr.?)	Nenni yaųrum, | nenni		Lullaby, my little one, lullaby,
	Yedi yïlda | bir bulduğum		[Whom] I found seven years past,
	Nenni guzum, | nenni.		Lullaby, my lamb, lullaby.
	2. Nenni çaldïm | sadesina,	a	[Hearing his voice I sang lullaby,
	Atlïm ïnmiş | odasïna.	a	My knight came down into his room.
	Cïğrïn[1] bunun[2] | babasïna,	a	Call his father,
(refr.?)	Nenni görpen, | nenni,		Lullaby, my tender one, lullaby,
	Yedi yïlda | bir bulduğum,		[Whom] I found after seven years past,
	Nenni yaųrum, | nenni.		Lullaby my little one, lullaby.

1) = çagïrïn. 2) According to the transcription on the spot. The record has something like dyarç
3) Dam means as well: room

	Ağït		Song of Mourning
1b.			
	1. Gaplan geldi | bağïrmaya,	a	The tiger reached the [age of] roaring,
	Yaşï değdi | yirmiye.	a	His age reached twenty.
	Her annenin | kârï değil	b	It is not possible for any mother
	Böyle yeğit | doğurmaya.	a	To give birth to such a brave one.
	2. Yüce dağda | çam yïkïldï,	a	On the high mountain the fir-tree fell,
	Dalï, budağï | yere döküldü.	a	Its boughs and twigs fell to earth.
	Kalk-sana(ya) | Sar' Ahmedim,	b	Arise, my Sarï Ahmed,
	Koca babayïn (sic) | beli büküldü.	a	The waist of thy grandfather is bent.
	3. Üzüm gara, | düzüm gara,	a	The grapes are black, the chain of sausages is b
	Salkïmcïğmï[1] | yüzüm gara.	a	- - - -[1] my face is black.
	Şimdi emim, | dayïm duyar,	b	Now my paternal and maternal uncles will
	Ağlamaya | yüzüm gara.	a	My face is [too] black for crying (of

1) The meaning of this word could not be established.

2

1. Evlerinin | önü gaya, a
Gayadan ba|χarlar aya. a
Havlıdakı | duru taya a
Bin, gidelim, | emmim oğlu. b

In front of their house is a rock,
From the rock they gaze on the moon
On the bay filly in the courtyard
Get on, let us go, son of my uncle.

2. Evlek kestim, | biber saçtım, a
Al öküzüm | çifte goştum, a
Ben bir halal | mala düştüm: a
Ben gidemem, | emmim gızı. b

I cut the beds, I sowed pimento,
I yoked my pair of brown oxen,
A lawful property I fell against,
I am not going, daughter of my uncle.

3

1. Sarbdır yayla|nın yolları, a
Kilîm do|kur ağ elleri. a
Çoksundunmu | gadir mevlâm, b
Mor perçemli | gelinleri? a

Steep are the roads to the mountain pasture,
Her white hands weave a rug.
Did you consider, my Almighty God, too many
The purple-tressed maidens?

2. Sarbdır yayla|nın yolağı,[1] a
Eksik dile|meñ[2] dileği. a
Nasıl medh eyleyem | böyle gü|zeli, b
Sürmeli hak|kın meleği? a

Steep is the bottom of the road to the mountain pasture,
Ask not for incomplete (impossible) desires
How should I praise such a beauty,
Painted eyed angel of God?

3. Yaylalarda | biter yonca, a
Gamışdan da | belin ince. a
Nasıl gıydın, | gadir mevlâm, b
On altı ya|şında gence? a

On the mountain pastures grows the clover,
Thy waist is more slender even than rushes.
How couldst thou not have mercy, my Almighty God
Upon a sixteen year old young [maid]?

[1] = ayağı. [2] = dilemeyin.

4

1. Seni vuran | dağlımıydı? a
Gurşuncuğu | yağlımıydı? a
Garşıdan düş|man geliyor, b
Elin, golun | bağlımıydı? a

He who slayed thee, was he a mountain dweller?
Was his little bullet oily?
Enemy comes from opposite,
Have thy hands, they arms been bound?

2. Seni vuran | Kürtmüyüdü ? a He who slayed thee, was he a Kurd ?
Gurşuncuğu | çiftmiyidi ? a Was his little bullet doubled ?
Garşidan düş|man geliyor, b Enemy comes from opposite,
Elin, golun | gütmüyüdü ? a Have thy hands, thy arms been lamed ?

5

Ağit		Song of Mourning
1. Gızlar toplan|dı mezere,	a	The maidens assembled at the grave-mound,
Ehmed oğra|mış nazara;	a	Ehmed expired from the evil eye;
Habar salın	gardaşına,	b	Send news to his brother,
Posta geli|yor bazara.	a	The post arrives until Sunday.
2. Yazlar geldi,	yazlar geldi,	a	Summer has arrived, summer has arrived,
Gatır ile	gazlar geldi;	a	The ducks arrived in groups;
Yekin, sürmel'	oğlum, yekin,	b	Arise, my painted [eyed] son, arise,
Top top oldu	gızlar geldi.	a	Maidens arrived in a mass.
3. Gani cıvıl	cıvıl akar,	a	His blood flows babbling,
Yaylanın sümbülü gozar;	a	The hyacinth of the mountain pasture is scenting,
Zalım imiş,	zalım duşman,	b	Cruel was the enemy, cruel,
Sol böğründen	gama sozar.	a	Into his left side he thrusts a dagger.

6

Ağit		Song of Mourning
1. Kapıya bay|rak dikmedim,	a	I did not kiss a flag on the gate,
İçeri ge|lin dıkmadım;	a	I did not push the bride inside;
Yerinek[1] gitti	Duranım,	b	My Duran went away disgusted,
Gınalı par|mak sıkmadım.	a	I did not press [any] henna fingers.
2. Allı bayra|ğını açın,	a	Unroll his reddish flag,
Çerkes atlı|sını seçin;	a	Chose his Circassien knight;
Ben oğlumu	everiyom,	b	I married my son,
Pırtısını	eyi seçin.	a	Chose well his linen.

1) = yerinerek

7a. Nenni

1. Ince-elekten | elediğim,	a	On whom I sieved from a fine sieve	
(1. refr.) Beben oy oy | oy oy,		My little baby, hey hey hey hey,	
Kum toprağa | belediğim,	a	Whom I swaddled with sand,	
(2. refr.) Yayrum nenni, | nenni, nenni, nen.		My little one, lullaby, lullaby, lullaby, bye.	
2. Seni hakdan | dilediğim	a	Thou whom I begged from God	
Mevlâm saña | bir can vërsin,	b	My Creator should give you a soul,	
2. refr.		2. refr.	

3. = 2.

7b. Oyun havasï — Dance Song

1. Deveyi defveye çattïm, bebeg oy (1. refr.)	a	I lined camel to camel, oh, my little babe,
Yularïn boyfnuma daktïm,	a	I swung the halter onto my neck,
Nennide, nennide, | nennide, nen.		Lullaby, lullaby, lullaby, bye.
2. Gayïn babamfdan hicap ettim, 1. refr.	a	I was ashamed before my father in law, 1. refr.
Bebek galdï, | diyemedim,	b	That the babe stayed here, I could not say,
2. refr.		2. refr.
3. Havada dufman yelişir, 1. refr.	a	Smoke curls in the air, 1. refr.
Çadïrda düşfman gülüşür,	a	The enemy is laughing in the tent,
2. refr.		2. refr.
[1] 4. Geri döndüm, baktïm ki ne: 1. refr.	b	I went back, what saw I: 1. refr.
Bebeği guşlar bölüşür,	a	The birds were tearing up the baby,
2. refr.		2. refr.
5. Yekin gara löküm[2], yekin, 1. refr.	a	Arise, my brown camel, arise, 1. refr.
Zilli çanlarïnï dakïn,	a	Put on your ringing bells,
2. refr.		2. refr.
6. Göç uruma giderkene, 1. refr.	b	At migration passing to the summit, 1. refr.
Bebeği dallardan sakïn,	a	Beware of the branches for the babe,
2. refr.		2. refr.

[1] St. 4–8 are not recorded. [2] = a camel older than five years

7. Göyün yüzü gar havasĭ, 1. refr.	a	⎫	The face of the sky is snowy, 1. refr.
Yayĭlĭr öskün[3] devesi 2. refr.	a	⎬	The camels of – – are dispersing, 2. refr.
8. Silini-silini ağlar, 1. refr.	b	⎪	Wiping himself he weeps, 1. refr.
Bebeğin beşik mayasĭ, 2. refr.	a	⎭	The yeast of the baby's cradle, 2. refr.

3) The meaning of this word could not be established. It is perhaps the name of a village.

8a.b.[1)]

1. Kurt paşa çıktı Gozana,	a	Kurt Pasha went out to Kozan,
Akĭl yetmez | bu düzene;	a	A mind cannot understand this arrangement;
Öldürmüşler | Guzanoğlu, var. oğlun,	b	Kozan-oğlu was killed,
Yasak mezerin | yazana. var. Yazĭk mezerin yazana.	a	It is forbidden to dig his grave.
2. Istambulun | âlimleri	a	The learned of Istanbul,
Ne zor olur | talimleri;	a	How difficult were their instruction;
Kör olasĭ | Derviş paşa, var. olasĭn	b	Blind should become Derviş Pasha!
Hep dul goydu gêlinleri. var. goydun	a	He made all the brides widows.
3. Göy yüzünde | dönen guşlar,	a	On the surface of the sky wheeling birds;—
Bu guşlar nerede gişlar?	a	Where do these birds hibernate?
Zabĭtlar süngü sokunca,	b	When the officers stab [with] their bayonets,
Ağam okumaya başlar.	a	My master begins to pray.
4. Mağarada | at oynağĭ,	a	In Magara the horses are exercised,
Ğirildĭ elimin deyneğĭ;	a	The cane of my hands broke;
Hatĭna bergüzar gitti	b	It was sent as a remembrance to the wife
Ağamĭn ganlĭ | göyneğĭ.[2)]	a	The bloody shirt of my master.

1) b. has st. 1 and 2 of a. as text, with the deviations marked as var.
2) = gömleği.

[3] 5. Garalĭ yağlik garasĭ,	a	The black parts of the black decorated kerchief,
Garişti Gozan arasĭ.	a	The district of Kozan rebels
Ünü böyük Gozanoğlu	b	The highly renowned Kozanoğlu
Ağ göğsü süngü yaresi.	a	His white breast: the wound of the bayonet.
6. Amanĭn böyle olurmu	a	Alas! is it possible:
Oğul babayĭ vururmu?	a	That a son should slay his father?
Padişahĭn zabitleri,	b	Officers of the Padishah:
Bu dünya size galĭrmĭ?	a	Will this world remain yours?

[3] St. 5 and 6 are not recorded.

c.

1. Sĭçan dolap|ta oturur,	a	The mouse lives in the cupboard,
Guyruğun' bal|la batĭrĭr,	a	It dips its tail into honey
Hizmetkâra | söz yetirir	a	It is pert to the servant,
Sösçü başĭ | gücücük sĭçan.	b	The chief of chatterers, the tiny mouse.
2. Gaplama gĭlĭç belinde,	a	A plated sword is at his waist,
Süngü dag mar|tin elinde.	a	A bayonetted gun is in his hand.
Dün gece Ha|lep yolunda	b	Last night on the road to Aleppo
Kervan almĭş | gücücük sĭçan.	a	The tiny mouse might have caught a caravan.
3. Sĭçan gelir | zurbayanayn,[1]	a	The mouse arrives with the robbers,
Beş yüz atlĭ | gürbeyineyn.[2]	a	With dung [carried by] on five hundred horses.
Ekmeğn' al' ga|çar torbaynan,[3]	b	Pilfering thy bread it runs away with the knapsack:
Cendarm olmuş | gücücük sĭçan.	a	The tiny mouse might have been a policeman.

[1] = zorba ĭla. [2] = gübre ile. [3] = ekmeyini alĭp kaçar torba ĭla.

d.

1. Ezmeyinen, | üzmeyinen,[1]	a	By trampling, by tormenting,
Yer[2] bulamam | gezmeyinen[3];	a	I cannot find a love by wandering [all over the earth];
Altĭn zaplĭ | gazmayinen[4]	a	Digging with a golden handled [spade],
Gĭzlar deşsin | mezerimi.	b	Let the maidens cut out my grave.
2. Mezerimi | derin̆ edin,	a	Make my grave deep,
Sular serpin, | serin̆ edin;	a	Sprinkle water, make it cool;
Emmim gĭzĭnĭ | imam edin,	a	Make the daughter of my paternal uncle priest,
Gĭzlar gĭlsin (sic) | cenazemi.	b	Let maidens perform the ceremony.

[1] = ezmeyile, üzmeyile. [2] = yar. [3] = gezmeyile. [4] = kazmayĭla.

8e.

1. Öküz aldĭm, | goşamadĭm,	a	I bought [an] ox, I could not yoke it,
Yeğid oldum, | yaşamadĭm.	a	I was a youth, I could not live.
Namusuma | ar geliyor:	b	Shame came to my honour,
Gelin, seni | boşamadĭm.	a	Bride, I could not divorce thee [from thy husband].
2. At içinde, | at içinde,	a	Amongst horses, amongst horses,
Ağĭr buxağlar içinde,	a	Amongst heavy fetters,
Eller yayla|dan geliyor,	b	The others are coming from the mountain pasture,
Hacĭ beğim | yog içinde.	a	My Hacĭ bey is not amongst them.

9

1. Bu almayĭ | kim dişledi?	a	Who bit into this apple?
Çevre yanĭn | gümüşledi?	a	[Who] silvered the edge of the embroidered handkerchief?
Bunu baña | bağĭşladi?	a	[Who] gave this to me?
(refr.) Bu alma bir | dost almasĭ.	r.	This apple is the apple of a friend.
2. Bu almayĭ | ben dişledim,	a	I bit into this apple,
Çevre yanĭn | gümüşledim,	a	I silvered the edge of the embroidered handkerchief,
Bunu dosta | bağĭşladĭm;	a	I gave this to [my] friend;
(refr.) Bu alma bir | dost almasĭ.	r.	This apple is the apple of a friend.
3. Bu alma bir | dalda bitti,	a	This apple was bred on a branch,
Dal dal oldu, | kolun attĭ.	a	The branch became a branch, it threw its arms apart
Bu almayĭ | kimler attĭ?	a	Who threw this apple?
(refr.) Bu alma bir | dost almasĭ.	r.	This apple is the apple of a friend.
Bu gün almayĭ | kimler attĭ?		Who threw the apple today?
(refr.) Bu alma bir | dost almasĭ.		This apple is the apple of a friend.
4. Bu alma düştü, | tekerlendi,	a	This apple fell down, it rolled apart,
Mahmud baña | fikirlendi.	a	Mahmud had fancies to me.
Alma aldĭm, | şekerlendi;	a	I took the apple, it became sugared;
(refr.) Bu alma bir | dost almasĭ.	r.	This apple is the apple of a friend.
Elim' aldĭm, | şekerlendi;		I took it (into my hand), it became sugared;
(refr.) Bu alma bir | dost almasĭ.		This apple is the apple of a friend.

10a.

1. Ala gözlerini | sevdiğim dilfber,		Oh charming one, whose light eyes I loved,
Senin baχışların | bana yar gelir.		Your gaze is to me [so dear as] a friend.
Bu dünyede yaụru | güzel sevmefyen		He who loves not a little beauteous one in this world
Ahrete hayfvan gelmiş | bün (sü) gider.		Came [here] as a beast and will leave as a fool to the other world.
2. Tilli mahramasın | atmış başıfna,	a	She threw her muslin kerchief on her head,
Gudiretten[1] galem | çekmiş gaşıfna;	a	On her eyebrows pen-etched by the Almighty;
Bir yiğitte düşmefyince eşifne	a	If a lad finds not his pair,
Ah dedikçe | yüreğinden | gan gelir.	b	Saying "ah", blood flows from his heart.

[1]) = kudretten.

11.

1. Avşar beğlerinde | gördüm bir | güzel,		At the Bey of Avşarı I saw a beauty,
Guzan arasına | çekmiş göfçünü.		She moved to the district of Kozan.
Nasıl medheyleyim | böyle gözeli:		How should I praise such a beauty:
Sırmaynan[1]) garıştırfmış saçını.	b	She mingled her hair with golden twine.
2. Her sabah sabah da | gendini | öger,	a	Every morn-morning she praises herself,
Altın saç bağı da | topuğun[2]) | döger.	a	Her golden tresses beat her ankles,
Sade gaşıynan[3]) | girpiği | değer	a	Alone her eyebrows and lashes are worth
Acem ölkesinin tahftın, tafcını.	b	The throne, the crown of Persia.
3. Mis goχuyor zülüffünün ufcundan,	a	Musk scent from the tip of her locks,
Öpeyidim al yafnağın' purfcundan!	a	Could I but kiss her in the middle[4]) of her red face!
Eğlenip galdığım | senin yüzünfden,	a	My diverting, staying away, is because of thee,
Üç beş sene bekleyeflim Hafcını.	b	Let us wait for three-five years in Hacın [?].
4. Garaca Oğlan der: | eğlendim, | galdım,	a	Says Karaca Oğlan: I amused myself, I stayed;
Muhabbet neyimiş | yenice | bildim;	a	What love is I learned recently.
Kimse dahletmesin: | miriden | aldım	a	Let none interfere: from the treasury I received
Üç beş sene güzellefrin pafcını.	b	The taxes of three-five years beauties.

[1]) = sırma ila. [2]) = topuğunu. [3]) = kaşı ila. [4]) According to the translation of Mr. A. Adnan Saygın (cf. Anadilden Dermelemeler: purc = blossom of tree).

12

1. Dinleyin ağalar | benim sözüfmü,	Listen masters, to my words,
Has bahça içinde | gül emmim oğflu;	A rose in a flower-garden is the son of my paternal uncle;
Emmim oğlu arabasın' | çekmiş gidifyor,	The son of my paternal uncle departs drawing his [funeral] car,
Bu gazaya allahdan | bilemem, oğflum.	[Whether] this accident [derives] from God, I cannot know, my son.

2. Yĕğit dara düşmüş, | boğazĭ ẋĭt|lar,	a	The courageous got into trouble, his throat rattles,
Çok da çabalamĭş: | bĭyĭğĭ ter|ler;	a	He has struggled much, his moustache is sweating,
Gelin, bakĭn ehali, | gazĭlmĭş yer|ler,	a	Come, people, see, the soil is dug,
Elinizde varmĭdĭr | bir emmim oğ|lu?	b	Is there [anyone like] the son of my uncle in your tribe?
3. Imam gelmiş goç | yĕğidi yuma|ğa,	a	The priest arrived to wash the ram[-like]-youth,
Yuyup onu dar me|zere goma|ğa[1];	a	After washing him to place him into a narrow grave
Dutmadĭ dillerim | „öldü" dĕma|ğa[2],	a	My tongue could not undertake to say: he died,
Billâha, dutmayor | dil, emmim oğ|lu.	b	By God, no tongue undertakes this, son of my uncle

1) = koymağa. 2) = demiye.

13a.

1. Bileydim de Derin|ciya (sic!) varmaz|dĭm,	a	Had I known, I should not have gone to Derince
Gelen belelara | garşĭ durmaz|dĭm,	a	I should not have withstood coming troubles
Çifte guzularĭ | garĭp goymaz|dĭm,	a	I should not have left the two lambs orphaned
Yuvasĭz galdĭ, | garĭp anam, | çifte guzular.	b	Nestless remained, my poor mother, the two lambs
2. Cĕnazemi | de sardĭlar | hayvana,	a	They wrapped my corpse and put it on the beast
El ettiler | Badarsaya, | mĕydana.	a	They pointed towards Badrasa, towards the square
Çifte guzularĭm | galdĭ gadir | mĕvlâma,	a	My two lambs stayed, my God Almighty:
Emaneti senin, | gadir mĕvlâm, | çifte guzunun.	b	Their guardianship is thine, my God Almighty, of the two lambs

13b.

1. Dĭğnen[1] ağalar da, | birem birem söyle|yim:	Listen, masters, let me tell from beginning to end
Afşĭrĭ çafşĭrĭ | yolun var, dağ|lar.	You have winding-twisty roads, oh hills.
2. Gamalaklu, garardĭçlĭ,[2] sekifli[2],	Gamalaks[3], junipers, sekis[3],
Selvili, sögütlü | çalĭn var, dağ|lar.	Cypresses, willows on your slopes, oh hills.
3. Ahar dağĭnda[2] gördüm[2] Maraş[2] beyi[2],	On Mount Ahar I saw the Bey of Maraş,
Engizekte derler | elin çoğu|nu.	They say the greater part of the tribe is in Engizeg
4. Beyti Saracĭgda | Göğür[2] dağĭ|nĭ,[2]	Mount Göğür is in Beyti Saracĭk,
Göğsün güzeli derler | elin var, dağ|lar.	You have a tribe called the Beauty of Göğsün, oh hills.

1) = dinleyin. 2) According to the transcription on the spot; the record has different yet unintelligible words. 3) Kind of trees. 4) Or perhaps < göğüs = breast ?

14.

1. Şahĭn dedicen[1] bir | curaca ğuş|tur,	a	What they call the falcon: it is a slender bird;
Güzel dedicen de | gözünen[2] ğaş|tĭr.	a	What they call the beauty: it is eye and eyelashes.
Ğadir mevlâm, | dosta ğavuş|tur,	a	Almighty God, let me see my [maiden] friend again,
Uzağ ise yaχĭn | eyle yolu|mu.	b	Were she distant, change my path close to hers.
2. Evvel altĭn idim, | şimdi tura|bĭm;	a	I used to be gold, now I am the dust of the earth,
Ayrĭ düştüm, nazlĭ | dostdan yĭ|radĭm.	a	I had to separate, I departed from my pretty friend,
Ğadir mevlâm, versey|din mura|dĭm,	a	Almighty God, wouldst thou have granted my desires,
Haramlara eli|mi | sürmezdim. (sic!)	b	I would not have stretched my hand into forbidden [ground].

1) = dediceğin. 2) = göz ile.

15.

1. Istanbuldan çĭktĭm | dĭrya yü|züne,	a	From Istanbul I went [sailing] on the sea,
Meylim düştü erme|niñin ğĭ|zĭna.	a	My sympathy has fallen for the daughter of the Armenian.
Yeme, içme, baχ yav|rĭnĭn gö|züne,	a	Eat not, drink not, look into the eyes of thy love,
refr.) Al beni terkiñe, | gidek[1], kürd | ōlu!	r.	Take me behind thee onto thine saddle, let us leave, son of the Kurd!
2. Ğanlĭ çyerkes şafah|layĭn u|yandĭ,	a	The blood[thirst]y Circassian has awakened at dawn,
Ağ goynağĭ[2] al ğan|lara be|lendi.	a	His white shirt is stained with red blood.
Buna çyerkes ğĭzĭ | nasĭl dayandĭ?	a	How can the young Circassian maiden endure it?
refr.) Al beni terkiñe, | gidek, kürd | ōlu!	r.	Take me behind thee onto thine saddle, let us leave son of the Kurd!
3. Ufaçĭk taşĭnan[3] | kale ya|pĭlmaz,	a	No fortress is built of small stones,
Cĭğĭp cĭğĭp[4] yar yo|luna ba|χĭlmaz;	a	Going out many times it is not the custom to gaze towards the path of my beloved,
Bir ben ölmeyine[5] | âlem yĭ|χĭlmaz, —	a	The world will not collapse by my death,
refr.) Al beni terkiñe, | gidek, kürd | ōlu!	r.	Take me behind thee onto thine saddle, let us leave son of the Kurd!
4. Ĭrgatçĭler sokmĭş | eline | elli[6],	a	The workmen have put gloves on her hands,
Çyerkes ğĭzĭ taχĭn|mĭş beşi bir|liği.	a	The young Circassian put on her golden five pound coin.
Alsam, gitsem eder|miyik dir|liğĭ? —	a	If I married thee and I departed, would we live well together?
refr.) Al beni terkiñe, | gidek, kürd | ōlu!	r.	Take me behind thee onto thine saddle, let us leave, son of the Kurd!

1) = gidelim. 2) = göyneği (gömleği). 3) = taş ĭla. 4) = çĭkĭp? 5) = ölmek ile.

6) = eldiveni.

16

1. Gapĭmĭzĭn önü | yüksek çefvirme,	a	A high hedge in front of our door
Kadir mëvlâm bu yĭlflik da afyĭrma!	a	My Lord, my God, do not separate us this year!
Mapiz olduğumu | yere dufyurma,	a	Let none hear of my being a captive,
Duyar Lëylâm, | ifafdëy çevirir.	b	If my Leyla heard of it, she would turn her words [from me]
2. Lëylâm, ğalk, gidelim | yolumuz | ĭrak,	a	My Leyla, arise, let us depart, our way is distant,
Ĭrağa dayanmaz, | derdli dir | yürek.	a	Distance it cannot bear: the heart is sorrowful.
Hacĭlar köyünü | bir kimden | sorak.[1]	a	Hacĭköy['s whereabouts] we can ask from someone.
Işte ğarip ğarip | gediyor | Lëylâm,	b	Lo! sadly my Leyla departs,
Garĭştĭ kürtlere, | gediyor | Lëylâm.		She has mingled with the Kurds, my Leyla departs.
3. Lëylâm, ğalk, gidelim | Hacĭköfyüne,	a	My Leyla, arise, and let us go to Hacĭköy,
Acemisin, güvenefmem hufyuna;	a	Thou art inexperienced, I have no confidence in thy nature;
Lëylâm, gurban olam[2] | usul bofyuna!	a	My Leyla, that I were a sacrifice for your pretty figure.
Işte ğarip ğarip | gediyor | Lëylâm.	b	Lo! sadly my Leyla departs.
4. Mavi çorap geymiş | lapçin ifçinde,	a	She wears blue stockings in her shoes,
Dökünmüş lâvanta, | goχar safçĭnda,	a	She has sprinkled herself with lavender, her hair is scente
Yë Lëylâ' yitirdim | kürtler ifçinde,	a	I have lost Leyla amidst the Kurds.
Işte ğarip ğarip | gediyor | Lëylâm.	b	Lo! sadly my Leyla departs.

1) = soralĭm. 2) = olayĭm.

17a.

1. Gedup gedup ger'afkana bakĭnfma,	a	In walking, do not gaze back,
Naz götürmez yürefciğim, ezginfdur,	b	My poor heart cannot bear [these] frivolities, it is shattered
|: Yanağĭna cĭhan[1] | teller sokunfma,	a	Do not put long threads on your face,
Yar elinden yareflerim azgĭnfdur :|.	b	Because of my beloved, my wounds are horrible.
2. Ben seni bilirim, | gücücekten güzelfsin,	a	I know thee, since thy childhood thou art beautif
Yed avcĭdan ceren | gibi tegerfsin,	a	Thou fleest like a gazelle from the strange huntsmar
|: Dostum neden melül | mahzun gezerfsin?	a	Friend, why dost thou wander sadly and afflictedly
Baş bir yanna ziliflerin[2] eyginfdur :|.	b	The head and the plaits of thy hair bowed to one sid
3. Der Karaca Oğlan: | dedim, oturfdum,	a	Says Karaca Oğlan: I have said it, I have stayed
Oturdum, da lâle, | sümbül bitirfdim;	a	I have stayed, I have grown tulips and hyacinth
Gendim Istanbuldan | ferman getirfdim:	a	From Istanbul I myself brought the written order
Her kesin sevdiği | vërilsin dëfyi[3].	b	Everybody's beloved should be granted [to everybody] according to i

1) = cĭğa. 2) = zülflerin. 3) = diye.

17b.

1. Dinleyin, ağalar,|Üçgözoğlu|manisini|söyleyem,		Listen, masters, let me relate the mani-song of Üçgözoğlu,
Mani sayĭlmaz da|öğd sayĭflĭr.		It cannot be reckoned as mani, it is reckoned as advice.
Her yĕğit ne bilir|sĭrĭn gĭymetim,		What does every lad know the value of [keeping] a secret:
Sĭr altĭn terefziye garfşĭ goyulur.	b	The [keeping of a] secret is placed against golden scales.
2. Yĕğid isterim ki|sözü gayim|ola üstüfne,	a	I demand [such] a lad who can hold his words back,
O ërer murafzĭna[1], dostufna.	a	He reaches his desire, his friend.
Deme yar eline,|o der dostufna,	a	Do not tell [anything], my dear one, to strange people, they relate it to their friends,
Bir ağĭzdan çĭkan|bĭñ ağĭz|yayulur.	b	What comes out of our mouth, is spread [by] a thousand mouths.

1) = muradĭna.

7c.

1. Zeytün beli|gürleyerek,		The trunk of the olive-tree collapses,
Ben gĭzĭmĭ|gelin ettim,		I turned my daughter into a bride,
Ben gĭzĭmĭ|gelin ettim,		I turned my daughter into a bride,
Üzengisi|parlayarak.		Her stirrup shining.
2. Gĭzĭn gĭzlarfĭn içinde	a	Amidst maid, maidens,
Yemen gĭnafsĭ saçĭnda.	a	On her hair the henna of Yemen,
Torlak mayaflar gibi sallanĭr,	b	She is swaying herself as a young female camel,
Zeytin belinin|içinde.	a	Olives are in her belt.
3. Arkasĭnda|çay[1] örgüsü,	a	On her back her hair-plait,
Buda Servefrin görgüsü.	a	In this is the experience (?) of Server.
Günamayĭn|emmi, dayĭ,	b	Scold her not, paternal, maternal uncle,
Gözellik Alflah vergisi.	a	Beauty is God's gift.
4. Evlerinin önü firez,	a	In front of their houses straw,
Aklĭnĭ çĭtlattĭn biraz;	a	Thou hast crazed thy mind a little.
Yüz gülgülü, dudak kirez,	a	[Her] face is smiling, [her] lips cherry [-like],
Bende verdim bir yosmayĭ.	b	I also have sold (= lost) a pretty [maiden].
5. Gelin gĭzlar, gelin gĭzlar,	a	Come maidens, come maidens,
Alt gapĭya durun gĭzlar;	a	Stand at the lower gate, maidens,
Serverimi öldü derler,	b	My Server died, they say,
Kefinini dürün gĭzlar.	a	Tuck up her pall, maidens.
6. Nerden gelirsin yelerek,	a	From where dost thou come panting,
Alnĭnĭn terin silerek?	a	Wiping the sweat of thy forehead?
Ben Serverime muska yazdĭrdĭm,	b	I had an amulet written for my Server,
Gece uyqusuz galarak.	a	Staying sleepless at night.

1) = saç; 2) St. 4–6 though recorded, are not transcribed from the record.

18.

1. Göy /: yüzünde bölük | bölük duma|lar :/,	Against the sky are cranes in groups,
Erken eyle, | şu halime | bak benim.	Be merciful, look here upon my state.
Şahin pençe vurdu, | ganatlarım | /: yareli :/,	The claws of a falcon pounced [thereon], my wings are wounded,
Şu siname | bir ok değdi | /: berk benim :/	This bosom of mine was strongly (?) struck by an arrow.
2. Şahin pençe vurdu, | ganatlarım | yareli, aman, yareli,	The claws of a falcon pounced [thereon], my wings are wounded,
Şu siname | bir ok değdi | /: berk benim :/.	This bosom of mine was strongly struck by an arrow.

19

1. Nice methideyim | sevdiğim se|ni ?		How should I praise thee, my beloved ?
Rumeli, Bosnayı | değer gözle|rin,		Thine eyes are worth Roumelia, Bosnia
Âlemde bulunmaz | ruh u ravanın,		In the universe the like of thy soul is not to be found,
Izmiri, Gonyayı | değer gözle|rin.		Thine eyes are worth Smyrna, Konya.
2. Alnına çekilmiş | güzel nişa|nı,	a	On thy forehead is drawn a lovely [beauty] sign,
Seni sevenlerin | artar fuğa|nı.	a	The wailing of those who love thee increases.
Karsı, Ahişkayı, | Erzurum, Va|nı,	a	[All] Kars, Ahişka, Erzurum, Van,
Balhı, Buharayı | değer gözlerin.	b	Balk, Bukhara, are worth thine eyes.
3. Kimsede görmedin | sendeki na|zı,	a	Never have I seen [such] playfulness as with thee,
Yemeni, Bağdadı, | Acem, Şira|zı,	a	Yemen, Bagdad, Persia, Shiras,
Bütün Gürcüstanı, | Mısır, Hica|zı,	a	Whole Georgia, Egypt, Hedjas,
Hindi, Hindistanı | değer gözle|rin.	b	India, Hindustan are equal to thine eyes.
4. Güzel gözlü göç yiğite naz o|lur,	a	The beautiful eyed youth is being flirted with,
~~[illegible]~~		
Vakti gelir, gül açılır, yaz o|lur.	a	[When] its time arrives, the rose blooms, it will be summer.
Mısırın haznasın | versem az o|lur,	a	Should I give the treasures of Egypt, it would be little:
Bütün Istanbulu | değer gözle|rin.	b	Thine eyes equal all Istanbul.
[1] 5. Der Karaca Oğlan[2]: | eylerim me|tin,	a	Karaca Oğlan[2] says: I would sing [thy] praise,
Bulsam yanağında | buse himme|tin.	a	If I would only find the favour of a kiss on thy cheeks.
Yüzbin şeher saysam | bilmez kıyme|tin,	a	Should I enumerate one hundred thousand towns, it would not explain thy value,
Büzbütün dünyayı | değer gözle|rin.	b	Thine eyes are worth the whole universe.

[1] not recorded. [2] Name of the supposed author of the text.

20

1. Pencereden mayil | mayil bakan | yar,	a	[My] darling leaning, leaning [and] looking out of the window,
Ciğerimi işk öfdüne[1] yakan | yar,	a	[My] darling lighting my entrails to the fire of love,
Ben ölürsem, sen kimflere bakan[2] | yar?	a	If I should die, who wouldst thou gaze at, my darling?
Bana senden oldu, | kime ne difyim?[3]	b	[This trouble] came to me from thee, what shall I say to whom?
2. Pencereden mayil | mayil bakafrim,	a	Leaning, leaning out of the window I gaze,
Ciğerini işk öfdüne yakafrim.	a	I light thy entrails to the fire of love.
Sen ölürsen, aksufrumu[4] yikafrim,	a	If thou wouldst die, I would wash out my aksur,
Öldürmeyin Mahmudu, | ben de ölüfrim.	b	Kill not Mahmud, I would also die.
3. Yüksek pencereden | yere bakilfmaz,	a	From the high window, one does not gaze at the ground,
Yüce merdivende, | aman, çikilfmaz.	a	High ladders one does not ascend,
- - - - -[5] bir ben ölmeyinen[6] | âlem yikilfmaz,	a	Surely from my death, the world will not collapse,
Bana senden oldu, | kime ne difyim?	b	[This trouble] came to me from thee, what shall I say to whom?

1) = aşk oduna. 2) = bakarsin. 3) = diyeyim. 4) According to the transcription on the spot; the record has a different, yet unintelligible word. The meaning of aksur could not be traced. 5) The record has here five unintelligible syllables, not transcribed on the spot. 6) =

21a.

	1. Bir emir gelse, de | kâhyalar afsilsa,	a	If only an order would come: the keepers should be hung,
	Şu dünyadan zürifyeti kesilfse,	a	Their generations should break in this world,
	Avradi dul galsa, | gizi basilfsa!	a	Their wives should remain widows, their daughters be surprised [in shame]!
(refr.)	Gaçaklarin baş düşfmani kâhyaflar,	r.	The chief enemies of runaways are [these] keepers,
(refr.)	Kâhyalar, deyuslar, | kerhanecifler!		[Oh! you] keepers, [you] cheated husbands, you brothel-people!
	2. Imamin evinde | tütün tütmefsin,	a	In the house of the priest smoke should not smoke,
	Kâhyanin evinde | oğlan yetmefsin,	a	In the house of the keeper, there should not be enough boys,
	Horantacak sabahflara çikmafsin!	a	The morn should not reach him with his household!
(refr.)	Gaçaklarin baş düşfmani kâhyaflar,	r.	The chief enemies of runaways are [these] keepers,
(refr.)	Kâhyalar, deyuslar, | dümbükler, elli-sekizler![1]		[Oh! you] keepers, [you] cheated husbands, you scoundrels, [you] fifty-eight[1] ones!

1) ه + ن + ب + ا = 5 + 50 + 2 + 1 = 58; ابنه = ibné = passive pederast.

3. Candarma gelmiş, de | bir geçi duftar,	a	The guard arrived, he grabbed a goat,
Kâhya der kine | dört tene yëfter,	a	Says the keeper: four more pieces will suffice;
Buğdayï, bulguru | hep una ğafar!	a	The corn, the wheatgroats, he mixes all into the flour!
(refr.) Gaçaklarïn baş düşmanï kâhyaflar,	r.	The chief enemies of runaways are [these] keepers,
Kâhyalar, dümbükler, | elli-sekizfler, kerhanecifler!		[Oh! you] keepers, [you] scoundrels, [you] fifty-eight ones, [you] brothel people!

21b.

1. Yörü dilber, yörü, | yolundan | galma,	a	Depart, my beauty, depart, stop not on thy way,
Her yüze güleni | dost olur | sanma.	a	He who smiles into every face do not fancy friend,
Ölümden gorχup da | sen geri | /: durma :/,	a	Fearing the death stay not behind,
Yeğidin alnïna | yazïlan | /: gelir :/.	b	What is written on the forehead of the brave, will be fulfilled
2. Ördek gölü beklër, | şahïn | gayayï; —	a	The duck dwells on the lake, the falcon on the rock; —
Ne-ğadar vasf eyflesem değer | bahayï.	a	For however much I value it, it would be worth its price.
Durnadan-mï alfdïn, gelin, | /: cïğayï :/?	a	From the crane didst thou buy, bride, [those] coloured feathers?
Bulamam üstüne | mahana,[1] | /: gelin :/.	b	I find no excuse for thee, bride.

1) = bahane

22

1. Havayï da | deli gönlüm, | havayï, aman, havayï,	a	Inconstant indeed is my crazy heart, inconstant, aman, inconstant,
Alïc' guşlar | yüksek yapar | yuvayï,	a	The birds of prey build their nests high,
Gaterlemiş[1] | türkmen gïzï | davayï.	a	The Türkmen maiden lines up the camels.
(refr.) Çekip gider | bir gözleri | /: sürmelim :/.	r.	She departs pulling them, my painted-eyed one.
2. Niçin düştüm | şu gözelin | ardïna, aman, ardïna?	a	Why did I fall towards this beauteous [maiden] aman, towards her?
Kendi göçsün, | biz gonalïm | yurduna,	a	She herself should move away, ourselves should settle in her land
Yïkïlasï | garlï dağïn | ardïna.	a	Behind the crumbling snowy mountains.
Aşïp gider | bir gözleri | /: sürmelim :/.	r.	Passing through, she departs, my painted-eyed one.
3. Ayağïna geyfmiş gïrmïzï | yemeni, aman, yemeni,	a	She has put the red shoes on her feet, aman, shoes,
Gel dostum, | galdïralïm aradakï | gümanï.	a	Come, my friend, let us stop [this] doubt twixt us,
Ağ topuk üsftünde sandal | tümanï.	a	Above her white ankles are her silk bloomers.
Döküp gider, | bir gözleri | /: sürmelim :/.	r.	Pouring [water], she departs, my painted-eyed one.

1) = katarlamiş.

23

1) 1. Ilk akşamdan doğdu bir sarı yıldız,	a	The first evening a yellow star arose,
Üç gün gılıç çaldı geceli gündüz.	a	For three days did the swords play night and day.
/: Yazılı defterde on iki bin gız :/,	a	Twelve thousand maidens are written in the list,
Güzelleri esirge /: Ahıskanın :/!		Save the beauties of Ahıska!
Yazılı defterde on iki bin gız,		
Güzelleri esirge Ahıskanın!		
2. /: Ahıskanın ardı | cığı dağ idi :/,	a	Behind Ahıska is a bare mountain,
Babam paşa, gardaşım bey | idi.	a	My father was pasha, my brother bey.
Böyle olmadan bize | ölüm yeğ idi,	a	Death was more desirable to us than this state,
Güzelleri esirge /: Ahıskanın :/!		Save the beauties of Ahıska.
Böyle olmadan bize | ölüm yeğ idi.		
Güzelleri esirgesin Ahıskanın!		
3. /: Adımı sorarsan | benli Emine :/,		Should you ask of me my name: [it is] beauty-spotted Emine,
Altın burma dakınırdım golluma.		I put golden bangles on my arm.
Yolumuz oğradı | ganlı zalim.		This was on our road, [oh] bloody murderer.
Padişahdan imdad | ister bu gızlar.		These maidens beg help from the Padishah.

1) St. 1, though recorded, is not transcribed from the recording.

24

1. /: Edem,		Hey!
Bu cerenin | sulakları | gayalı :/,	a	The drinking-pool of this gazelle is rocky,
Gayasında | lele, | sümbül dayalı.	a	Tulips, hyacinths lean onto its rocks.
2. /: Edem,		Hey!
Şeker yimiş | dudakları | boyalı :/,	a	She has eaten sugar, her lips are coloured [with it],
Seherde garşıma | geçti bir ceren.	b	At dawn a gazelle came towards me.

25 Agıt — Song of Mourning

1. Dedenin de | döşü enli,	a	The bosom of Dede is broad,
Nenni Boyraz | oğlum, nenni!	a	Lullaby, my son Boyraz, lullaby!
2. Öldürürler, | guzum, sizi, (var. yavrum,)	b	They will kill thee, my lamb, (var. my little one,)
Eskiler evvelden kelli.1)	a	- - - - - - - - - - - - - 1)

1) The meaning of this line could not be established.

3. Evimizin | uğru ekin,	a	Before our house are sprouts,
Yëkin gora[2] | Dedem, yëkin!	a	Arise, my - - -[2] Dede, arise!
4. Ağlamaya | ar ediyom,	b	I am ashamed to weep,
Duşmanların | evi yakın.	a	The house of the enemy [is] near.

2) The meaning of this word could not be established.

26

1. Uçtu da şafhanım, uçtu,	a	My falcon flew away, flew away,
Uçtu, da derÿayı gëçti.	a	It flew away, it passed even over the sea.
2. Göynüm bir gözele düştü,	a	My heart fell to [the love of] a beauty,
Zarv edecek | malım yoktur.	b	I have no fortune to spend.

3. = 2.

27

1. Her kës sevdiğini | yanına | gëtirdi,	Everybody brought his beloved beside him,
Sallan, geç garşıma, | nazı[1] | menekşem.	Sway yourself, come in front of me, my coquette violet.
2. Annacından gelen | gücücük gelin,	Little bride coming from the opposite [side],
Bir saat garşımda | durabilinmi[2]?	Couldst thou stay with me for an hour?
3. Divane göynümün | talibi[3] | sensin,	Thou art the desire of my crazy heart,
Gırıldı ganadım, | sarabilinmi[4]?	My wing has broken, couldst thou bind it?

1) = nazlı. 2) = durabilirmisin. 3) = talebi? 4) = sarabilirmisin.

28

1. Şu cerenin suvakların gezmeli,	a	The drinking-pool of this gazelle must be sought,
Galem alıp gaşın, | gözün | yazmalı.	a	Thine eyebrows, thine eyes must be written taking a pen.
2. Gırmızı öğnüklü,[1] | sarı çizmalı,	a	Red-aproned, yellow-booted [maiden],
Seferde urma[2] | geldi | o ceren.	b	At dawn this gazelle came to the summit.

1) = önlüklü. 2) = seherde (u)ruma.

3. Kak gedelim Garafmana aşaği,	a	Arise, let us go to the bottom of Karaman,
Iki baci gïvrak | bağlar | guşaği.	a	The two sisters tie their belts coquettishly.
4. Bize derler: Gâvïrdağïn uşaği.	a	We are called the youths of Gâvïrdağ.
Seferde urma | geldi | o ceren,	b	At dawn this gazelle came to the summit,
Aglïmï başïmdan | aldï | bir gelin.		A bride has taken my mind from my head.

9

1. Deriye indim, | daş bulafmadïm,	a	I went down to the brook, I could not find a stone,
Bür yüzük yapdïrdïm, | gaş bulafmadïm,	a	I had a ring made, I could find no gem,
2. Gendime münasip | eş bulafmadïm.	a	I could not find a companion fit to me.
Tez gel, ağam, tez gel, | gatï darfdayïm,	a	Come quickly, my lord, come quickly, I am in great need,
Garip bülbül gibi | ah-ï-zarfdayïm.		Like an unfortunate nightingale, I complain bitterly.

0

1. Karşïmdan geliyor | gözelin | biri,	a	Opposite comes one of the beauties,
Yüzüne vurmuş da | şavkïnïn | nuru, sürmelim, dost. (refr.)	a	The brightness of her light struck her face, my painted eyed one, friend. (refr.)
2. Haddini tanï da, | sen öyle | yörü,	a	Learn thou also to know thy limits, proceed,
Eller azgïn olmuş, | dil değer | saña, refr.	b	Everyone became furious, [their] tongues reach thee, refr.
1) 3. Gözel olan al velesin bağlanïr,	a	Her pretty red parade-veil she puts on,
Gözeller sayesinde gönül eylenir, refr.	a	Beside beauties the heart rejoices, refr.
4. Garbï değimiş gavak gibi ïgranïr,	a	She sways west-wind touched poplar-like,
Deñsiz olur yörüyüşü gözelin, refr.	b	The walk of the beauty is often restless, refr.

1) St. 3 and 4 are not recorded.

1

1. /: Garsïda | kürt evleri :/,	a	Opposite are the houses of the Kurds,
/: Yayïlur | develeri :/, hey, anom, hey! (1. refr.)	a	Their camels are dispersing, ho, my mother, ho (1. refr.)
2. /: Oturmuş | goyun sağar :/,	b	She sat down, she is milking the sheep,
/: Terlemiş | memeleri :/, hey, güzel, hey! (2. refr.)	a	Her breasts are sweating, ho, beauty, ho! (2. refr.)

32

1. |: Duda mërdifman gurdum, vay vay :|, — a
|: Yare söylafma durdum, of of :|. — a

I leant a ladder to the mulberry, hey, hey,
I greated my beloved, oh, oh.

2. |: Yarïm guïbefte gitti, vay vay :|, — b
Yidi yïl befkyar durdum, of of. — a

My beloved went to foreign lands, hey, hey,
I stayed for seven years bachelor, oh, oh.

(refr.) Dolanïr, | Ëda, | sallïnïr, | Ëda,
Saç topuğa | dolaşïr, | Ëda.

She is strolling, Eda, she is swaying, Eda,
Her hair falls until her ankles, Eda.

3. |: Këlëm ektim | bayïra, vay vay :|, — a
|: Yël yaprağïn | ayïra, of of :|! — a

I have sown cabbage on the slope, hey hey,
That the wind separates its leaves, oh, oh!

4. |: Iki hasret | bir yirde, vay vay :|, — b
Mëvlâm gayït | gayïra, vay vay! — a

Two separated in one place, hey, hey,
My God protect them with care, oh, oh!

1) 5. Bostanda mïsïrïm var, — a
Dibinde hasïrïm var. — a

There is maize in the vegetable garden,
At the foot of it is my mat.

6. Ittin köpeyin ölu! — b
Neremde kusurum var. — a

Son of a dog, of a bitch!
In my something there is insufficiency.

1) St. 5 and 6 are not recorded.

33 Kïna türküsü — Henna Song

1. |: Bismillah | yëdin | gïnaya :|, — a
Sağ ëlin | vërsin | gïnaya. — a

Tell Bismillah during the putting on of the henna,
She should give her right hand during the putting on of the he…

2. Çağïrïn, | gelsin | anaya, — a
Yar, ëlin, | gïnañ | gutlu olsun, — b
Bunda dirfliğin | datlu olsun!

Shout, she should come to her mother,
[My] darling, blessed be thy hand, thy henna,
May thy life here be sweet!

3. |: Hatladï, | çigdï | ëşiği :|, — a
Sufrada | galdï | gaşïğï. — a

She skipped, she crossed the threshold,
Her spoon has stayed on the table.

4. Gïz anafsïnïñ | danïsï; — — a
Yar, ëlin, | gïnañ | al olsun, — b
Bunda dirfliğin | bal olsun!

The daughter is her mother's only one; —
[My] darling, that thy hands, thy henna be vermill…
That thy life here may be honey!

5. |: Mërcimek | egdim, | bittimi :|? — a
Dâlinde | bülbül | öttümü? — a

I have sown lentils, have they sprouted?
Has the nightingale sung on the branch?

6. |: Gïz, anañ | seni | unuttumu? — a
2a volta: | 'nutdumu?
Gïz, gïnañ | gutlu | olsun! — b

[My] daughter, has thy mother forgotten thee?
[My] daughter, blessed by thy henna!

4

1. Maraşda guftu,	a	In Maraş a box,
icinde oftu,	a	~~~~ therein its grass,
Nişanlĭñ köftü.	a	Your betrothed is wicked.
/:) Geldin gelifnim,	r.	You have arrived, my bride,
Geldin, geldin | gelinim,		You have arrived, you have arrived, my bride,
sen sefa gelfdim!		welcome!'
2. Narĭn ağafcĭ,	a	The tree of the pomegranate,
narĭn ağafcĭ,	a	the tree of the pomegranate,
Gĭz, gelin, bafcĭ.	a	Maiden, bride, sister.
refr.	r.	refr.

5

1. Zabahdan oğfradĭm ben bir | /: geline :/,	a	At morn I paid a call on a bride,
Bal bulamĭş | dodağĭna, | /: diline :/.	a	She smeared honey on her lips, her tongue.
2. Harcedeyim | bunca malĭ | /: yoluna :/,	a	I would spend so much fortune for thee,
Az gelirse, | datlĭ canĭ | /: vërmeli :/.	b	Would it seem little, I must give [my] dear soul.
3. Zabahdan oğradĭm ben bir /: geline :/,		At morn I paid a call on a bride,
Gelin sultan olmuş elin /: üstüne :/.		The bride became Sultan over her tribe.

1) St. 3, though recorded, is not transcribed from the record.

6

1. Ner[e]de ydin çĭktĭn | yolum üsftüne?	a	Where werst thou, [that] thou comest onto my path?
Can dayanmaz | şu güzelin | /: gasdine :/.	a	The soul cannot resist the intentions of this beauty.
2. Gel, abdestal, | sen imam ol | /: üstüme :/,	a	Come, wash thyself, become priest, for me,
Sağlĭğĭmda | cenazemi | /: gĭl galan 1) :/.	b	Carry out my death ceremony [yet] whilst I live.
3. Benim dostum çĭkmĭş | yola, otufrur,		My [maiden] friend has come out onto the path, has there sat down,
Ağlayarak | aklĭcĭğnĭ 2) | /: yitirir :/.		She loses her little mind weeping.

1) = artĭk. 2) = ak[illegible]ĭlcĭğĭnĭ.

7

1. Bey oğluyum, | ben hatalar | işledim,	a	I am son of a bey, I committed faults,
Hayrĭ goydum, | da şere | başladĭm.	a	I gave up the good deed, and gave myself to crimes.
2. Öpem derken | al yanaklar | dişledim	a	Saying "Let me kiss" I bit red faces
Ağrĭmadan | çekilesi | dişineyn 1).	b	With my teeth which ought to be drawn for [caused] pain.

1) = dişile.

3. Senin için | terk eyledim | silamĭ,	a	For thee I left my birth-country,
Sarf eyledim | bütün olan | varĭmĭ.	a	I spent my whole existing fortune [I had].
4. Kim ağlatmĭş | benim nazlĭ | yarĭmĭ?	a	Who made my naughty darling cry?
Girpiklerin | top top olmuş | yaşĭnan[2]?	b	Her eyelashes became fully-full with tears.

2) = yaşĭla.

38

1. Inerler, giderler | Çemişözüne,	a	They descend, they are going to Çemişözü,
Hökünüp[1] salarlar | yavrĭ | sözüne.	a	Loading they send the little one to its promise.
2. Ne zaman baksam da | dostĭn | yüzüne,	a	Whenever I look into the face of my friend,
Duman çökmüş, | çöl götünür | gözüme.	a	A fog descends, a desert appears before my eyes.

1) < yökünmek = to load

39

1. Yazĭn geldiği | neresinden | bellüdür?	a	How does the coming of the summer reveal itself?
Gonca gülün | yapracĭğĭ | dürgündür,	a	The little leaves of the ~~summer~~ rosebuds are folded,
Dürgündür, | dürgündür.		Folded, folded.
2. Soğuk furmuş | ötselemiş | yüzünü,	b	The cold has beaten his face, has torn it,
Benim gönlüm | bir Leylaya | furgundur,	a	My heart is the wounded one of a Leyla,
Furgundur, | furgundur.		The wounded one, the wounded one.
3. Yazĭn geldiği | neresinden | bellüdür?		How does the coming of the summer reveal itself
Ne ded' ola | boz bulanĭk | dereler,		What had said the grey troubled streams,
Dereler, | dereler?		Streams, streams?
4. Her kes sevdiğini alĭn | yatĭnca		When everyone taking his beloved goes to rest:
Arttĭ derdim, | yeniledi | yareler,		My pain augmented, the wounds reopened,
Yareler, | yareler.		The wounds [reopened], the wounds [reopened].

40 Oyun havasĭ — Dance Song

1. Galadan eniyordum,	a	I came down from the fortress,
Çağĭrsan dönüyordum.	a	If you called me, I would return.
(refr.) { Yar cim-dallĭ[1], cim-dallĭ,		Darling of the djim-dal [-clothes],
Sar cim-dallĭ, cim-dallĭ. }		Embrace the djimdal [-clothed] one.
2. /: Derdimden kirbid oldum :/,	b	From pain I have become [thin as] a match,
Üfürsen yanĭyordum.	a	Wouldst thou blow [on me], I would burn.
refr.		refr.

1) = a kind of embroidery (with patterns of ج [= cim] and د [= dal]?).

3. /: Cim-dallĭ çarfşĭsĭnda:/		At the market of djimdal-clothes
Yar oynar qarfşĭsĭnda.		The darling dances opposite [me].
refr.		refr.

1

1. Köprünün alftĭ tiken,	a	Under the bridge are thorns,
refr.) /: Yēşillim:/, afman, aman;		My darling in the green dress, aman, aman;
Yaqdĭn beni | gül iken,	a	Thou burnst me in my rosehood,
refr.) /: Efendim:/ eğflēn, eğlēn.		My mistress, enjoy thyself, enjoy thyself.
2. Allah da sefni yaqsĭn,	b	Allah should also burn thee,
refr.) /: Yēşillim:/, afman, aman;		My [darling] in the green dress, aman, aman,
Üç günlük geflin iken,	a	When thou artst a three day bride,
refr.) /: Sürmelim:/ eğflēn, eğlēn.		My painted-eyed one, enjoy thyself, enjoy thyself.
3. = 2.[1]		
4. Köprünün alftĭ buzlar,	a	Under the bridge are ice[-floes],
refr.) /: Yeşillim:/, afman, aman;		My [darling] in the green dress, aman, aman;
Top gediyor | yĭldĭzlar,	a	The stars move in groups,
refr.) /: Efendim:/, afman, aman.		My mistress, aman, aman.
5. Gene aklĭfma düştü,	b	They came to my mind again,
refr.) /: Yeşillim:/ eğflēn, eğlēn,		My [darling] in the green dress, enjoy thyself, enjoy thyself,
Fincan göbekfli gĭzlar,	a	The girls with the cup-like navels,
/: Sürmelim:/ eğlēn, eğlēn.		My painted-eyed one, enjoy thyself, enjoy thyself.

[1] Instead of /: aman:/ there is /: eğlēn:/.

2

1. Ormanĭn boz | gĭracĭ,	a	The grey fallow fields of the woods,
Çift gezer ifki bacĭ.	a	Two sisters are walking together.
Şahan olsam, | avlasam	b	Were I a falcon, I would hunt
Goyundakĭ | turacĭ.	a	The pheasant in thy bosom.
2. Galadan infdim düze,	a	From the fortress I came down to the plain,
Su bağladĭm | nerkise.	a	I sprinkled water onto the narcissi;
Yedi yĭl hizfmat ettim	b	Seven years did I serve
Bir gömür gözflü gĭza.	a	A coal-eyed maiden.

3. Gideyim yolfca, yolca,	a	Let me go from road to road,
Yolun çiçefği morca.	a	The flower of the path is bluish.
Güzel gel, bir | öpüş vër,	b	[My] beauty, give me a kiss,
Harmana galfsïn borca.	a	Let it stay a borrowed one till harvest.
1) 4. Bir avucuk küşneyim,	a	I am a small handful of vetch,
Bir gïzïnan eşneyim.[2)]	a	I am the comrade of a maiden.
Gïzïn babasï düymüş (sic),	b	The father of the maiden heard of it,
Hiç ardïna düsmeyim.	a	[Rather] should I never follow her.

1) Not recorded. 2) = eşim.

43a. Oyun havasï — Danse Song

1. Ay gider, ufca gider,	a	The moon passes on, it passes towards the horiz
Bezirgen gefce gider;	a	The merchant walks at night;
Ağ mëmenin | üstünden	b	Across thy white breast
Doğru yol hafca gider.	a	A straight road leads to pilgrimage.
2. Değermen öfnü çiçek,	a	In front of the mill flowers,
Orak getifrin, biçek[1)].	a	Bring a sickle, let us cut them down.
Ben dostumu | bilirim:	b	I know my friend:
Orta boylu | mor çiçek.	a	She is a medium sized mauve flower.

1) = biçelim.

43b.

1. Haydi!		Go!
Galeden infdim iniş,	a	From the fortress I came down the slope,
mendilim doflu yimiş;	a	my handkerchief is full of fruit
Yara saldïm, | yimemiş,	b	I sent it to my darling, she did not eat:
yar gendi gelfsin dimiş.	a	"Let him come himself" the darling sai
Aman, aman, | pusarïk,	a	Aman, aman, the sulky one,
başta durmaz | bu sarïk,	a	this turban stays not on the head,
Doldur sevdiğim | gadehi,	b	Fill, my love, the glass,
belki yolda | susarïk.	a	perhaps we shall thirst on the road

2. Haydi!		Go!
Indim guyu | dibine,		I descended to the bottom of the well,
guyu dibi | sazĭmĭş;		at the bottom of the well are reeds,
Yalan değil, | sevdiğim		It is not a lie: my beloved
gömür gözlü | gĭzĭmĭş.		is a coal eyed maiden.
Ah çinçinim, | çinçinim,[1]		Oh! my çinçin, my çinçin![1]
öpem ağzĭn | içini;		let me kiss the inside of thy mouth;
Öperken ifşĭrmişim,		Kissing, should I bite it,
sen bağaşla | suçumu!		forgive me my sin!
3. Su gelir, hillendirir[3],	a	Water is coming, refreshing,
bağçayĭ güllendirir;	a	it enroses the garden;
Bu sevda nasĭl sevda?	b	This love, what kind of love is it?
Ahrazĭ dillendirir.	a	It makes even the mute talk.
Gala galadan garşĭ,	a	Fortress opposite fortress,
galanĭn içi çarşĭ;	a	inside the fortress is a market [-place];
Eğil bir yol öpeyim	b	Bend down, that I should kiss you
dosta, düşmana garşĭ.	a	in front of friend [and] enemy.

1) çinçin is a pet word. 2) Not recorded. 3) Probably = hallandĭrĭr = refresh.

3d.

1. Urfanĭn boz | gĭracĭ,	a	The grey fallow field of Urfa,
çift gězer ifki bacĭ;	a	two sisters are walking coupled;
Şahan olsam, | avlansam	b	Were I a falcon, I would be on a chase
goynundakĭ | turacĭ.	a	for the pheasant in thy bosom.
Urfa, Urfa | uc olur,	a	Urfa, Urfa is on the border,
dyomlaleri[1] | tuc olur;	a	its meltings (?) are of bronze;
Galĭn verip | evlenmekte	b	To give bridal money at marriage
ergenlere | güc olur.	a	for the youths, it is difficult.
2. Galanĭn arfdĭ tiken,	a	Behind the fortress a thorny [place],
yaktĭn beni | gĭz iken.	a	thou burnst me in my maidenhood.
Allah da sefni yaksĭn	b	God should burn thee also
üç günlük geflin iken.	a	when thou art a three days old bride.

1) This word is recorded; probably a distortion of dökmeleri which was transcribed on the spot.

3. Galanĭn arḟdĭ tandĭr,	a	Behind the fortress a small oven,
yandĭr, allaḟĭm, yandĭr;	a	burn me, my God, burn me,
Beni bir çift | guş ëyle,	b	Transform me into a couple of birds,
yarĭn göğsüḟne gondur.	a	place me on the bosom of my love.

44 Oyun havasĭ — Dance Song

1. Dud ağacĭ | dut verir,	a	The mulberry tree gives mulberries,
yaprağĭnĭ | gït verir,	a	leaves it sparsely gives,
Ergen oğlan, | büyük gïz,	b	The youth, the grown maiden,
sarĭldĭkca | dat verir.	a	their embrace gives flavour.
(refr.) Şu yanna dönḟder beni,	a	Turn me this way,
bu yanna dönḟder beni;	a	turn me that way;
Sağ yanĭmda | yarem var,	b	On my right side I have a wound,
yarĭme gönḟder beni.	a	send me to my beloved.
2. Tut koyunun | yünlüsün',	a	Hold the [most] woolly of the sheep,
debüğnürse | büğnüsün',[1]	a	if kicking let it kick;
Ser güzelin | eyisin,	a	Of the beauties, upset the best,
alnĭda çifte | benlisin.	a	who has double beauty spots on her forehea
refr.		refr.
3. Şu dere deḟrin dere,	a	This brook is a deep brook,
kölgesi seḟrin dere;	a	a brook with cool shadows;
Ğïzlara duḟzak kurdum,	b	I have sat a trap for the maidens,
korkarĭm geḟlin gele'[2].	a	I fear, a bride will come.
refr.		refr.

[1] Perhaps a distortion of debinirse debinsin?

[2] = gelecek.

45

1. Gura gurmuş | yol üstüne | çĭkrĭğĭ,	She merely put her spindle on the road,
Aydĭn havaḟsĭna büker | ipliği,	She spins her twine according to Aydĭn custo
(1. refr.) ëlḟler, ëller,	oh strangers, strangers,
Amanĭn dërḟler, dërler, | horazĭm nenḟni, nenni,	|: They say: | aman, my cock, |: lullaby :|,
Keleşim nenḟni, nenni, | bir danem nenḟni, nenni.	My nice one, |: lullaby :|, my only one, |: lullaby
2. Evlerinin | önü, aman, | idrişah,	In front of their house, aman, are geranium
Boyu uzun, | gendi şah,	Her figure is slender, she herself is Shah,
(2. refr.) ëlḟler, ëller, ëlḟler, ëller,	oh |: strangers, strangers;
Amanĭn dërḟler, dërler, | horazĭm nenḟni, nenni,	|: They say :|, aman, my cock, |: lullaby :|,
Bir danem nenḟni, nenni, | keleşim nenḟni, nenni.	My only one, |: lullaby :|, my nice one, |: lullaby

3. Evlerinin | önü armut | alanĭ,		Before their house is the orchard of pear trees,
Ananĭ eşek | siksin | yeni buldun | belanĭ,		The ass should f... your mother, now thou found thy punishment,
1. refr.		1. refr.
in print only: s....		

6

1. |: Menevşe bulfdum derede :|,	a	I found violets at the brook,
|: Sordum, evlefri nërede :|.	a	I inquired where their house is.
2. |: Üç-beş güzel | bir-arada[1] :|.	a	Three [or] five beauties together.
r.) Dilber, dilber, | canĭm dilber,	r.	Darling, darling, my soul, darling,
Canĭmĭn yayflasĭ dilber,		The mountain pasture of my soul, darling,
Gönlümün eğflesi dilber.		The entertainer of my heart, darling.
3. |: Gara çanafğĭn[2] yaprağĭ :|,	a	The leaf of the çanak is dark,
|: Dibinden alfdĭm toprağĭ :|.	a	From its foot I took [this] earth.
4. |: Dilber güzelfler aplağĭ :|.	a	The chubby one of the beauties is charming.
refr.	r.	refr.

1) = beraber. 2) Çanak is probably the name of a plant. The dictionary Anadilden Derlemeler, however, gives the following meaning: a sort of a ditch or pit on a hill side.

7

1. |: Sandiğĭmĭ | açamadĭm, Leyle :| la la,	a	I could not open my chest,
Ciğimizi | seçemedim, Leyle.	a	I could not choose my dowry.
2. |: χadër χĭzmet | böyle imiş, Leyle :| la la,	b	Fate and destiny was thus:
Bir χĭz alĭp | χaçamadĭm, la la.	a	Taking [with me] a maiden I could not run away.
3. |: Güllü çorap | örmemişim, Leyle :| la la,	a	I have not knitted rosy stockings,
Ayağma | gimemişim, Leyle.	a	I have not put them on my feet.
4. |: Çoχ mëmeler | ellemişim, Leyle :| la la,	a	Many a breast have I patted,
Böyle mëme | görmemişim, la la.	a	Such a breast I have not seen.
5. |: Ağ daşĭn alftĭ deniz, Leyle :| la la,	a	Sea beneath the white stone,
Ak sayalĭ[1] | χĭz neñiz?	a	The maiden of the white embroidered dress, what is she to you?
6. Koğun, gitsin mahalleden,	b	Chase her away, she should go away from the quarter,
Ne bet kodĭ, ne beniz.	a	She has left no face colour [in the people].

1) Saya = işlemeli üst yeleği. 2) St. 6–8 not recorded.

1. Kapīn kapuma baxar,	a	Thy gate faces my gate,
Ateşīn beni yaxar.	a	Thy fire burns me.
2. Etme bu kötülüğü,	b	Do not commit this wickedness,
Gine yüz yüze baxar.	a	Face will anew regard face.

48a.

1. Mavilim | Daşbaşında	a	My blue-dressed [darling] one at Taşbaşı,
Inceli | fes başında, | mavilim. (refr.)	a	Pearly fez on his head, my blue-dressed [darling] (refr.)
2. Xīz, niyeñ | ağlamīyon[1]?	b	Maiden, why dost thou not weep?
Nişanlīñ | gīxh yaşında, | mavilim. (refr.)	a	Thine bridegroom is forty years old, my blue-dressed [darling] (refr.)
3. Mavilim, | ğak,[2] gidelim,		My blue-dressed [darling] one, arise, let us depart
Fênarī | yak, gidelim, | mavilim (refr.)		Light the lantern, let us depart, my blue-dressed [darling] (refr.)

1) = ağlamayor musun. 2) = kalk.

48b.

1. Mavilim | hirk idiyor,	a	My blue-dressed [darling] tills the soil,
Hirgini | terk idiyor, | mavilim. refr.	a	He quits his labours, my blue-dressed [darling] one (refr.)
2. Hirgin başīnī yësin!	b	Thy labourings should destroy thy head!
Yarīn elden gidiyor, | mavilim. refr.	a	Thy beloved is slipping from thy hands, my blue-dressed [darling] (refr.)
(refr.?) Gīz mavilim, /: mavilim :/!		My blue-dressed maiden, /: my blue-dressed one :/.
Çal dauülcī /: daūlī :/,		Beat, drummer, /: the drum :/,
Çal zurnacī /: zurnayī :/!		Blow, piper, /: the pipe :/!
3. Mavilim, | kalk, gidelim,	a	My blue-dressed [darling] one, arise, let us depart,
Fênerī | yak, gidelim, | mavilim. (refr.)	a	Light the lantern, let us depart, my blue-dressed [darling] one (refr.)
4. Gözële | doymag olmaz,	b	One cannot be satiated of a beauteous maiden,
Bir çala | bak, gidelim, | mavilim. (refr.)	a	Look [around] a little, [then] let us leave, my blue-[dressed] [darling] (refr.)

49a. Yağmur duası

Yağmurcuğum, | yağı vir,
Kuyucuğum, | dolu vir!
Ekmek getir, | yiyelim,
Gaytan getir, | giyelim,
Allah, allah | diyelim!

Üşüdüm, üşüdüm, | üş oldum,
Bir topacık | kiş oldum.
Kişimi elimden | aldılar,
Beni yola | saldılar.
Yolda bir yu|mak buldum,
Yumağı ebe|me virdim,
Ebem baña | darı virdi,
Ben darıyı | guşlara virdim,
Guşlar baña | ganat virdi,
Ganatlandım, | göye ucdum.
Göy baña yağ|mır virdi,
Ben yağmırı | yire virdim,
Yir baña çi|men virdi,
Ben çimeniği | goyuna virdim,
Goyun baña | guzu virdi,
Bindim, gittim | Garasuya.
Garasuda | ganlar akar,
Iki bülbül | baña bakar.
Getirin ganını: | icelim,
Aksëraya | göçelim.
Aksërayın | kilidi, —
Gece geler | kim idi?
Emmin oğlu | Musacık,
Golu, budu | gısacık,
çık çık çık.

Ben guzuyu | beğlere virdim,
Beğler baña | at virdi,

My little rain, rain away,
My little well, fill thyself!
Bring bread, let us eat,
Bring braid, let us dress,
Let us say God, God!

I was freezing, I became cold,
I became a little cheese dumpling.
They took my cheese from my hand,
They put me out on the road.
On the road I found a spool,
I gave the spool to my mid-wife,
My mid-wife gave me millet,
I gave the millet to the birds,
Birds gave me wings,
I became winged, I flew to the sky.
The sky gave me rain,
I gave the rain to soil,
Soil gave me verdure,
I gave the verdure to sheep,
The sheep gave me [a] lamb,
I leapt on, I went to Karasu.
[Much] blood flows at Karasu,
Two nightingales gaze at me.
Bring their blood: that we may drink,
Let us take the road to Aksaray.
Aksaray has a lock, —
Last night, the arrival, who is he?
[My] uncle'son, little Musa,
His arms, his thigs, are shortish,
-ish, -ish, -ish.

I gave the lamb to the masters,
Masters give me [a] horse,

49b. Yağmur duası

Teknede | hamur,
Arabada | çamur,
Vir allahïm | sulu sulu | yağmur,
[1] Topal gïzïn gïçïna yağmur!

Rain-begging Song

Dough in the basin,
Mud in the carriage,
Give, my God, watery-watery rai
Rain on the buttock of the lame girl!

[1] This line is spoken.

49c. Yağmur duası

Bodi, bodi,[1]
Neden ōdi[2]?
Bir gaşïcak sudan | ōdi.
Yağmur gïzï yağ | ister,
Palta, kürek bal | ister,
Goç, goyun gurban | ister,
Göbekli harman | ister,
[3] Ver allahïm, ver bir sulu sulu yağmur!
Ekin ektim evlek | evlek,
Sular döktüm külek | külek,
Yedi, içti hacï | leylek,
[3] Ver allahïm, ver bir sulu sulu yağmur!

Rain-begging Song

Duck, duck,
Of what didshe die?
She died of a little spoonful of water.
The daughter of rain demands oil,
The axe, the shovel demand honey,
The ram, the sheep demand sacrifices,
The big bellied one demands crops,
Give, my God, give watery-watery rai
I sowed seeds from furrow to furrow,
I poured water by buckets to buckets,
The migratory stork has eaten, has drunk
Give, my God, give watery-watery rain

[1] Nobody on the spot knew the meaning of this word. In the vilayet of Yozgat it mea ördek, according to the dictionary Anadilden Derlemeler. [2] = öldü.

[3] This line is spoken.

49d. Yağmur duası

Bodu, bodu,[1]
Anan nëden | öldü?
Bir gaşïcak sudan | öldü.
Ayağ'ïm çamïr | ister,
Boğazïm hamïr | ister.
[3] Gastï[2], yer yarïldï,
Saban gïrïldï.
Ver, allahïm, ver
Sulu sulu yağmur,
Ver, allahïm, ver!

Rain-begging Song

Duck, duck,
Of what did your mother die?
She died of a little spoonful of water.
My feet demand mud,
My throat demands dough.
He dug, the soil rent,
The plough broke.
Give, my God, give
Watery-watery rain,
Give, my God, give!

[1] See remark [1] to N° 49c. [2] = kazdï. [3] These lines are spoken.

Nenni

1. Nenni yau̯rĭm, | nenni,
Nenni diyi | beledim,
Al bağĭrdaχĭ | doladĭm,
Yau̯rĭm nenni, | nenni!
Sënye hakdan | diledim,
Guzum nenni, | nenni!

2. Nenni didim | bëşiğine,
Yau̯rum nenni, | nenni!
Devlet konsun | eşiğine,
Yau̯rum nenni, | nenni!

3. Beğin oğlu | döşeğine,
Yau̯rum nenni, | nenni,
Nenni guzum, | nenni!

4. Nenni didim | nësine,
Yau̯rĭm hu | hu hu;
Sëlam söylen | dayĭsĭna,
Yau̯rĭm nenni, | nenni!

5. Mama getir | dayĭsĭ,
Cici getir | babasĭ,
Yau̯rĭm nenni, | nenni!

Lullaby

Lullaby, my little one, lullaby,
I swaddled her, saying lullaby,
I encircled her with red ribbon,
My little one, bye, lullaby!
I besought God [to give] thee [to me],
My lamb, bye, lullaby!

I said lullaby to her cradle,
My little one, bye, lullaby!
May good fortune come to her threshold,
My little one, bye, lullaby!

May the son of a Bey be thy bed-mate,
My little one, bye, lullaby,
Lullaby, my lamb, lullaby!

I said lullaby to her something,
My little one, heigh, heigh, heigh;
Say greetings to her uncle,
My little one, bye, lullaby!

[Her] uncle: bring [her] pap,
[Her] father: bring [her] gee-gaws,
My little one, bye, lullaby!

Ağĭt

atĭrmişler | yazĭmĭ, | guzum oy,
icin gibi | yau̯rĭm, yau̯rĭm, | da oy oy,
arĭ saçĭ, guzum, | sicim gibi, | yau̯rĭm oy.
elin gardaşlarĭm | yau̯rĭma, oy oy,
ğlĭyalĭm | bacĭm gibi, | yau̯rĭm oy!
Mezerin' de | yol üstüne | gazsĭnlar,
fol üstüne | goysunlar, | yau̯rĭm oy!

They have laid down my spring, my lamb, woe,
Like a camel, |: my little one :|, woe, woe,
The hair yellow, my lamb, like string, my little one, woe.
Come my brothers, to my little one, woe, woe,
Let us weep like my elder sister, my little one, woe!
Dig the tomb over the road [side],
Over the road [side] lay him [down to rest], my little one, woe!

52

1. Sivrisarĭñĭ altĭ,	a	The lower part of Sivrihisar; —
Gelinler ëſsir aldĭ.	a	The young brides he has enslaved.
Atineden | gyelmezdim,	b	I would not have come from Athens,
Ahmet bëy syebeb | oldu, Nazĭk,	a	Ahmed bey was the cause, Nazĭk.
(refr.) Nazĭk, | gül memeler | ezik,		Nazĭk, the rosy breasts crushed,
(refr.) Nazĭg, | üç yaûrĭya | yazĭk.		Nazĭk, pity for the three little ones!
2. Gidin bulutſlar, gidin,	a	Pass, clouds, pass,
Papaza ñaſzar ëdin.	a	Watch over the priest.
Çocuxlarĭ | sorarsa,	b	If he asks news of the children,
Deñizi tarif | ëdin, Nazĭk,	a	Show the sea[-road], Nazĭk,
(refr.) Nazĭg, | üç yaûrĭya | yazĭk.		Nazĭk, pity for the three little ones!

53

Yüce dağ başĭnĭn | dört yanĭ | yoldur, dört yanĭ | yoldur,	a	There are paths on the four slopes of the summit of the high h[ill], there are paths on the four slope[s],
Doldur Sunam[1], doldur, | suyunun | doldur, suyunun | doldur.	a	Pour, my Suna[1], pour, pour out thy water, pour out thy water.
Yolunun üstüne | yatam, uſyuyam, yatam, uſyuyam,	b	Let me lie on thy path, let me sleep, let me lie, let me sleep,
Mevlâyĭ syeversyen, | gel, beni | galdĭr, gel, beni | galdĭr.	a	If thou lovest God, come, wake me, come, wake me.
(refr.) Dumanlĭ | dağlar, boranlĭ | dağlar, gül yüzlüm ağlar.		Hazy hills, stormy hills, my rose faced one is weeping.

1) This word is possibly not a name, but implies: slender one.

54

1. Yarĭn bayram derler,	Tomorrow [is a] holyday, they say,
|: Al giyer | eller :|	|: The people dress in red :|,
Bir âdet goymuşlar: | gutl'olsun derler.	The custom is brought in: they say "hail!"
2. Yaz bahar ayĭnda	In the month of summer-spring
Açĭlan | güller, | aman, da | güller,	Blooming roses, aman, roses,
Güller nazlĭ yardan | baña bir | haber!	Roses, [give] me news of [my] coquettish dar[ling]
3. Yaz bahar ayĭnda | açĭlan | güller,	In the month of summer-spring blooming ros[es]
Güller nazlĭ yardan | baña bir | haber!	Roses, [give] me news of [my] coquettish darli[ng]

55a.

1. Hasan dağı, | Hasan dağı,	a	Mount Hasan, Mount Hasan,
Senden yüce | dağ olmamı?	a	Is there no mountain higher than you?
Seni yaylı | yan güzelin	b	The beauty, resting on thee
Al yanağı | bal olmamı?	a	Is her red cheek not [sweet as] honey?
2. Aman, güley | memelerim,	a	Aman, my rosebosoms,
Canım, güley | memelerim!	a	My soul, my rosebosoms!
Kör olası | terzi başı,	b	Blind be the chief of the tailors,
Ne sık dikmiş | düğmelerim!	a	How tight he sewed my buttons!

55b.

1. 2. = № 55 a. 1.

3. /: Aman güley | memeleri :/,	/: Aman, her rosebosoms :/,
Çeşilmeyor[1] | düğmeleri.	Her buttons do not unbutton.

1) = çözülmiyor.

55c.

1. 2. = № 55 a. 1.

3. Yavrım güley | memeleri,	The rosebosoms of my little one,
Gızım güley | memeleri,	The rosebosoms of my maiden,
Çezilmiyor[1] | düğmeleri.	Her buttons do not unbutton.

1) = çözülmiyor.

55d.

1. Hasan dağı, | Hasan dağı,	a	1. 2. = № 55 a. 1.
Senden yöce | dağ olmamı?	a	
2. Seni yaylı | yan gözelin	b	
Al yanağı | bal olmamı?	a	
3. Aman, güley | memeleri,		Aman, her rosebosoms,
Tohul[1] güley | memeleri.		Her tiny rosebosoms.

1) = tifl.

56

1. Garamandan | gelir iken, a
Yandīm, Garamandan | gelir iken
Ayağīma | battī tiken. a

2. Ayrīlīk tir | belimi büken. a
(refr.) Ağlama cīvanīm | çerkes gīzī,
Sen al geyin, | ben gīrmīzī,
Çīkalīm da dağlarīn başīna,
Sen gül topla, | ben nergizi.

Coming from Karaman,
I enflamed, coming from Karaman
A thorn stuck into my foot.
The separation bowed my body.
Weep not, my young Circassien maiden,
Put on crimson thou, [and] I red,
Let us go to the summit of the hills,
Thou pick roses, I narcissi.

3. Garamanīn | alt yanī guyu, a
Yandīm, Garamanīn | alt yanī guyu,
/: Guyudan çekerler suyu :/. a

4. O yarīmīn | eski huyu. a
(refr.) Oynama cīvanīm | çerkes gīzī,
Sen al geyin, | ben gīrmīzī,
Çīkalīm da dağlarīn başīna,
Sen gül topla, | ben nergizi.

In the lower part of Karaman a well,
I enflamed, in the lower part of Karaman a
/: From the well water is scooped :/.
This is an old habit of my darling.
Dance not, my young Circassien maide
Put on crimson thou, [and] I red,
Let us go to the summit of the hills,
Thou pick roses, I narcissi.

57

1. /: Garşīda kürd | evleri, a
(refr.) ğöy ver elle|rim, ğöy ver :/,
Yayīlīr de|veleri, a
(refr.) gelin, elle|rim ğöy ver.

2. /: Sâlīnīr, su|ya iner, b
(refr.) ğöy ver elle|rim, ğöy ver :/,
Türkmenin ma|halari, a
(refr.) gelin, elle|rim ğöy ver,
Türkmenin ma|halari,
(refr.) keklik, elle|rim ğöy ver.

3. /: Garşīda ga|u̯īn[1] yerler,
(refr.) ğöy ver elle|rim, ğöy ver :/,
Biz de varsaχ | ne derler ?
(refr.) Gelin, elle|rim ğöy ver.

[1]) = kavun.

Opposite are the houses of the Kurds,
free my hands, free them,
The camels are dispersing,
young bride, free my hands.
They walk swayingly towards the water,
free my hands, free them,
The cattle of Turkmen,
young bride free my hands.
The cattle of Turkmen,
my partridge, free my hands.
Opposite they are eating melon,
free my hands, free them,
If we also were there, what would they s
young bride, free my hands.

58

1. Hopladım, geçtim bağa, a
başım değdi | yaprağa; a
Gelin seni | almazsam, b
girmem gara | toprağa. a

refr.) Aman gelin | ne diyon![1]
Aman gëlin (sic!) | ne diyon?
suna boylum | ne diyon?
Asker oldum, | gidiyom[2]
ifademe | ne diyon?

I leapt, I went forward in the vines,
my head touched a leaf,
Bride, if I do not marry thee,
I shall not get into the black earth.

/: Aman, bride, what dost thou say :/?
my slender-figured one, what dost thou say?
I became a soldier, I am departing,
what dost thou say to my explanation?

[3] 2. Galadan iniyordum, a
çevirsen dönüyordum; a
Işkından kirbid[4] oldum, b
üfürsen yanıyordum. a
refr.

I came down from the fortress,
if thou wouldst turn back, I would return;
From thy love I became [as thin as] a match,
wouldst thou blow [on me], I would burn.

1) = diyorsun. 2) = gidiyorum. 3) Not recorded. 4) = aşkından kibrit.

59

1. /: Oğlanın | ëlinde | şişe tapafsı :/,
Irgalama, | calkalama | eşek sıpafsı!
refr.) Ne güzel oğflan, | yanası çofban.

2. /: Oğlanın | bëlinde | dapancası | var :/,
Galdırma fisftanı, | gül bağçesi | var.
refr.

/: In the hand of the lad the cork of a bottle :/,
Wriggle not, jiggle not, foal of an ass!
What a handsome lad, would the shepherd burn.

/: On the waist of the lad is his revolver :/,
Take not off [your] clothes, there is a rosegarden.
refr.

Notes to the Texts

8c. *Compare with Kúnos, *Oszmán-török népköltési gyütemény*, No. 7, pp. 382–384.

31. *Var. Kúnos, No. 244, p. 229.

40. *Var. No. 58.

42. *Var. No. 43d.

43b. *Var. Kúnos, No. 107, p. 199.

43d. *Var. No. 42.

45. *Var. Kúnos, No. 67, p. 192: second stanza. N.B.—According to the Kúnos translation, *şah* is bough!

58. *Var. No. 40.

Bibliography

Bartók, Béla. *Hungarian Folk Music.* London: Oxford University Press, 1931. [Cited as *Hung. Folk Music.*]

— "Collecting Folk Songs in Anatolia," *Hungarian Quarterly* (Budapest), Summer, 1937. [In revised form as No. 26 in *Béla Bartók Essays* (ed. Benjamin Suchoff), Faber & Faber, London, 1976.

[— *Slovak Folk Songs.* Bratislava: Academia Scientiarum Slovaca, 1959 (Vol. I), 1970 (Vol. II), ? (Vol. III).]

[— *Rumanian Folk Music* (ed. Benjamin Suchoff). The Hague: Martinus Nijhoff, 1967 (Vol. I: Instrumental Melodies; Vol. II: Vocal Melodies; Vol. III: Texts), 1975 (Vol. IV: Carols and Christmas Songs [*Colinde*]; Vol. V: Maramureş County).]

— and Kodály, Zoltán. *Folk Songs (Transylvanian Hungarians).* Budapest: The Popular Literary Society, 1921.

— and Lord, Albert B. *Serbo-Croatian Folk Songs.* New York: Columbia University Press, [1951].

Hornbostel, Erich v. *Musik des Orients* (Album of recordings and notes), No. 19, Odeon 0-5168.

Kolessa, Philaret. *Melodien der ukraïnischen rezitierenden Gesänge (Dumy).* Beitrage zur ukraïnischen Ethnologie, Vols. XIII–XIV, Lemberg, Ševčenko Society, 1910, 1913.

Kuba, Ludvík. *Slovanstvo ve svých zpevech.* Pardubice, Poděbrady, Praha, 1884–1929.

Kúnos, Ignác. *Oszmán-török népköltési gyűtemény.* Budapest: Hungarian Academy of Sciences, 1889. [Cited as *O-t.n.g.*]

— *Ada-Kálei török népdalok.* Budapest: Hungarian Academy of Sciences, 1906.

A Companion to Hungarian Studies. Budapest, 1943.

Anadilden Derlemeler. Ankara, 1932.

Afterword

by Kurt Reinhard

THE FIRST TWO VOLUMES of the series of folk songs published by the Conservatory of Istanbul appeared ten years before Bartók's journey to Turkey. Of the fourteen volumes published prior to 1936[1] only four songs are included from the region visited by Bartók.[2] These four songs—unlike those in Volumes 3–13, which were collected on the spot and then personally notated by music specialists during four collecting trips—were sent to those specialists for inclusion in the publication; their authenticity, therefore, is by no means warranted. Thus Bartók, despite the abundant literature about Turkish folk music in general, could obtain little information about the musical situation in the Adana province.[3]

1. *Anadolu Halk Şarkıları*, İstanbul Belediyesi Konservatuvar Neşriyatından. Vols. 1–2 (1926) with preface by Rauf Yekta Bey, Vols. 1–7 in Arabic script and with the title *Chansons populaires Turques*. Vol. 1 published again (no date) in Roman script. Vols. 3–4 (1927) with prefaces by Cemal Reşit Bey, Vol. 5 (1927) with preface by Ekrem Bessim Bey. Vols. 6–12 (6 and 7: 1928, 8–12: 1929) without preface; Vol. 8 on in Roman script. Mahmud Raghib (subsequently M. R. Gazimihâl) gives a comprehensive survey of all the volumes published till then in Vol. 13 (1930). Vol. 14 was published in 1931.

2. Vol. 2: Three songs from Adana, pp. 41, 43. Vol. 6: A song from Kozan (Adana *vilayet*), p. 2.

3. Veysel Arseven, *Açılamalı Türk Müziği Kitap ve Makaleler Bibliyografyası* (İstanbul, 1969). This work lists 22 books and 35 essays, as well as single songs, to 1936. From 1937 to 1945 (the year of Bartók's death) 35 books and 201 essays were published, but one can assume that Bartók had access to very few of them. Because of the language difficulties, moreover, probably only those which include music examples would have been of use to him. On the other hand, it is beyond doubt that the sudden growth of the number of essays published in Turkey since 1936 can in part be attributed to the increased interest of Turkish specialists in their own folk music, which was sparked by Bartók's journey.

Regarding this literature, it is of an absolutely descriptive character and is not conceived in the spirit of ethnomusicological style analysis. In fact, it is composed for the most part of ethnographic studies which partly deal with the subject of music, including occasional notations; reproductions of melodies with scanty annotations or none at all; or pure monographs.[4] Although the last-named category does include morphological subjects,[5] Bartók could hardly use them as a starting point: the Turkish folk songs that had been collected till that time were not analyzed topologically as Bartók had done with his own material.[6] And that is precisely the reason why he was invited by the ruling party, the Halk Partisi,[7] "to lecture in Ankara on ethnomusicology and to help it start a collection of its own folk music."[8]

Prior to his short collecting trip in South Turkey, Bartók prepared for the visit by listening to records kept in Istanbul Conservatory, which were shown to him by Adnan Saygun the day after Bartók arrived there. Three collections were on display: the seventy-nine wax discs recorded by the Conservatory team during its fourth journey in 1929;[9] about sixty records, comprising 120

4. Among the publications purely on music and works by known music writers, e.g., eight works by M. R. Gazimihâl, three by S. Y. Ataman, and one by A. Saygun are included here.

5. M. R. Kösemihal (= Gazimihâl), *Türk Halk Muziklerinin Tonal Hususiyetleri Meselesi* [On the Tonal Peculiarities of the Turkish Folk Music], İstanbul, 1936; Kösemihalzade (= Gazimihâl), *Polifonik Türkülerimiz Meselesi* [On the Polyphony of our Folk Songs], "Millî Mecmua," 1933; Ahmed Adnan (Saygun), *Türk Halk Musikisinde Pentatonizm* [Pentatonicism in the Turkish Folk Music], İstanbul, 1936.

6. M. R. Gazimihâl at one time voluntarily declared to the present writer that the Turkish literature on folk music, till then, is not of purely scientific character.

7. Bartók uses the term Halkevi in his Preface, which means "People's House," the designation of the cultural centers set up at that time to be used for the national education.

8. Béla Bartók, *Auf Volkslied-Forschungsfahrt in der Türkei* [Folk Song Collecting in Turkey], *Musik der Zeit* (ed. by Heinrich Lindlar), Vol. 3: *Béla Bartók*, published by Boosey & Hawkes, Bonn, 1953, pp. 23–26.

9. It was on this journey that recordings were made for the first time. A list of them is given in Vol. 13 of the folk song series described in fn. 1, above. The 155 melodies published there, however, were notated on the spot by ear, rather than transcribed from the recordings. The melodies in the other volumes were similarly published.

songs,[10] made by the Columbia Corporation on behalf of the Conservatory; and the already existing, industrially pressed records which had never been placed on sale but were stored in the Conservatory's Archive.[11]

A special, more or less independent, folk song archive was established in 1936 at the recently founded State Conservatory at Ankara. The reason for inviting Bartók—initiated by L. Rásonyi, M. R. Gazimihâl, and A. Saygun—was extended in order to obtain an experienced collector of folk songs as expert adviser.[12] From then on and for a long period of time excursions were organized each year from Ankara for recording purposes: at first on soundfoil, later on by means of magnetic tape. The collection grew to approximately 10,000 recordings under the direction of Muzaffer Sarısözen, head of the Archive for many years. The institute was closed for a long time after the death in 1963 of this able folk song connoisseur; it was temporarily administered by Gültekin Oransay, and at the present time most of its activities are suspended—including the organizing of field trips for the collecting of folk songs. The Turkish Radio has partly assumed this task since 1967, and on several occasions has sent teams to make tape recordings in different regions of Turkey.[13] Other initiatives have been made by the privately founded "Milli Folklor Enstitüsü" in Ankara.[14] Finally, we may mention the endeavors of the present writer and

10. A list of these commercial records is also included in the Appendix (pp. 12–13) of Vol. 13 of the folk song series described in fn. 1, above (see also fn. 11, below).

11. No catalogue was ever published of this collection, nor of the art music records in the collection mentioned in fn. 10, above.

12. For this and further details concerning Bartók's stay in Turkey, in addition to his own report (see fn. 8, above), refer to A. Saygun's illustrated essay, "Bartók in Turkey," *The Musical Quarterly*, No. 37 (1951), p. 5.

13. The first report is *Folklor Derlemesi I*, Türkiye Radyo Televizyon Kurumu, Ankara, 1968.

14. See the publication listed in fn. 3, above.

his pupils, who have written scholarly works[15] and numerous articles in Turkish publications.[16]

Bartók's brief sojourn in Turkey, and the "model work" in the realm of ethnomusicological field research he performed, are undoubtedly a decisive milestone in the development of Turkish musical folklore. The exact notation of the texts, provided by his travelling companion, Adnan Saygun; the minute interrogation and observation of the authorities; auditions of the singers and instrumentalists in their customary settings; the aim at a possibly complete picture of the existing musical folklore in a comparatively restricted area; choice of the plain of Adana where, still at

15. Of the eight field trips undertaken by Kurt Reinhard thus far (1955, 1956, 1963, 1964, 1966, 1967, 1968, and 1970), four were devoted exclusively and three partly to the study of Turkish folk music in connection with tape recording. The publications that resulted from this activity, and which deal solely with the folk music in South Turkey, are: "Zustand und Wandel der bäuerlichen Musik in der türkischen Provinz Adana [State and Development of the Peasant Music in the Turkish Province of Adana], *Sociologus*, 1956; "Types of Turkmenian Songs in Turkey, *Journal of the International Folk Music Council*, 1957; "Tanzlieder der Turkmenen in der Südtürkei" [Dance Songs of the Turkmen in South Turkey], *Kongreßbericht der Gesellschaft für Musikforschung Hamburg 1956*, 1957; "Ein türkischer Tanzliedtyp und seine außertürkischen Parallelen" [A Turkish Dance Songs Type and its non-Turkish Parallels], *Baessler Archiv*, 1960; "Trommeltanze aus der Süd-Türkei" [Drum Dances from South Turkey], *Journal of the IFMC*, 1961; "Zur Variantenbildung im türkischen Volkslied, dargestellt an einer Hirtenweise" [On the Way Variants Come into Being in the Turkish Folk Song, Demonstrated by a Shepherd's Song], *Festschrift Heinrich Besseler zum 60. Geburtstag*, 1961; *Türkische Musik*, Berlin, 1962; "Die gegenwartige Praxis des Epengesanges in der Türkei" [The Present Practice of Epic Songs in Turkey], *Beiträge zur Kenntnis Südosteuropas und des Nahen Ostens*, II, 1967.

Also Ursula Reinhard, "Vor seinen Häusern eine Weide . . ." [A Pasture Before His Houses . . .], *Volksliedtexte aus der Süd-Türkei*, Berlin, 1965; Jens Peter Reiche, "Stilelemente süd-türkischer Davul-Zurna-Stücke" [Stylistic Elements of the South-Turkish Davul-Zurna Pieces], *Jahrbuch für musikalische Volks- und Völkerkunde*, 5, 1970.

16. In addition to the works included in Arseven's bibliography (see fn. 3, above)—973 items until 1967—mention should be made of the publication *Müziki Mecmuası*, published by Etem Tungör, and the ethnographical periodical *Türk Folklor Araştırmaları*; both magazines contain articles on Turkish folk music.

that time, numerous and hardly acculturated Yürüks[17] were to be encountered; the attempt to induce women to sing; and many other aspects reveal the experienced music folklorist who also knows how to proceed in an exemplary way.

Although this experimental model in the *vilayet* of Adana only lasted eight days (18–25 November 1936), and, moreover, though Bartók used—for certain practical reasons—the technically inadequate Edison phonograph with its wax cylinders limited to about two minutes of recording, the resulting melodic typology Bartók describes in *Turkish Folk Music from Asia Minor* is simply amazing. The fact that his insights are still valid, in this first, methodically founded study on Turkish folk music, is supported by the experiences and cognitions of the present writer, which in part resulted from the latter's journey to Turkey in 1963 in connection with these lines. These findings, together with those derived from abundant examinations of a rich collection of technically superior sound recordings, prompt us to offer here—without the slightest intent to diminish the great scientific merit of Bartók's work!—a number of supplements and rectifications.

It seems obvious, because of the above-mentioned restrictions of Bartók's undertaking, that his declared chief aim: "to find out if there were any relation between Old Hungarian and Old Turkish folk music" could not be fully implemented. He found decisive proof for this thesis in the Turkish-Hungarian parallels he en-

17. Yürük literally means "quickly walking," figuratively "migrant," and in the present case designates the population of nomadic shepherds who do not, however, as Bartók presumes, take up their summer abode only in the Taurus Mountains, but also in other areas of South and Western Turkey from which they can reach the frost-free coast in winter. The selection of the Adana plain was particularly of advantage, since a significantly large number of nomads are to be found here. More importantly, also located here are ethnic groups who call themselves Turkmen and, like the Yürüks, are divided into tribes (*aşiret*) which are comparatively little intermixed. *Aşiret*, erroneously spelled by Bartók without dot (ĭ) over the "i" in his Note to melody No. 24, is not the denomination of a certain tribe but that, generally, of a nomadic one. In fact, it is most frequently used in connection with the name of the tribe.

countered during his preliminary examinations and even at his first village recording.[18] He undoubtedly would have compiled further evidence for the present study, despite the scantiness of material for comparison, had he had access to the Hungarian material in the Budapest collection.[19]

Further evidence of the kinship of the Turkish and Hungarian folk music, in terms of common country of origin, is perceptible in the fact that the *parlando* and *tempo giusto* style types, recognized as basic for the Hungarian folk songs, are quite similar and easily demonstrable in the Turkish melodies. The Turkish concepts *Uzun hava* (Bartók's classification Groups 1–12) and *Kırık hava* (Groups 13–17) could therefore be logically applied to the listing in Bartók's chapter on structure of the melodies.

The concept *Uzun hava* is very comprehensive, even if it is not always used as a specific name by the executants. It comprises in its widest sense all vocal as well as instrumental nonharmonic melodies, classified here by Bartók in the so-called *parlando* groups. In a narrow sense one has to mean by it all the *parlando* melodies of bigger size, having a composite structure, and interspersed with sustained tones or flourishes. According to the data derived from recent research of Turkish folk songs, it is no longer possible to uphold the idea that *Uzun hava* is a pattern rarely met with (see Bartók's comments about melody No. 62).

18. The two recordings of 16 November mentioned by Bartók in his Preface, and the first recording in Osmaniye (melody No. 8a.) are referred to here, about which Bartók writes in his report (see fn. 8, above): "I hardly believed my ears. It is a variant of an old Hungarian melody!"

19. See Bartók's remark in his Introduction where 13,000 Hungarian melodies are mentioned. A statement of similiar comparison is contained in an essay by Bence Szabolcsi, published in English translation, "Eastern Relations of Early Hungarian Folk Music", *Journal of the Royal Asiatic Society*, 1935. A work of Bruno Nettl can be quoted here in regard to the relationship of Hungarian music to that of the Cheremissians, as advocated by Bartók, *Cheremis Musical Styles*, Bloomington (Indiana), 1960. A. Adnan Saygun offers a first contribution to the topic at hand, which was initiated by Bartók, in his essay "Quelques réflexions sur certaines affinités des musiques folkloriques turque et hongroise," *Studia Musicologica* (Budapest), v, 1965.

There is also the question of whether the laments (*ağıt*) of narrower range are to be included, since a number of recordings of the present writer have dual class names, for example, *Uzun hava* and *ağıt*.

The *Bozlak*, however, whose meaning Bartók could not establish (see the Note to melody No. 21b.), undoubtedly belongs here. *Bozlak* is an ambiguous concept, indeed. It might be said generally that it has for the most part eleven-syllable text lines, definite structural form, and is topically related to the love songs.[20] Bartók's Note to melody No. 62 also discloses that the concepts *Uzun hava* and *Bozlak* are often mentioned together. Here the instruments perform this originally vocal type, and Bartók is not particularly astonished at that, but in the preceding melody (No. 61) he questions whether the performance of a vocal melody by instruments is exceptional. The answer may be that the method is not so unusual. Texted melodies are often played on the flute, oboe, and *saz*. In many cases there are even frequent efforts to imitate the peculiarities of a singing voice, while on the other hand taking liberties made possible only because of the lacking interconnection with the text.[21]

The *Kırık hava* is the opposite of the *Uzun hava*, that is, the former is comprised of pieces in *tempo giusto*. Although this concept has no universal use, it is nevertheless very characteristic that *Kırık* means "broken"; thus it seems obvious that the *Uzun hava* is to be considered as the normal type, whose free-flowing melos is somehow dismembered in the *Kırık hava*. According to this

20. See Kurt Reinhard, *Türkische Musik* (pp. 16ff.), where a facsimile of this *Bozlak* recorded by Bartók (melody No. 21b.) is shown. The *Musical Lexicon* of M. R. Gazimihâl (*Musiki Sözlügü*, İstanbul, 1961) does not mention this concept, nor can an all-encompassing, valid definition be obtained from Ferruh Arsunar, *Anadolu Halk Türkülerinden Örnekler* (Ankara, 1947), Vol. I, chapters 3 ("*Türkmen Bozlaği*") and 4 ("*Avşar Bozlağı*").

21. See Kurt Reinhard, "Zur Variantenbildung . . ." (details in fn. 15, above). With regard to the special importance of the *Uzun hava* in the repertory of *Davul-Zurna* performers, see Reiche's essay (fn. 15).

definition it is also obvious that all genuine dance melodies belong to this style group. If Bartók expressed a different opinion in his explanations to melody Nos. 43b.c., it is because he did not know what *Halay havası* means. *Hava* only means melody, and *Halay* is a noncompulsory form spread over almost the whole of Turkey. The Rain-begging songs also belong in this category, in a certain way, although Bartók lists them separately (Group 18) after the *tempo giusto* pieces. Melody Nos. 49a.b. are strictly metrical; 49c.d., however, can be traced back to simple meters. These songs, Bartók observes, resemble the children's songs of southeast and west Europe. But even Nos. 42, 44, and 48 give evidence of a certain resemblance, and still more convincing would be their comparison with a dance-song pattern, possibly of Kurd origin, met with in the Turkish-Arabic borderland.[22]

In view of Bartók's classification of his material solely according to musical criteria, it is all the more proper for him to discuss in detail his selection of text lines of seven, eight, and eleven syllables as the most important text structures. These structures are not regularly linked to certain melody types or to certain topical attributes of the melodies. However important this subject may be, lack of space precludes our dealing with it in detail here. Texts with seven-syllable lines belong mostly to the dance songs, the *Kırık hava* respectively. Those with eight-syllable lines appear in the *tempo giusto* pieces as well as in the *parlando* songs, while those with eleven-syllable lines belong exclusively to the latter group. These eleven-syllable lines are indeed used in high style folk poetry; but persons composing and generally singing such well-shaped folk songs, whose lines are for the most part worded with eleven syllables and are of slightly more elaborate melodic structure, as

22. See Kurt Reinhard, "Ein türkischer Tanzliedtyp . . ." (details in fn. 15, above). A more substantial knowledge of Turkish Rain-begging songs is hardly to be obtained nowadays, since these supplications are rarely sung anymore. In fact, not one example of this genre is to be found in the very comprehensive material of Reinhard from 1955, 1956, and 1963.

a rule had and have no town education, as Bartók infers. On the contrary, they often are illiterate. Those who have been taught to write, to compose, and to sing as a main or subsidiary occupation —generally by someone else—of course reach a higher standard of education than the rest of the villagers.

Some of the songs qualified as heterometric (Groups 11, 12, 17), as well as the manifestly corrupted melodies of Group 19, can be traced back to one of the forms with more usual structure of the text lines. One must somewhat modify Bartók's observation that texts and melodies are interchangeable. For the most part only different texts are linked to the same melody and not vice-versa. This circumstance, moreover, holds true not only for simple melodies but with the lengthy *Uzun hava*, too. It is even customary for popular poets (*âşık*) to use the same melody or, at least, the same melodic pattern with different poems.

The limited time of observation and the restriction to one region necessarily led Bartók to consider that certain musical phenomena were only typical of the Yürüks. But the habit "to sing in as high a pitch as possible, at the top of one's voice" is also met in other parts of Turkey. That it is particularly characteristic in South Turkey verifies the experience that it is the musical speciality of numerous pastoral tribes. It is quite probable that the very loud and high-pitched beginning of the songs is a reminiscence of the kind of shouts necessary for the mutual communication between herdsmen. In this regard the thesis of Carl Stumpf comes to mind: that the music of mankind has on the whole developed originally out of shouts of information of this kind.[23]

Bartók's inference that "the Turkish rural folk music does not know proper upbeats" should not be generalized, since there are an adequate number of instances in which upbeats are fitted to the

23. Carl Stumpf, *Die Anfänge der Musik* [The Origin of Music], Leipzig, 1911. According to the belief of Turkish experts, the beginning of many songs is emphasized in the above-mentioned way, because the singers need to express something decisive with their words.

actual text.[24] Such upbeats often occur in incomplete measures, for example, on the second quarter in a 4/4 measure or in a 9/8 measure (*aksak*). On the other hand, it is just those pseudo-upbeats mentioned by Bartók that offer proof that the upbeat was not only unfamiliar to the Turks but was often artificially created.

Vibrato, called pulsation according to ethnomusicological terminology and described by Bartók as "observed nowhere else" and "ascribed to the influence of Arabic urban music," is to be met with all over the world and is a typical singing style of many performers in India.

Even at the present time it is difficult to induce Turkish women to sing in front of a microphone, particularly uneducated peasant women. Religious inhibitions are just as obstructive as the male prerogative of not tolerating the public appearance of women. It is also in the home that a certain restraint is observed, even if the folk song collector is a female. Should one or another woman sing, it will rarely be a lullaby; this genre is of specific intent, and the lullaby would lose its evil-preventing force if not sung to a baby. The questions asked by Bartók about women's performance can be answered approximately as follows: women's repertory is not basically different from that of men, it is only more limited, although it comprises lullabies and special female dance songs, which are as a rule not sung by men. In many regions it is preferable for the women to sing the laments. The feminine style of singing, on the other hand, is far different. The high-pitched singing, in which preference is given to the high diapason, is missing completely. There is much less flourish, and pulsations and emphases are rarely met with. Although women do sing the *Uzun hava* pattern with eleven-syllable text lines, it is done in a simpler and particularly in a quieter way, also. The custom described by Bartók in his Note to melody No. 40 probably stems from the

24. See the various folk-song publications (among others, those included in fn. 1, above) and several publications of Reinhard (fn. 15).

traditional obligation of women to show great restraint musically; therefore, since they played no instruments, whenever a drum accompaniment was required they substituted a household utensil instead.

Another difficulty experienced by Bartók is still to be encountered in remote villages. There the researcher will stumble on cases of fear of losing the voice, because of tape recording.

Bartók's chapter on musical instruments may be completed with these points: In Turkey it is understood that *gayda* also means bagpipe. It is questionable whether this word, as used by the Yürüks, denotes their concept of melody. Bartók was probably erroneously informed about that. The designation *kemençe* (the Turkish form of a Persian word), also current in Arabic areas, is used in Turkey for widely varied stringed instruments. In the southern part of the country there were specimens of both types of lutes, referred to as long-neck and short-neck lutes by organologists. Since Bartók describes an instrument which greatly resembles a violin, one might presume that the instrument in question is one of the many bastard shapes. Although in former times even the nomads (Yürüks), having very little luggage, carried along bow instruments, this type is no longer encountered in south Turkey in nomad camps or among the settled inhabitants. *Cura* is the smallest type of *saz*, the Turkish long-neck lute.

The custom of accompanying the dance with the oboe and the drum is popular in nearly all Islamic countries and is spread as far as the Balkans. The players, nearly always professional musicians, are for the most part gypsies—at least in the cultural area previously or at the present time under Turkish dominion. It is quite probable that the gypsies imported the instruments from India. The chief executant of the inseparable pair of instrumentalists is the drummer. He often joins the dancers or performs artistic, frolicsome gestures, while the oboist generally and indifferently stands apart. The drummer, who receives first mention in the Turkish denomination, decides on the pieces to be played. His cord-strung, large, double-membrane drum arrived in central Europe during the course of the Turkish wars and developed here to its present form as the bass drum. The bell oboes, turned out of one piece, have the same shape all over the Near East, although size varies. There is a widespread custom of blowing without interruption: during a sustained note the tongue is fed air from a tank created by the inflated cheeks, at the same time respiration takes place through the nose.[25]

The designation *Il bey* (No. 36), baffling to Bartók, presumably means a song from the epic *Elbeylioğlu*.[26] The word *Garip* or *Garib* in Nos. 54 and 64 is the name of a folk poet (*âşık*) who lived in the sixteenth century. There is no contradiction that Bartók places No. 54 in Group 19 (indeterminable structure). The eleven-syllable text-line structure preferred by *Âşık* is only slightly muddled. The following text correction is possible:

Yarın bayram derler al giyer eller,
Bir âdet koymuş kutlu olsun derler.
Yaz bahar ayında açılan güller,
Güller nazlı yardan bana bir haber.

These four lines constitute one verse. Bartók has numbered the verses according to the melody sections, although his perception of the text structures and the relation between text and melody was correct in principle. In other words, he divided the text verses incorrectly—an occurrence that will be found in several other instances.[27]

The identification of the composers of the songs recorded by Bartók is probably not possible, since names are given only at the beginning of the penultimate verse and were therefore not re-

25. About *Davul-Zurna* performance, see Felix Hoerburger, *Der Tanz mit der Trommel* [The Dance with the Drum], Regensburg, 1954; also J. P. Reiche's essay (fn. 15).

26. See Wolfram Eberhard, *Minstrel Tales from Southeastern Turkey*, Berkeley and Los Angeles, 1955.

27. For example, Nos. 24–33, 35–38, and 48a.

corded on phonograms which hold only about two minutes of performance time. The fact that these songs might be performed as purely instrumental music, possibly as dance music, is of no importance whatever.

Some place names mentioned by Bartók have changed since 1936. In certain cases, too, erroneous administrative functions have been applied to some towns. Adana is the capital of a province (*vilayet*) which was previously named Seyhan but is now called by the name of its capital, as are all Turkish provinces. (Bartók twice designates Seyhan as the capital, too.) Kadirli and Osmaniye are not *vilayet* but district towns (*Kasa*) in Adana province. The place named after the castle of Harun al-Raschid—the castle was there at one time—is Haruniye (not Harunie), and the village in this small district (Nâhiye) has the official name of Tabaklarköy. The designation *köy* (village) is occasionally affixed, unofficially, to other place names. Maraş, the title of piece No. 26, is a provincial capital whose name was chosen for a certain dance. Antep (No. 37) today bears the name of Gaziantep.

The Abdals (see melody Nos. 61–66), a tribe verifiable as far as Turkestan, constitute in Turkey—particularly in the area of Gaziantep—nothing more than a special kind of gypsies engaged in music, mostly in *Davul-Zurna* playing.[28] That is the only reason that various notions have been derived from this denomination.[29] With regard to the meaning of *abdal* as "itinerant singer," the word has become an honorary title, used by many outstanding folk song poets, such as Pir Sultan Abdal (sixteenth century). The Ulaş aşiret (tribe) (Nos. 7b., 8a., 10, 42) no longer supplies the main quota of Osmaniye inhabitants. It should be borne in mind that the denomination of nomadic tribes is abandoned a few years after settlements are established, then the name sinks into oblivion.

28. See P. Pelliot, "Les Abdals de Painap," *Journal Asiatique*, 1907; and A. von Le Coq, "Die Abdal," *Baessler Archiv*, 1912.

29. See Heuser-Şevket, *Deutsch-Türkisches Wörterbuch*, Wiesbaden, 1953.

Today there still is a village Ulaş not far from Osmaniye, where the inhabitants refer to themselves as kin of the Ulaş aşiret.

Bartók's travelling companion has been writing his last name as Saygun for a long time. The last name of Dr. Hamid Zübeyr, mentioned by Bartók in his Preface, is now Koşay; he is no longer head of all the museums in Turkey and recently retired after serving as director of the Ethnographical Museum in Ankara. He and Ishak Refet are the authors of the last item (published in Ankara in 1932) in Bartók's Bibliography. (Koşay and Orhan Aydın [now Açıpayamlı] collaborated in the publication of a complementary second volume, Ankara, 1952.)

Finally, these remarks on some of the performers: Basri Demir (No. 55c.) was still living in 1963. Mahmud Bekiroğlu (Nos. 43b.c., 60) was also still alive, in Osmaniye. The full name of Kır İsmail (Nos. 18, 23) is İsmail Güngör. Kır means grey: he had a long grey beard, and the denomination served to highlight the minstrel out of the multitude of men with the same name. In 1963, even at the age of seventy-eight, he was able to declaim uncommonly well; in fact, he was one of the last bards or minstrels in the entire area. He performed for a fee at weddings or other festivals, reciting the ancient Turkish folk epics (*halk hikâyeleri*) in which were interspersed songs of the kind Bartók recorded there. These pieces were of the *Uzun hava* type, with eleven-syllable text lines, whose lengthiness can be attributed to the fact that they are recited as parts of very voluminous epics and by professional minstrels. A minstrel reciting this kind of heroic poem, though illiterate, of course cannot be considered as a representative of simple peasant music, according to Bartók's meaning. On the other hand, all other songs with eleven-syllable text lines are "folk" or "peasant" songs in a narrow sense. The still viable, large group of lofty folk poetry constitutes an exception, even though it is sung by the rank and file.[30]

30. Additional data concerning Kır İsmail will be found in Eberhard (fn. 26 above), who recorded this "itinerant minstrel" in 1951; and in Reinhard (fn. 15 above), who recorded him in 1955, 1956, and 1963.

The present writer salutes the publication of this book, and he expresses his gratitude and, in all certainty, that of his colleagues to the Estate of Béla Bartók in New York, to its indefatigable trustee Dr. Benjamin Suchoff, who knew how to overcome energetically all obstacles, and last but not least to the publisher.

The reader may have found in the foregoing essay an illustration of why Bartók's last scientific work could not have become the definitive, all-encompassing monograph on Turkish folk music. There are, however, two cogent reasons why this late, posthumous publication is to be appreciated as an ethnomusicological asset.

First of all, it is a foregone conclusion that all of Bartók's research works must be brought within public reach, particularly in view of the fact that many people share the opinion of the present writer that Bartók was not only one of the greatest composers of our century but also an equally significant ethnomusicologist.

Secondly, this final Bartók work demonstrates and corroborates once again, and in a most representative way, the analytic and typological methods of folk-music research set up by Bartók, in part jointly with Ilmari Krohn. Despite the further developed outlook that has meanwhile occurred, one cannot contest the premise that Bartók, decades ago, and with his exceedingly exact, scientific system of workmanship, had anticipated the ideas and methods of modern structuralism. Indeed, this system, modified accordingly, is still applicable today.

Appendix

LEXICOGRAPHICAL INDEX OF TURKISH VOCAL MELODIES

THE PURPOSE of this computer-derived tabulation is to provide the reader with a simple and rapid method of locating individual melody sections of the Turkish vocal music examples in this publication,[1] or of comparing them with others for possible borrowings.[2]

In order to make comparisons with other materials, it is only necessary to calculate the first seven (or less) intervals of a given melody section or incipit. This calculation should omit from consideration the chromatic quality of the obtained intervals, repeated notes, and rests. Ascending intervals should be indicated by a plus

1. Instrumental melodies have been omitted from this index; problems concerning their contour, music representation, and programming procedures are under investigation by the present writer.

2. The melodies have been encoded in the Ford-Columbia Music Representation which was developed for computer applications by S. Bauer-Mengelberg. The tabulation was compiled by means of the GRIPHOS (General Retrieval and Information Processor for Humanities-Oriented Studies) procedure which was developed by Dr. Jack Heller, Professor of Computer Science, State University of New York at Stony Brook. The reader interested in specifics concerning this computer application to Bartók's Turkish material should consult *Computers and the Humanities*, Vol. 5, No. 2 (1971), p. 110, and Benjamin Suchoff, *A* GRIPHOS *Application to Bartók's Turkish Folk Music Material*, *Spectra* Monograph No. 1 (Center for Contemporary Arts and Letters, State University of New York at Stony Brook, 1975).

sign, descending ones by a minus sign (for example, an ascending diatonic scale would yield an interval sequence of +2 +2 +2 +2 +2 +2 +2; half-steps and whole steps are designated alike as seconds). The derived calculation can then be compared with the interval sequences published here. If a complete match is found (or a significant subset of an interval sequence) or a similar contour, refer to the respective melody in the Turkish music examples for further analysis.[3]

To facilitate use of the Index the following explanation of column headings is offered:

Index No. Lexicographical order of the 209 string interval sequences, in which plus precedes minus and lesser precedes greater intervallic size.

Interval Sequence. The melodic contour of a melody section (carried to a maximum of seven positions) expressed in plus or minus numeric figures. Index number 36, for instance, displays an interval sequence of ascending and descending seconds exclusively (+2 -2 +2 -2 +2 -2 +2).

Class. The class to which the given melody section belongs, as numerically designated by the author in his Introduction (p. 36, above).

Melody No. The Turkish vocal melodies as numbered by Bartók in this volume.

3. Further details regarding data-processing techniques in Bartókian folk song research will be found in Suchoff essays titled: "Bartók, Ethnomusicology and the Computer," Institute for Computer Research in the Humanities *Newsletter* (New York University), Vol. IV, No. 4, 1968; "The Computer and Bartók Research in America," *Magyar Zenetörténeti Tanulmányok* [ed. Ferenc Bónis], Vol. III (Editio Musica, Budapest, 1973); also in *Journal of Research in Music Education*, Vol. XIX, No. 1, 1971; "Computer Applications to Bartók's Serbo-Croatian Material," *Tempo* (London), No. 80, 1967; "Computerized Folk Song Research and the Problem of Variants," *Computers and the Humanities*, Vol. 2, No. 4, 1968; "Computer-Oriented Comparative Musicology," *The Computer and Music* [ed. Harry B. Lincoln], Cornell University Press, 1970; "Some Problems in Computer-Oriented Bartókian Ethnomusicology," *Ethnomusicology*, Vol. XIII, No. 3, 1969; also in *Revista de etnografie şi folclor* (Bucharest), Vol. 14, No. 5, 1969; also in *Muzsika* (Budapest), Vol. XIII, 1970.

Content-Structure. Melody sections of different content are distinguished by capital letters A, B, C, or D, depending on the number of different structures in a given melody.[4]

Index No.	Interval Sequence	Class	Melody No.	Content-Structure
1		17	48a.	A[5]
2	+2+2+2−2	1	4	A
3	+2+2+2−2+2−2−2	2	21b.	C
4	+2+2+2−2+2−2−2	19	53	A
5	+2+2+2−2−2	1	1b.	A
6	+2+2+2−2−2+2−3	2	16	C
7	+2+2+2−2−2+2−5	2	16	B
8	+2+2+2−2−2−2	2	19	B
9	+2+2+2−2−2−2−3	13	43d.	B
10	+2+2+2−2−2−4+3	1	7b.	A
11	+2+2+2−2−3+2+2	13	43b.	B
12	+2+2+2−3−2	1	8a.	B
13	+2+2+2−4−3	4	26	A
14	+2+2−2+2−2	19	56	A
15	+2+2−2+2−3	2	16	A
16	+2+2−2−2−2	1	5	A
17	+2+2−2−2−2	1	7b.	B
18	+2+2−2−2−2	1	8c.	B
19	+2+2−2−2−2	2	15	D
20	+2+2−2−2−2	2	21b.	A
21	+2+2−2−2−2+2+2	13	43d.	A
22	+2+2−2−2−2−3	1	8b.	B
23	+2+2−2−2−2−3−2	2	21a.	B
24	+2+2−2−2−4	1	8a.	D
25	+2+2−2+3−2−3+2	13	44	A

4. It should be noted that content-structure has been editorially determined.
5. A seven-syllable melody section comprised of repeated notes (d^2) only.

Index No.	Interval Sequence	Class	Melody No.	Content-Structure
26	+2+2−2−3	1	8e.	A
27	+2+2−2−3−3+2	6	30	B
28	+2+2+3−3−2−3−3	6	30	A
29	+2+2+3−3−3+2+2	13	43d.	C
30	+2+2−4−2	12	38	C
31	+2−2	1	3	C
32	+2−2+2	17	48b.	A
33	+2−2+2−2	2	18	A
34	+2−2+2−2	18	49c.	A
35	+2−2+2−2+2	4	25	A
36	+2−2+2−2+2−2+2	18	49d.	B
37	+2−2+2−2+2−2−2	2	15	B
38	+2−2+2−2+2−2−2	12	36	A
39	+2−2+2−2−2	19	51	A
40	+2−2+2−2−2−2	2	15	C
41	+2−2+2−2−2−2−2	2	10a.	B
42	+2−2+2−2−2−2−2	2	19	C
43	+2−2+2−2−2−2−2	17	48a.	B
44	+2−2+2−2−3	1	8d.	A
45	+2−2+2−3−3	17	48b.	B
46	+2−2+2−4−3	1	8d.	B
47	+2−2−2	13	41	B
48	+2−2−2	13	41	C
49	+2−2−2+2−2	12	39	B
50	+2−2−2+2−2	2	22	A
51	+2−2−2+2−2+2−2	2	18	D
52	+2−2−2+2−2−3	2	14	C
53	+2−2−2+2−3	16	47	B
54	+2−2−2+2−4	12	36	C
55	+2−2−2−2	10	34	A
56	+2−2−2−2	13	40	B

Index No.	Interval Sequence	Class	Melody No.	Content-Structure
57	+2−2−2−2−2	1	1a.	B
58	+2−2−2−2−2	1	8d.	C
59	+2−2−2−2−2	2	12	B
60	+2−2−2−2−2	2	17c.	D
61	+2−2−2−2−2	2	21a.	C
62	+2−2−2−2−2	5	29	B
63	+2−2−2−2−2−2	2	17a.	C
64	+2−2−2−2−2−2	2	17b.	C
65	+2−2−2−2−2−2−4	2	10a.	A
66	+2−2−2−2−2−3+2	2	22	D
67	+2−2−2−2−2+4	3	24	A
68	+2−2−2−2+3+2−2	2	12	C
69	+2−2−2−2−3	1	8a.	C
70	+2−2−2−3	1	1b.	B
71	+2−2−2−3−2	5	28	B
72	+2−2+3−2−2	2	13b.	A
73	+2−2+3−4	2	13a.	C
74	+2−2−3	1	3	A
75	+2−2−3	1	9	C
76	+2−2−3	2	21b.	D
77	+2−2−3+2−2	1	1b.	C
78	+2−2−3+2−2−2	3	24	B
79	+2−2−3−2	1	7a.	C
80	+2−2−3−2−2−3	1	3	D
81	+2−2−3−2−3−2	2	11	C
82	+2−2−3+3−2−2−3	13	44	D
83	+2−2−3−3	2	17c.	C
84	+2+3+2−2−2−2−2	13	43d.	D
85	+2+3−2+2−2	19	50	A
86	+2−3	12	39	C
87	+2−3+2−2−2	5	28	A
88	+2−3+2−3+2−3	1	7a.	D
89	+2−3+2−3+2−3	1	8e.	B

Index No.	Interval Sequence	Class	Melody No.	Content-Structure
90	+2−3−2	1	2	D
91	+2−3−2−2	13	43a.	B
92	+2−3−2+3−2−5	5	27	A
93	+2−3+3−3+2−2−2	2	17a.	D
94	+2+4−3−2	8	32	A
95	+2−4	1	1b.	D
96	−2	2	12	A
97	−2+2	16	47	A
98	−2+2+2+2−6−2	2	20	C
99	−2+2−2	1	4	C
100	−2+2−2	2	13a.	A
101	−2+2−2+2+2−2	9	33	A
102	−2+2−2+2+2−2	9	33	B
103	−2+2−2+2−2+2−2	12	37	A
104	−2+2−2+2−2+2−3	12	37	C
105	−2+2−2+2−2−2	13	43b.	A
106	−2+2−2+2−3+3−4	5	29	A
107	−2+2−2−2	18	49b.	A
108	−2+2−2−2+2+2−2	2	17a.	A
109	−2+2−2−2+2−2	1	4	D
110	−2+2−2−2−2	2	22	C
111	−2+2−2−2−2+4−2	13	44	C
112	−2+2−2−2−3	12	38	B
113	−2+2−2−3	1	2	A
114	−2+2−3+2−2−2−2	5	27	B
115	−2+2−3−2	1	1a.	C
116	−2+2−3−2	1	8c.	C
117	−2+2−3+3−2−2	2	17b.	A
118	−2+2−3+3−2−3	1	8b.	A
119	−2+2−4−3−2	2	20	D

Index No.	Interval Sequence	Class	Melody No.	Content-Structure
120	−2−2	13	43a.	A
121	−2−2	2	20	A
122	−2−2+2	7	31	B
123	−2−2+2+2−5	2	13b.	B
124	−2−2+2−2−2	1	2	C
125	−2−2+2−2−2	1	7b.	B
126	−2−2+2−2−2	2	11	D
127	−2−2+2−2−2	2	17b.	D
128	−2−2+2−2−2−2	10	34	B
129	−2−2−2	1	5	D
130	−2−2−2	1	6	D
131	−2−2−2	2	23	A
132	−2−2−2+2−2−2	14	45	B
133	−2−2−2+2+3−2−3	7	31	C
134	−2−2−2−2−2+2	15	46	B
135	−2−2−2+3−2−2−3	13	44	B
136	−2−2−2−3−2	1	8b.	C
137	−2−2−2−3−2−2	1	3	B
138	−2−2+3−3−2+2	2	11	A
139	−2−2−3−2−2	2	20	B
140	−2−2−3−2−2−2	11	35	D
141	−2−2−3+3−2−2	8	32	B
142	−2−2−4+2−4	2	14	D
143	−2+3+2−2−2−3	2	19	D
144	−2+3−2−2+2−2	1	5	C
145	−2+3−3+2−4	9	33	C
146	−2−3−2+2−3	12	38	A
147	−2−3−2−3	4	26	B
148	−2−3+3+2−2−3	14	45	C
149	−2−3−3	2	23	B
150	−2−4	12	37	B
151	−2−4+2−3	2	13a.	B

Index No.	Interval Sequence	Class	Melody No.	Content-Structure
152	+3	11	35	C
153	+3	13	41	A
154	+3+2−2	14	45	A
155	+3+2−2−2+2	15	46	D
156	+3+2−2−2−2−2	13	42	B
157	+3−2+2	7	31	A
158	+3−2+2−2+2−2−2	2	18	B
159	+3−2−2	2	21a.	A
160	+3−2−2+2−3−2−2	2	14	B
161	+3−2−2−2	1	8a.	A
162	+3−2−2−2	2	16	D
163	+3−2−2−2	2	19	A
164	+3−2−2−2+2	13	42	C
165	+3−2−2−2+2	15	46	C
166	+3−2−2−2+2−2−3	2	17b.	B
167	+3−2−2−2−2	2	22	B
168	+3−2−2−2−2+2+2	2	21b.	B
169	+3−2−2−2−2−2−2	2	17a.	B
170	+3−2−2−2−3−2	2	17c.	B
171	+3−2−2−2−5−3	1	9	D
172	+3−2−3	2	15	A
173	+3−2−3−2	12	39	A
174	+3−2−3+4−2−3	18	49d.	A
175	+3+3−2	1	6	A
176	+3+3−2	13	42	A
177	+3+3−2+3−2−2−3	19	55a.	A
178	+3−3−2+2−3	13	42	D
179	+3−3−2−2	2	11	B
180	+3−3+3−2+2−3	2	17c.	A
181	−3	1	1a.	D
182	−3	1	7a.	B
183	−3	19	54	A

Index No.	Interval Sequence	Class	Melody No.	Content-Structure
184	−3+2−3−2+2−2−2	2	21a.	D
185	−3−2+4−3	1	9	B
186	−2−3−4	13	43a.	C
187	−3+3−2−2	15	46	A
188	−3−3	2	14	A
189	−3−4+4	18	49a.	A
190	+4	11	35	A
191	+4	13	40	A
192	+4+2−2	18	49c.	B
193	+4+2−2−2−2+2−2	19	58	A
194	+4−2+2−2−2−2	19	55c.	A
195	+4−2−2+2+2−3	1	1a.	A
196	+4−2−2+2−3	1	6	B
197	+4−2−2−2	1	5	B
198	+4−2−2−2−2−2	1	8c.	A
199	+4−3−2+2−2−6	12	36	B
200	+4−3−2+4−3−2	1	7a.	A
201	+4−3+3	1	9	A
202	+4−3+3−3−2	19	55b.	A
203	+4−4+4+2−2−2−2	19	57	A
204	−4	11	35	B
205	−4	2	18	C
206	−4−2+3	2	23	C
207	+5−2+2−2−2−3	19	55d.	A
208	−5+3−2−2−2	1	2	B
209	+6−2+2−2−2+2	19	59	A

INDEX OF FIRST LINES

TURKISH TEXTS

ENGLISH TRANSLATIONS

GENERAL INDEX

Library of Congress Cataloging in Publication Data

Bartók, Béla, 1881–1945.
Turkish folk music from Asia Minor.

(New York Bartók Archive studies in musicology; no. 7)
Bibliography: p.
Includes indexes.
1. Folk music, Turkish—History and criticism. I. Suchoff, Benjamin. II. Title. IV. Series: Béla Bartók Archives. Studies in musicology; no. 7.

ML3757.B37 781.7'561 75–23186

ISBN 0–691–09120–X